Joyce & Lorne

May you be blessed as you read about my students

2011, 03, 28

Charles Hart

Radically Changed

37 Real Life Inspirational Stories

Christopher Wilson

authorHOUSE®

AuthorHouse™
1663 Liberty Drive
Bloomington, IN 47403
www.authorhouse.com
Phone: 1-800-839-8640

The stories are recollections of the author and are presented as inspirational works of real people in real situations. Any additions or omissions are presented without malice.

First published by AuthorHouse 7/14/2010

ISBN: 978-1-4490-8147-8 (e)
ISBN: 978-1-4490-8146-1 (sc)
ISBN: 978-1-4490-8145-4 (hc)

Library of Congress Control Number: 2010901284

Printed in the United States of America
Bloomington, Indiana

This book is printed on acid-free paper.

C. Wilson and his wife are co–founders of Jesus Cares Ministry in the Philippines and in Canada. The ministry supports a preparation school which enables disadvantaged children to gain entrance into grade one and prepares needy children for a life time of learning. It also supports Manila Boys and Girls town, the toddlers village and the Home for the aged. Many of these boys and girls and the aged have been abandoned and put out on the street to beg. They are taken from the street and placed in a home which cares for them. Our volunteers also provide food for the squatters and meals for hungry children.

To learn more about this mission work - email jesuscares@live.ca

TABLE OF CONTENTS

INTRODUCTION

Radically Changed

People from all walks of life come to our Bible College in the Downtown Eastside, on the Skid Row of a large city.

The College is affiliated with a Mission which operates seven days a week feeding men and women with the Word of God and a free meal. It is where the students from the College receive hands on experience in preaching, witnessing to people from the street and leading worship in song. When in the Mission they carry out responsibilities as assigned by the Senior Pastor.

It starts with cleaning and stacking chairs after a service and setting up chairs for each service. They are then promoted to working in the kitchen, preparing and serving food and drinks. From there they start booking worship leaders and preachers for two services every day.

In the second year they preach, lead worship and play their instruments. In the third year they learn administration skills such as assisting the treasurer, updating the web site, publicity and other administrative tasks. All the time ministering to people from the street and caring for people in the community.

I was invited to the Mission as a volunteer in the kitchen. My wife and I were doing a prison ministry along with one of the leaders of the Mission who insisted we become part of their ministry.

Each day on the way to the Mission and Bible College can be a stressful experience as it entails walking through a maze of people on the street. It involves trying not to bump into people or get knocked down by the residents of the street, who mill around with no consideration for others. Sometimes they back up without looking and bump people who are passing by. At other times two men will argue and the innocent ones get pushed around in the scuffle. Others are wheeling grocery carts with their worldly possessions through the throng, running into those who will not get out of the way. Cyclists, who have no regard for pedestrians cause people to scatter. Those selling their stolen goods often stand in front of pedestrians trying to force them to buy. Others, set up merchandise on a blanket which you dare not step on. Dealers sell their drugs and users shoot up in doorways.

It is considered to be the worst part of a large city, the most dangerous street in the country. Known for its violence and crime.

The Mission is a safe haven for those who come off the street.

Twice daily, the music at the Mission is gospel songs sung by different musicians playing the guitar, violin, piano and drums. I enjoy the variety and get into the mood of worshipping my Lord and Saviour in a peaceful setting.

When the Bible College was instituted, I enrolled. I was accepted as a student and completed the program. Upon graduation, I was told I should preach regularly which was quite a shock as I had never envisioned myself as a preacher.

Soon, I was a Pastor in charge lining up speakers and teams coming to the Mission.

I later became the assistant treasurer and then the treasurer. I was asked to be a teacher at the College. I had taught in the pubic school system for twenty-six years and had a Master's Degree so they knew I was qualified.

From there I was given the honour of being a Pastor and am addressed as Pastor Christopher.

I have spent fourteen years in the downtown core as a pastor and teacher. I am still teaching and preaching as it is my calling and I enjoy being with the students and staff.

I have been radically changed by these experiences and I would like to share how others have been changed to the same degree.

Our Bible College has had as many as twenty graduates a year, who then go out to do ministry as they are called by God.After studying one year, students are commissioned and receive a diploma. After two years they are eligible to apply for ordination and they receive a diploma in various studies, depending on their major.

After three years of studies and upon completing all requirements, they receive a graduation diploma and start their ministry Some stay with the Mission and become Pastor's in Training.

Others start their ministry in various fields and in many different ways. We help support most ministries for the first year.

Some students do not graduate on the three year program, but they have kept the faith and shared the Good News of the Gospel in various capacities. We recognize these individuals as an integral part of the College and encourage them to keep reading their Bibles and praying for the guidance of the Holy Spirit in order to know the will of God for their lives and their ministry. We believe all Christians have a ministry.

Many students come to class on days when they are not working or when they are waiting to start another job. Others just drop in to say hello, share their stories of what Jesus is doing in their lives and tell of their triumphs in their ministry. Some of these are classified as casual students and work for years on their program of studies and eventually graduate.

Our Mission and Bible College on skid row has changed many lives.

It is still changing lives and will continue to do so.

The names of the students I write about have been changed to protect their identity. All facts given in private are strictly confidential and are not recorded in the book.

'Radically Changed', is written without prejudice and is an inspirational book meant to inform the reader about lives which have been changed by coming to the Mission and the Bible College in the Downtown eastside on the skid row of a large city.

From those who spent one session to those who spent three years of College and more years as pastors in training, all have been changed to some degree by the Word of God and their relationship with Jesus the Christ. Most have been filled with the Holy Spirit.

Of the hundreds of students I have taught, I chose thirty-seven whose stories I feel are interesting and at times profound and will touch the hearts of the readers just as they have touched my heart.

In the downtown core there are many street children. I have talked to some of them and have had a few in the College. One of these street children stands out in my mind because of his accomplishments.

CHAPTER ONE

JACK

A Street Boy

2 Timothy 2:1-"You then, my son, be strong in the grace that is in Christ Jesus. Endure hardship with us like a good soldier of Christ Jesus."

My wife and I were introduced to the prison ministry by an ex convict who had given his life to Christ Jesus while in prison.

When he was released he got in touch with everyone he knew and everyone his wife knew and started a fellowship for released prisoners at his home.

The fellowship is primarily for those who have been recently released from prison and who don't have family or friends in the immediate area.

My wife and I were invited to his home to listen to these men's stories and encourage those who are often starting a new life on the outside.

The reason we were invited is that the ex convict's wife and my wife attended a Bible Study Fellowship. His wife was a leader and my wife was in her class.

The ex convict knew that those released from prison needed encouragement, from caring people who will show them love and concern. He had experienced what it was like to be released from prison and not have a safety net.

He also introduced my wife and myself to a prison ministry.

He put us in touch with a group that did this ministry once a month on a Sunday afternoon and evening. The church that sponsored this ministry has a bus which they let those in this ministry use.

We joined this prison ministry and got to know the regulars. It was great fun riding the bus as we would sing gospel songs and fellowship on our way to the Correctional Centre and also on our return trip to the big city.

This is where we met the young man, Jack. He was one of the key persons as he was friendly with the leader of the ministry and all the participants. He was the one to get the singing started and to make sure that everyone was introduced and were getting to know each other.

He came and sat with my wife, Kristina and I. We shared where we went to church and what we did for a living. At that time I was not in the ministry and was working part time as well as volunteering in a hospital. I had taken early retirement and was free to volunteer and make a difference in the community.

When he heard that I was a volunteer, he insisted that I come and volunteer at the Mission where he did his ministry. He told me where it was located. I knew that this was one of the worst and most dangerous streets in the city.

I told him that when I drove down that street, I locked the doors of my car and rolled up the windows and got out of there as quickly as possible.

He laughed and assured me that it was safe as long as I didn't make eye contact with anyone and as long as I didn't hold my nose because of the smell, and didn't act like a big shot.

After much thought and several discussions with my wife, I volunteered.

The first evening I was walking from the bus stop to the Mission. On the way, I was stopped on the street by a big man who kept saying, "rock, rock." I tried to get by him but he blocked my way. He told me, "I know why you're here. It's for your girls isn't it?" When I told him I was going to the Mission, he moved aside and tried peddling his 'rock cocaine' to other buyers.

At the Mission, I learned that two years before my coming to volunteer, Jack was a street boy. He was hustling for a living and sleeping in the squats, living hand to mouth. Later, Jack told me of some of his experiences on the street. Some which he was proud of and some which he was ashamed of.

That evening, before the service, Jack and I were joined at a table by two others. Jack told us that he had eight young people on the street whom he has cared for and who he still has contact with. He explained,

"They are so fragile, so easily pushed around. I'll take you down there and you'll see for yourself."

I nodded my approval but deep down I felt l would rather decline the offer of walking the streets and going into vacant run down buildings occupied by vagrants who would mug you and rough you up for drug money.

During the service that night, Jack gave his testimony.

I learned from his testimony that his father was an alcoholic and was abusive to his wife and his two sons. At the age of fifteen, Jack went onto the street, tired of being beaten and abused. He explained, "It turned my stomach when I had to watch my mother being yelled at for no reason and often being slapped and punched."

Jack told us he wanted to intervene but his mother told him to stay out of their problems. She knew he would be beaten if he came to her rescue.

Jack had charisma, which drew people to him, and he had a following on the street.

Jack told us that one day, he heard singing from the Mission and got into the line-up. He was drawn to the Mission by the music. Once inside he was amazed to see happy Christians who showed love for each other and love for those who came off the street.

He said, "The Senior Pastor greeted me and invited me to come back and be part of the Mission. I liked to sing and I could talk. I felt I would get along fine as part of this ministry."

A month later, on the bus, going to the prison ministry, Jack told us that he became part of the Mission, working in the kitchen and making a difference. Occasionally, he said, he slipped back onto the street Once he told us he came to a counsel meeting a bit high. "The staff looked at me and shook their heads. I was reprimanded and told I shouldn't do that."

Jack still had his friends from the street and felt an obligation to care for them and make certain that they were not being abused or mistreated.

He was challenged by the staff of the Mission to give up his street life.

Jack tried his best to fit in with the Christians and walk a straight path. He got some used clothes at another mission and tried his best to be presentable. He is a tall, well built and handsome young man, which was to his benefit. He also had a ready smile and a word of affirmation for those he ministered to.

I later learned that one day he was on drugs and came to the Mission. He almost lost his standing in the ministry. It was decided he be given a last chance. After that episode, Jack took charge of his life. He became a new person, a new creation in Christ.

I became a steady volunteer at the Mission. Every time I came, Jack was happy to see me and he introduced me to everyone in sight.

I worked in the kitchen and did whatever cleanup was necessary. At times I carried boxes of food and whatever was donated to the Mission.

With the Mission in high gear and people giving their lives to Christ Jesus, the Senior Pastor realized there was a need for a community home, a dormitory for men who desired to live with other Christians and enjoy their fellowship.

A short distance from the Mission and College, there was a crack house.

It was closed down by the police after a man was beaten and killed in it. His body was thrown face down in the back yard. The house had been vacant and sealed off for months.

This house was ideal for a dormitory as it was only a block and a half away from the Mission. The Pastor spoke to the owner of the house and made arrangements to pay a reasonable rent in return for our renovating and cleaning up the mess.

It meant people from the Mission had to pitch in and help remodel the filthy and run down house. It happened quickly as at times there were crews of twenty or more men and women volunteering to renovate and repair the three story building.

Jack became the captain of the house. They called him the captain as he wore a captain's hat which he had picked up in a thrift store.

A year later, Jack was faced with a situation he had not envisioned. The Pastor of a church in a better part of town, asked if we could manage to take a convict into our dormitory and have him work in the Mission and go to the Bible College. At a staff meeting there was a lot of discussion but the Pastor from the church answered every concern. According to him this man was not violent but he did need supervision.

The proposal had to go through the courts as he was serving time in a Correctional Centre.

The Senior Pastor attended the court hearing and assumed responsibility for the man's actions and his supervision.

Jack told me he was quitting if convicts were going to be placed in his care. I encouraged him to stick in there and see what this man was like. I reminded him of all the nice people we visit during the prison ministry. He agreed that most of them are decent and just needed another chance.

When Tim came to the Mission, Jack and I were pleasantly surprised. He was one of the men we had visited on our last three visits at the prison ministry. Jack was ready to welcome him and make him part of the family of God.

Tim only had a year and a half left in his sentence. During that time he learned to play the guitar and sing gospel songs. He also enrolled in the Bible College. The study was not all new to him as he had belonged to the church whose minister had him sent to our ministry. He settled in and learned a great deal as our teaching is in depth and enlightening to those who take it seriously.

His time at the Mission and the Bible College went by without any problems. I learned from him that he was raised in an affluent home and had connections with some well known and respected people in the city.

I also learned that his crime was the result of his association with persons who tricked him into making big money illegally. He served his time for the crime.

Upon serving his sentence, he went back to the jail to be officially released.

When the Senior Pastor posted a notice on the bulletin board stating that a Bible College was enrolling students for September, I asked if I could enrol. He smiled and told me that I would be most welcome. I had gone to church for years but I had never gone to Bible College.

Jack also came to the Bible College for a short time and was given the role of pastor in training. With Jack, it was all or nothing at all. He accepted Jesus as Lord of his life and was filled with the Holy Spirit. Shining his light for all to see.

He couldn't wait to be baptized, which happened in the ocean one cold December day. There was a big celebration. All the students and some members of the Mission came to see Jack go under the water and come up a new person. His mother and brother attended along with an aunt and uncle and two cousins. It was a reunion for Jack and his family. Six of his street kids came. They were introduced to all who were present.

At the Mission, after the baptism, a big meal was served and everyone congratulated Jack.

Jack made a full commitment to the Mission and College. After a year of Bible College, he became a preacher and took over the responsibility of scheduling the preachers for the morning services. He was totally devoted to this ministry.

I have shared many memorable experiences with Jack.

On a field trip to a small city, Jack decided he would do his own ministry. He gathered the children and the teens together and had a fun day. He enlisted our help in preparing games the kids could play. This took ingenuity as our materials were limited. I made a list of things that could be gathered in the community and in the wilderness area adjacent to the church in which we were staying on our outreach. It was called a treasure hunt. The children and teens were in groups of three. It was not new to the kids so my instructions were few.

My wife made a board game and they had to spin a bottle and act out what it pointed to. There was lots of laughing as some had to act like clowns and others had to act like preachers and teachers, other like they were riding a horse or walking a tight rope.

Jack drew a picture of a monkey. The kids were blindfolded and had to pin a tail on the monkey.

Later, Jack gathered the kids together and told some Bible stories. They were given Bible verses to memorize. A candy was given to those who memorized and to those who made an attempt at memorizing even one or two verses.

It was always fun to work with Jack as he drew people to him and treated them with respect and dignity.

In the morning, he did his exercises which included a five mile run. I joined him for the exercises but I could only do a one mile run to begin with.

At meal times being a six footer and muscular, he had a good appetite. People smiled when at breakfast he would eat porridge, six eggs with lots of toast and coffee.

It was always pleasant when Jack was on an outreach.

Another time we went to a native reserve. Those who attended the service were the older members of the community. Jack would form a small group or go one on one and charm those who were in his presence.

We ministered together for a few years, while he was getting his life together. He was always busy as people asked him to come and help when they were in trouble or in difficult situations.

He adopted a family which was often in crises. There were four young sons and a daughter. He became their uncle and their best friend.

In the middle of the night or anytime, the mother of these children would phone Jack and ask for his help to solve their marital or financial problems.

Jack told me that her husband was hanging around with prostitutes. His wife told Jack that these young prostitutes gave her husband favours as he had no money. I didn't want to know all the details, but Jack unloaded them on me.

Here is a thirty-three year old man fooling around with prostitutes and defiling his marriage. His wife is asking a nineteen year old boy, Jack, to intervene and straighten out their marital and financial problems.

The miracle is that the problem with the prostitutes was resolved as a result of a lot of prayer and intercession. The man admitted his mistake and asked forgiveness. He went so far as to ask if he could come to Bible College and prepare for ministry.

Jerry did come to the Mission and Bible College for three years. He played the guitar and led worship. He stopped drinking and was good to his wife. It was great to see a person give up their earthly desires and desire to serve the Lord.

Jack kept working in their lives. He would drive the family to the Mission. The kids liked the hot dogs and the juice. They would line up to get two or three hot dogs as they were often hungry.

This family lived in native housing which is very nice and affordable.

Upon first year graduation and being commissioned, which means sent out, Jerry started a house church in the native housing complex. He gathered a number of families together and taught them what he had learned at the College. He also enlisted the help of Jack to come and teach. His house church flourished and grew.

God worked mightily through the ministry of Jack, and those who prayed that there would be a change in Jerry's life. God worked a radical change in his life.

He not only had his house church but he also ministered in the Mission.

His is another story.

Jack and I had fun together as there was always something new and often strange and different as we ministered at the Mission.

Jack took me to where his young street kids hang out. He introduced me to Shadow, who was taking his place as their protector. He was sixteen and already a man in charge of younger and older people on the street. They didn't frequent skid row but hung out in a different part of the city.

I had the privilege of talking to the kids he hung around with. Most of them were running from abusive or controlling homes. Some are as young as thirteen and fourteen years old, living on the street and on the run from the authorities. If they are caught they will be sent to foster homes or detention centres.

I was asked to take a fourteen year old girl to the hospital as she had a terrible cold. Jack was working and I had a car which they needed. The group was afraid her cold might turn into pneumonia and she would die.

It made me sad to know that they often slept in buildings with no heat or water.

I witnessed how they lived in abandoned buildings. I figured I'd do this young girl a favour and have her returned to her parents.

While she was waiting for the doctor to diagnose the degree of her cold, I spoke to a nurse. She told me that she had no authority to send her home. She gave me the phone number of a social worker.

I called and told the social worker her story. The worker explained that the girl would run and avoid treatment if she knew what I was doing.

She did tell me she would try to intervene, but she had to be careful.

The boy, Shadow, was waiting with the girl. He asked me what I was doing talking to the nurse and using the phone? It put me on the spot. I had to tell the truth. I told him I was concerned for the welfare of the girl and her living on the street.

He told me bluntly, "Esther is not going home. Her father sexually abuses her." He went on to tell me to mind my own business.

I nodded in agreement and after the girl was admitted to a ward, I went back to the Mission.

That night, Jack was giving the message. I was there in charge of the service. A man, who was under the influence of alcohol, came into the Mission. He started speaking out and disrupting the service. I moved over and asked him to be quiet and have some respect for God's house.

For some reason, he took offence to Jack's preaching, or more than likely it was to the Word of God which convicted him. I kept asking the man to be quiet. He motioned for me to get lost.

Finally, he stood up. I thought he was leaving. Instead, he picked up a chair to throw at Jack. He had the chair over his head. I backed off in case he would throw it at me. All the volunteers and members were praying that he would come to his senses and put the chair down.

The man pulled the chair further back over his head, lost his balance and came tumbling backwards, sprawled on the floor, with chairs banging and clanging.

Amazingly, Jack never skipped a word of his sermon.

Some young guys ushered the man out the door..

After one year at the College downtown on skid row, Jack enrolled in the more prestigious Bible College. His credits were transferred to the new Bible College as our College is affiliated with the Prestigious Bible College. Both belong to the same denomination.

This more prestigious Bible College's fees are astronomical as compared to the fee of five dollars a week at the downtown east side Bible College.

Our tuition fees are low because we operate in a low and sometimes no income area. Students who cannot afford tuition fees are often subsidized by supporters of the College.

Jack got a job to support himself. He worked as a cleaner in a dealership.

Hard manual labour for four years.

Jack was not satisfied with anything lower than an 'A' in every subject.

He kept active in the Mission, taking on responsibilities he had time for.

Quite often he would phone me up and ask if I could cover for him at the Mission or at the College as he had an essay due or was studying for an exam. I never refused as I knew how much his studies meant to him.

During this four year period, Jack preached every week and was given teaching assignments in the Bible College downtown; as long as they didn't conflict with his studies.

Being in leadership, he attended counsel meetings and was on the Board of Directors. By now he was well versed in the operation of the Mission and the College. He brought forward new ideas which were related to his research at the prestigious College. A few of them were acted upon and made a difference. As a result we set up counselling as an ongoing part of the ministry.

Upon graduation at the prestigious college, we were invited to attend his going out ceremony. Compared to our graduation ceremony, it was much more formal. A number of people from our downtown College and some former graduates attended. Jack's contingent was the loudest and most boisterous when Jack received his diploma.

People at the other tables laughed when they saw how happy our group was and how informal

The fact that Jack worked so hard and finally achieved his goal, gave great joy to those who cared so deeply for him.

His ordination, a short time after graduation, was cause for another celebration. This one took place at the Mission. His mother and brother attended along with his father and other relatives and friends. Everyone was interested in his future.

Jack forgave his father and visited him as often as he could. His mother was forced to move away from the marriage and his father was all alone.

Most had hopes that Jack would go into the ministry and they could then be part of his congregation.

Jack was also encouraged to do a Youth Ministry as he was in his early twenties. He had worked with the teen ministry, which our Mission conducted in another part of the city. It was also a tough area with lots of crime and youth gangs.

The reports from that ministry indicated that the kids loved Jack and the program. Jack told us point blank that he didn't like working with teens.

"They're a bunch of brats who need a good kick in the butt," Jack stated.

Having missed out on that ministry, we were looking forward to his planting a church on a reserve or in a small town. We have had many denominations ask for our graduates to plant churches or be associate pastors or youth pastors.

When we put planting a church to Jack as a ministry, he told us that wasn't his calling.

He said he liked small group Bible studies, which he was part of for years before graduation. He told us he wanted an informal setting for his ministry.

We gave him the green light to do a house ministry or whatever he was called by God to do.

The next year, Jack met a lady, a legal secretary, who loves him and they were married.

Now that Jack had the responsibility of supporting his wife and future family, he had decisions to make. His wife had a career and he had only a few pieces of paper saying he was a graduate of a prestigious Bible College and that he was an ordained and licensed Pastor.

My wife and I had Jack and his wife over for supper and talked. He knew that I had been a teacher in the public school system. He asked me what I thought of his becoming a teacher. I reminded him that he told us he didn't like kids. He corrected me and told me he didn't like teens. He went on to say he'd like to teach grade three or four.

I told him if that was his dream and his calling, go for it.

He enrolled in university the next semester.

I kept in touch and he told me how happy he was, and how grateful he was to his wife for supporting him during the four years he was going to university.

He is now a teacher in the Pubic School system teaching at the elementary level.

They are the parents of a beautiful daughter. We are still in touch but we are both busy. Jack has his Bible study group and plans on having a House Church when he is more settled in his teaching career.

He told me he needed to get enough money together to buy a big house and open it up to those who need an informal church setting. He plans to give them enough spiritual information so that they can make a decision for Christ as their Lord and Saviour, and also do a ministry of their own.

Jack went from being a Street boy, hustling on the streets and getting into trouble with alcohol and drugs, to an ordained minister and teacher.

A radical change in his life. All this because of the Mission which took him from the streets and brought him to Christ.

The Bible College gave him a start in his quest for more knowledge and understanding of the word of God. He learned biblical truths and spiritual doctrines.

His life has been radically changed for the better and has been blessed by God Almighty.

CHAPTER TWO

BEN

Gang Member

Romans 1:6,7, "And you also are among those who are called to belong to Jesus the Christ. Grace and peace to you from the Lord Jesus Christ."

On an outreach into the interior, we met BEN. He was in a smaller city at a Mission similar to ours.

We did a few services at this Mission and told those present about our Downtown Eastside Mission, Bible College and Christian dormitory. Some of the students on the outreach gave their testimony which drew Ben to our group.

Ben was impressed by our students and their commitment to Christ Jesus. He told me that he would like to come and live in our dormitory and go to College.

At a service in the small city Mission, Ben gave his testimony which really rocked everybody. There were only the College students and thirty or more men and women from the street who heard his testimony.

He explained that he was the son of a Roman Catholic priest who fell in love with a nun and got married. This marriage was against the rules of their church.

Ben told how he was raised in an overly religious home.

He stated that he sort of believed in a God and he often heard the name of Jesus Christ spoken in the home but he really didn't connect. It was like something surreal and far out. He blamed his father for this disconnect as his father tried to force his beliefs and values on him."

He told in his testimony, "When my mom and dad had prayer times, which happened five or six times a day, I had to be there and give up any opportunity of being on a school team or engaged in any club or outside activities. I felt like a stranger in my own home. For some reason, they felt I should be a priest to make up for their short comings," he stated, and thought for a moment.

"Being a priest, like my father, turned me off completely. He read his Bible continually and then turned around and gave me a rough time. I wondered where he got permission in the Bible to turn on his own son and take away all his privileges and his right to choose his friends.

When I complained to my mother, she'd backed up my father and tell me it was my fault that there was friction in the family. It got to the point where I didn't want to associate with my mother or my father.

The only freedom I had was when I was at school. I used this freedom to get into trouble. Not bad trouble but I was sent to the principal's office for minor infractions of the rules. When I turned up at the office, the vice-principal would say, "Not you again, Bennie? What did you do this time?" I'd tell him, "Nothing, really. The teachers like to pick on me." He'd laugh and try to lecture me and give me his best advice. He'd ask, "Do you want me to give you my best advice?" I'd tell him he could give me anything he liked. He'd tell me to smarten up and get my self in gear. Take control of my life and get a career. I'd thank him for his advice and go and do the same stupid things over again and again.

After school, I'd hang with some neat guys. They got me smoking and if they could get into their father's liquor cabinet, we'd get bombed, stinking drunk," he smiled at the thought.

"One day, I made the mistake of going home before I was completely sober. Alcohol gives a person the ability to say what they think regardless of the outcome. I told my father and my mother exactly what I thought of them, pointing out their faults and their weaknesses. At the time, I thought I was doing them a favour, letting them know what I thought. I was grounded for a month.

This led to my idea of leaving home and being on my own.

In rebellion, I dropped out of high school in grade eleven.

I thought I had hit it lucky when I was on the street and talked to this guy in a black leather jacket. I admired his jacket and wanted to know what the badges and patches represented.

He took a liking to me and invited me to a restaurant for coffee and something to eat. He asked me where I was staying. I told him wherever I could find a place to lay my head. He invited me to stay at his apartment until I could get some cash together and get on my own.

He warned me about staying on skid row. He told me I'd end up either dead or with my head so screwed up from drugs, I'd be a zombie.

Because I wasn't working, he gave me a few jobs; like going to the bank to deposit money and things like that. I began to learn the ins and outs of the rackets. It didn't matter to me if it was legal or illegal.

I stayed in the gang and was accepted as one of the bright and rising stars," he smiled

"The leader of the gang taught me new tricks and ways of making it big. They trusted me as I still had my Christian values and perspectives with regard to being honest and trustworthy. This impressed them as they didn't trust many people in the Motorcycle Gang. I was able to move up in the organization quickly as I didn't cheat, lie or steal.

I find it hard to believe that I stayed with them for over fifteen years. Making big money and spending nearly all my money. I kept a couple of thousand in the bank for a rainy day.

The hundreds of thousands of dollars I made went down the drain. Drinking, partying, hanging with women and anything I desired and I could pay for.

I stayed in the gang for a number of years, seeing things which I wasn't able to tell about. I was involved in a numbers racket, in drug delivery and other dealings. They had prostitution under their control and related activities, which I managed. I didn't agree with everything I was forced to do, but I had no choice as I was part of the gang.

One thing I resented was when they made me be present when hits (killings) were carried out.

At first it made me ill, but it was only when they told me why they had to make the hit, that I understood.

I was told, "He's a wise guy, causing trouble, see. He's got to go."

The crunch came when they told me I should make a hit on a member of another gang.

I knew the procedure. What to say and how to get the guy to own up to what he had done. I rehearsed it over and over in my mind. The problem was I knew the guy that was taking the hit. He was a young guy with too much ambition. He tried to branch out on his own. Start his own gang. That was not the way it's done if you wanted to stay alive.

Our gang always had a drink at a bar before making a hit. The alcohol took the edge off of what was to transpire.

I knew the bar we were going to. We hung out there, and many deals came down over the years in that bar. It was there that we celebrated deals which made thousands and at times millions of dollars in dirty money.

I thought about what I should do. I planned to run. I knew it would involve money so I withdrew all my savings.

I had to get out of this deal. I couldn't make the hit. I still had some Christian values which had been instilled in me by my mother and father.

Before we went to the bar, I phoned a taxi and told him to wait at the side of the bar we were attending. I gave him the time to be there. He knew me as I used his taxi quite often and gave him big tips.

I drank a few drinks, then went to the washroom at the back of the bar. From there I slipped out the back door and ran to the side of the bar and got into the taxi and was on my way.

I got to the airport and booked a flight on the next plane out. Fortunately, there had been a cancellation in first class and I filled that seat. It took me to a smaller city. I then took the bus to where I am now. And to where I was fortunate enough to meet you guys and girls from a big city Mission and Bible College. You guys are super and I can't wait to go to that city of yours and live with real Christians."

After two weeks, Ben came to live in the dormitory and be part of the Mission and the Bible College. He phoned and I met him at the bus station and drove him to the dormitory.

In the bus station, I noticed that Ben was uneasy and kept looking at the door and scrutinizing all who came into the depot. He also took an interest in all the passengers getting off the Greyhound buses that were arriving.

I asked why he was so uneasy. He told me he always looked behind him for fear of being recognized and killed by the gang. "I have this phobia," he explained.

I understood where he was coming from. I gave him some advice. I told him not to give that same testimony at the Mission and not even at the Bible College. It's a great and interesting testimony, but you could be in big trouble if the wrong person acts on it in order to make money by turning you over to that gang or an affiliate.

Ben nodded and told me he understood.

Ben came to the Mission and really enjoyed the service. He told me later that this is what Christianity is all about. Having fun and enjoying each other and doing something for others, rather than cloistering yourself and praying aloud ten times a day.

"My parents keep telling God how great He is.

God knows He's great, you don't have to tell him every hour or so. And you don't have to tell God how horrible you are. He knows your thoughts before you think them. For sure he knows my thoughts, but they're changing for the better from now on."

I understood where Ben was coming from. He was still resentful toward his parents. I knew he needed some inner healing and some love and affection.

Ben enrolled in the Bible College. He was not new to the scriptures. There was a carry over from his early training at the hands of his father and mother. Still, there were new things to learn and a great atmosphere in which to learn them.

The students were always caring for each other and interested in what others thought on the topics being taught.

Ben was most interested in the Historical books of the Old Testament. He told the class that his Father was so fixated on his breaking the vows of his church that he focussed on forgiveness and repentance rather than on the lives of the great patriarchs, who are found in the Old Testament.

He started by naming a few. "I particularly like Abraham and Jacob and Joseph. I also like Samuel and David, Isaiah and Ezekiel to name a few." He got bogged down as there were so many men and women in Old Testament times that intrigued him. He came to the conclusion that we can learn a great deal from the mistakes and accomplishments of those who are committed to God Almighty.

A couple of students shared his conclusions and added that we can learn from the lives of others today. Even those in our own community. This led to a research project. Each student was to become aware of and write an essay on a person in our country or in our community who is making a difference in the lives of others.

Ben told of how this love and concern for each other was completely different from his life which was so steeped in crime and debauchery. He agreed that his life was a perfect example of a life gone wrong.

He then told the class, "My life was a mess, but now I'm on the right path. I knew all along that God had a plan for my life, but I stifled God's plan when I got running with the devil Now the devil is under my feet and I'm running along the path of righteousness."

There were many, Halleluiahs and amens.

After class, the students all came and shook the hand of Ben and offered congratulations.

Ben did his stint with putting up the chairs in the Mission. He also swept and mopped the floors. From there he was promoted.

Ben worked in the kitchen and did what he was taught to do by the head of the kitchen. He dealt with people from the street with caring and concern.

He needed the kitchen to be clean and organized. He was always wiping and scouring. The person in control of the kitchen was a bit messy, but one of the better students in the College..

Ben had compassion for those who came to the Mission for food. Soon he was breaking the rules in order to make the people from the street happier.

The street people knew he was breaking the rules by giving refills and giving extra goodies to those he knew and was friendly with.

His stint in the kitchen ended when he took a box of Christmas candies and let the men take as many as they wanted. He had been told to give four to each person. Some got twenty or more and others were left without any. This caused jealousy and rebellion among those from the street. It led to a fight when one man demanded that another man give him what he thought was his share.

I was in the office and heard the shouting and name calling. The head of the kitchen and a helper came banging on my door.

When I heard the accusations and the list of misdemeanours levelled at Ben, I had to step in and ask Ben to move away from the kitchen.

Like many of the students, Ben had bought a guitar and was learning to play and sing. I told him to practice his guitar for a few days until the hostilities blew over.

Three days later, I assigned Ben to his new duties. I made him the maintenance man of the Mission and the College. He told me he had no idea how to use a hammer or a screwdriver. Ben lamented, "I can't do plumbing, carpentry or electrical maintenance."

I told him he only had to ask for help, with an announcement from the pulpit. The men who come off the street will help you if they have the skills and have the time."In that way you watch them and you will learn."

When we ask for such help, we always find someone who has these skills. They're usually happy to put in a few hours for the Lord.

The first project that Ben took on was putting a half door at the entrance to the kitchen and wash rooms He made an announcement asking for someone to help. A laid off carpenter, told him he would help but he needed a skill saw. Ben asked me where he could get a skill saw.

I had one at home and thought twice about it but I offered to bring it down the next day. That day, I was disturbed by the whining of the skill saw and the pounding of hammers. I went out to look and to my surprise the door was almost ready to hang. Ben told me they needed a couple of more cuts of the saw and a bit of sanding and painting.

Two days later, I heard through the grape-vine, that my skill saw had been stolen from the men's dormitory. Ben didn't tell me and neither did anyone else from the dorm. I wrote it off as something that happens on skid row. If it isn't locked up or nailed down, it will be lifted and sold for the purchase of drugs. Ben finished his first year and was commissioned.

At the graduation ceremony he was all smiles. He kept repeating, "I'm commissioned. I can't believe it. I'm really commissioned to go out and preach and teach and lay hands on the sick and they will get well."

Roy teased and asked, "Are you going to pick up rattlers and drink poison?"

Ken laughed, "Not likely."

Ben worked hard and completed his second year.

The time went by quickly. Thanks to Ben and his crew, the Mission was repainted, the tiles were replaced and it was refurbished. It was definitely in much better shape after Ben got though renovating and rebuilding.

He also took his duties as maintenance man to the dorms and did what was necessary to make them safer and looking brighter and cleaner.

By the end of the second year, Ben was able to play the guitar and he had learned a number of gospel songs. Many he heard sung by other worship leaders. He was always asking for the words to gospel songs he liked and wanted to learn.

He was now a pastor in training, which meant he was called upon to preach and keep order in the Mission. He was also learning administrative skills necessary in the operation of a church and a mission.

Ben was able to give up drinking and drugs, but try as he might he couldn't quit smoking. He was encouraged to do so by all the staff and by many of the volunteers, but it was not possible.

He asked me if smoking would interfere with his ministry. I told him it might cost him a few postings, but I didn't know God's plan for his life.

During the second year he took a liking to Becky, a student who had started at the Mission and College the same year he did. There is more to his story in the next chapter..

CHAPTER THREE

BECKY

Victim

Revelation 21:3, "Now the dwelling of God is with men, and He will live with them. They will be his people and God himself will be with them and be their God."

Becky came to the Mission and Bible College after going through a terrible ordeal. She told about this ordeal in her testimony to the Mission and added some more when she gave her testimony at the Bible College.

"I grew up in a home where I was given no knowledge and understanding of the Bible, or of God and Jesus. The only time I heard these names was in cursing and swearing," she laughed.

"Everything in the Mission and the College is new to me. In the College others know what the teacher is taking about, but I have to learn so much. Every day I marvel at the greatness of God Almighty and the Lord Jesus the Christ. See, I've learned a lot in these two weeks. She laughed he infectious laugh.

My one regret is that I can't pass this great knowledge on to my husband.

If I had known what I know today about the great and mighty God we serve, and our Lord Jesus the Christ, things might have been different in our marriage and in our relationship," she paused to think.

"When my son was born, the doctor told us he'd have to have open heart surgery to close a hole in his heart. It couldn't happen until he was over two years old. Those were two grief filled years watching my son suffer and knowing any day he might die.

I brought him down to the Children's Hospital. He had to stay for four months. I didn't understand why, but the doctors found another problem and they had to wait to do more surgery.

I wanted to cry out for help. I was so lonely living down here and not knowing hardly anyone. The ones from my reserve, who live down here, are those who party and do drugs and stuff.

I got in touch, with a couple, but I wasn't interested in their life style. They partied a lot and gossiped, played bingo and were lazy.

The only people I could talk to were the parents of other children in the hospital. We stayed with our children most of the day. The nights were long and lonely.

When Jason was to be released, I thought we'd go home by bus. I found out that the trip took fourteen hours. I knew it wouldn't be possible.

By plane it was much faster.

The problem was there would be a five hour wait for the bus to take us home to our village.

I phoned and asked my husband to come and pick us up, but he was working that shift. I called my father and he came to drive us the sixty miles home.

Jason was so pleased to see his grandpa, but he couldn't understand where his father was. He really loves his father," she smiled, remembering.

"You might wonder why I slur my words to the point where many people can't understand me. Also why I drag my right foot. And why I can't write with my right hand.

On the way home, about thirty miles out of town, a farm truck came out of a crossing and hit the back end of our car. It careened us over into the next lane where a car hit us broadside.

I was knocked unconscious and was in a coma a for a week or more. When I came out of the coma I didn't understand why I had casts on my arm and leg and why I was in traction. I felt terrible pain in my legs and feet. My right hand and arm had been broken and I had a terrible head ache.

I still get sharp pains but they're not as frequent.

The doctor told me I had fourteen broken bones which were healing nicely. I was thankful to be alive. My husband and Jason came to visit a few times.

When the accident happened, Jason was in a car seat and had minor injuries. Glass from the broken window cut his face and his hands but they were healing.

My father got the worst of it and he is now in a wheelchair. I knew this would be devastating for him as he loves to hunt, fish and pick wild berries.

I was told I'd have to stay in the small city for a few months as I would need rehabilitation therapy and would have to learn to walk and talk all over again. You think its bad now, but you should have seen me and heard me speak before therapy. The worst thing that came as a result of the accident is that my husband looked at me and was not able to love this invalid he saw in a wheel chair. He told me he wanted to remember me as I was before the accident. In my slurred speech I told him I was the same person. He couldn't understand my talking. He shook his head and walked away taking my son with him.

He went to live with his brother on another reserve. I had to go to court to get visiting rights to see my son.

When I came out of rehabilitation, I went and lived with my parents as my husband's house was taken by the band office and given to another family. I had nothing left to live for. I was lonely and the village kept reminding me of the past. I decided I had to leave and make a new life for myself.

A woman in my village told me about this Mission on skid row. She told me how the people who ran the Mission welcomed her and set her straight. "They preached to me and gave me the facts," the woman explained.

"I'm here and have been for a few weeks and all she told me has come true.

It's been a slow process, this healing, but some day I'm going to preach and sing and dance," she said in her slurred speech.

People clapped and were moved by her testimony.

She added, "Now I have Jesus and His Father, who will comfort me and bring joy into my life.

I know that I'm responsible for my own happiness. I don't need a husband who doesn't love me and looks at me with pity. I don't want anyone to pity me. I'm OK and I'm a whole person who is in recovery."

Becky laughed her infectious laugh and everyone was relieved as they thought they should give her special attention. Now they knew they could treat her as one of the family of God.

Becky took her place in the kitchen where everyone starts. It's a good place to meet people and hang out. There's lots of work but with many hands its not slavery.

She could only serve with her left hand but she didn't let that stop her.

At a counsel meeting there are sometimes extra tasks which are filled by volunteers. Every time one of these jobs was put forward, up went the hand of Becky.

She loved to do whatever she could for the Mission and the Bible College.

She became a delight to work with as she always wore a smile. Her laughter came spontaneously as she was filled with the joy of the Lord and gave thanks to Jesus in all circumstances.

Her first year went by quickly. She learned to adjust to the life of a student. There were essays and sermons to write as well as learning to play the guitar and sing gospel songs which were new to her.

She was given the honour of giving the acceptance speech at graduation. By now her speech was almost understandable.

The speech, at graduation, was interspersed with bouts of laughter and some side comments, which were humourous.

During summer break, Becky went back to visit her aging parents. She had visiting rights to her son. Her sisters and brothers had families and she got to know her nieces and nephews. She still missed her husband.

They met and had a long talk. She told him about the Mission and the Bible College. He apologized for moving away from their marriage. She forgave him as she knew that was necessary for her future development as a Christian.

I learned all about her summer. We had a long talk after she returned to begin her second year at the College. She brought some smoked salmon for my wife and a souvenir for me. It's a hand carved small replica of a paddle based on what they use to propel their canoes. I keep this in a place of honour in my office.

In November of that second year, it was put forward at a Counsel meeting, that we should open the Mission all night for people from the street. It came from the students who had compassion for men and women who had to sleep out on the street in the freezing cold of winter.

We had instituted such a measure before. It wasn't that successful.

Becky was one of the chief proponents. She was backed up by a number of students including Ben,who wanted to take part in the project.

I was not agreeable as we didn't have the proper equipment such as floor mats, blankets, pillows and washroom facilities for both men and women. However, I did not voice my opposition as I felt that if they wanted it; they had to support it. I told them to hand me a proposal as to how they were going to proceed and what measures they had envisioned to make it a success.

A couple of students told me to advertise it and open the door. "We can take it from there," they stated.

I told them we must know where we're going and how we will get there. I received the proposal and went over it with a nucleus of six students with Becky as their spokesperson. We had to make a few adjustments, after which I gave them the green light.

There were to be two people on each shift. One had to be a man as we were dealing with mostly men from the street. Becky asked if she could be the third person as she loved to be there to serve. That was vetoed, but she was given visiting rights with the volunteers until two o'clock in the morning. Then she had to go home with an escort for safety.

Becky asked, "What if I don't have an escort?"

"Then you don't visit."

Becky thought that was unreasonable.

They had agreed to serve coffee and sweets until two o'clock and then lights out. They opted to have the doors open all night as some men from the street didn't want to sleep early. I opposed that suggestion, but with a vote it was passed.

Things ran smoothly for the first two months. Those who signed up fulfilled their duties. Every morning a report was written in the day-book telling how many people came in and what problems they encountered, as well as what good things were said about the operation.

I signed for cleanup duty at seven in the morning after the men had gone. Quite often the men weren't gone and I had to wake them up and get them on their way. I was called a few names which I can't repeat, but that was to be expected.

I swept up needles which were used to inject drugs, along with empty wine bottles, dirty socks, empty chip bags cardboard on which they slept and anything that needed to be discarded.

Becky liked it when Ben was scheduled as her partner during the night shift.

The two of them now sat side by side in class. They were comfortable in the company of each other.

After the lesson, they compared notes and discussed what was taught. Ben was by far the superior student as he had had much more biblical instruction at home and in a church setting.

He was very gentle with Becky and never brought to her attention that she was lacking in motor skills or mental ability. He took her hand written essays and sermons, edited them and typed them for her on the computer. He also taught her to play the guitar. They practised after class and were always laughing and joking.

The night shift reports indicated that some people from the street were becoming aggressive. At a counsel meeting, I brought up the matter. Some thought it was not that bad. Becky told the group that they had to be a bit less rigid and treat these people with more respect.

This met with opposition from some who had been cursed, spit on and had things thrown at them. Becky told them to be more loving.

One outside volunteer from another church, asked, "How can you show love to a person who swears at you and calls you names, which I won't repeat." He was asked to repeat the names he was called. He repeated them but they aren't fit for print.

In the Spring of that year, a preacher from the Island came to preach some sermons at the Mission. He was a bachelor looking for a wife. His ministry on the Island was growing and he was in big demand as a travelling evangelist. He stayed at the co-ed dormitory where Becky lived. He engaged her in conversation and took her to dinner at a fancy restaurant. That night he proposed marriage to her.

She was confused. He was older and very overweight. He did not match her idea of a mate for life. Yet she didn't want to hurt his feelings.

The next day Becky was at the door of my office waiting for an interview.

She told me what had happened. Ending with, "What should I do?"

I asked her if she loved him. She said, "No, but I feel sorry for him."

I told her marriages aren't that successful if they are based on pity.

"What can I do?" she asked in exasperation.

"Tell him the truth."

She started to laugh. "It's really silly isn't it?" I agreed.

There was no more dating and no marriage.

Spring was beginning to replace winter. We were coming closer to graduation. The flowers were beginning to open although there was still frost at night.

Becky and Ben were seen walking in the park and spending time together.

The night shift was still happening. There were still a number of men and a few women who came to the Mission to drink coffee, eat and sleep.

I wasn't aware of it, but only one man, Ryan ,came to do his shift. The rule was there had to be two people on duty every night.

He tried to get others to come but all were busy studying for exams.

Things went well until four in the morning, three men came and demanded coffee and something to eat. Ryan told them coffee ended at two. They told him they wanted coffee. He told them he was sorry, "It's the rule."

One man reached across the counter and punched Ryan in the chest. Ryan realized that things were getting out of control. He demanded that they leave. By now people on the floor were beginning to wake up. Afraid that they would join these three in their protest, Ryan reached for the phone to call 911 and get the police.

The one who punched him, reached in and tore the phone wires from the wall. Ryan looked and saw a man take a sawed off baseball bat from his bag. He started banging it on the counter. Ryan told them, "Hang in, I'll put on the coffee." When I read the report, I called an emergency meeting. That ended the night shift.

Becky and Ben, along with all the students, wrote their finals and went into their next years study.

It was interesting to note the changing of one's personality from being in the world to being spiritual. When Ben came into the Mission and the Bible College, we soon realized that he had a short fuse. He would fly off the handle at the least provocation. As he became directed by the Holy Spirit he was more tolerant.

In his third year, Ben was put in charge of the kitchen. He chose Becky as his second in command.

During the third and final year, Ben and Becky started making plans for after graduation. Ben was adamant that he was going to plant a church. Becky felt that she just wanted to be a pastor's wife and support her husband.

Planting a church became a great undertaking for Ben and Becky. In the Mission and in the College, they could be heard planning their lives together.

Both Ben and Becky had applied for ordination. Becky, being a first nations lady, was almost assured of ordination as ordained pastors are needed on many of the reservations.

I was not so sure of ordination for Ben as he had a rather shady past. I was pleasantly surprised when he passed the interview and was granted ordination.

They were really happy to be ordained. They were definitely in love with each other and were getting it all together.

I was not surprised, after Easter, to get the news that they were getting married. Becky asked if I would give her away. I joked and told her, "As long as Ben doesn't give you back."

Ben was with Becky and told me that would never happen. He missed the humour.

They had a minister friend do the ceremony. I agreed and watched them make the arrangements. They came for advice once or twice but for the most part they and the students brought it all together.

The wedding took place with a large gathering of friends and College students, as well as students from previous years.

The wedding took place at the Mission, which was decorated for the purpose. By this time, Becky had learned to play the guitar and sing. Ben and Becky sang a duet and played guitars at their wedding.

After a short honeymoon at a resort town, it was studying for finals.

Ben and Becky told me they wanted to plant a church.

We had been to a small Island town on an outreach and later went to this town for an Easter Rally in the auditorium on the reserve.

They told me that they had fallen in love with this town and the people they had met.

The two of them gathered a team of eight interested persons together from the Mission and the College, to help in the church plant.

I questioned the selection of a few of their team and asked why they had chosen these persons as two had not been to Bible College.

Ben didn't like my interference as to his selection and made it known. I backed off.

I wasn't invited to the new church opening. I guess they didn't want me to rain on their parade.

Becky later apologised and told me Ben was being cruel.

The church flourished for a few years. I heard good reports and was part of the church in that I was the acting treasurer and handled the finances as they were affiliated with our College and we were supporting them.

Ben and I had a few disagreements over how much they had collected and over some of the contributions. I told him I can only record what I have received and record the information he had provided.

Some time later, the team fell apart because of inner turmoil and bickering. Ben and Becky kept the church going by asking for the help of outsiders. But problems began to surface and the church folded.

Ben and Becky kept ministering in house churches on Native reserves. They also had a home church ministry in the house of our contact person. This went on for some years.

Being in a car accident on the highway, coming back from a house church meeting on a reserve, caused complications for Ben. Two ribs were cracked and his right arm was broken. He started to go downhill. His respiratory problems from smoking became more severe.

Over the next few months, his problems became more complicated and his breathing was more difficult. Many inhalers were needed to keep him alive and assist in his breathing .

One evening, Becky heard him coughing but did not respond

"He often has these coughing spells," she told a few of her friends. According to Becky, the coughing stopped abruptly. Ben died and the Lord took him home.

Becky has continued the ministry and is still reaching out to people on the reserves and in the town. Meeting their needs as much as possible.

We have taken outreaches to her town and have been billeted in her home.

She had a marriage proposal from one of our former part time students.

Upon asking others from the College and her friends in the town where she lives, what they thought, she decided to remain a widow.

A widow with a ministry of joy and laughing to cheer up people and bring them to Christ Jesus.

Ben and Becky both overcame many obstacles and were both radically changed by coming to the Lord.

Ben going from escaping religious persecution to becoming a servant of God.

Becky going from no knowledge of a loving Lord and Saviour, to being dependent on Jesus and the Holy Spirit for her joy, peace, and love.

CHAPTER FOUR

CURTIS

Week End Addict

Psalm 15:1 , Lord, who may dwell in your sanctuary? He whose walk is blameless and who does what is righteous and speaks the truth."

CURTIS was a weekend addict. He and his friends would come down to the eastside on skid row on a Friday night to buy their crack cocaine, marihuana, crystal meth or whatever their choice of drugs, and then go home for a drug binge.

Curtis had a good job and was climbing the corporate ladder. He was employed in a dealership and was on salary plus a big commission. He had a good sized bank account and money to burn. It was this money to burn that financed his purchases on skid row every Friday night.

His friends were also well off young men in their early twenties. They were all well educated and upwardly mobile. They came from good homes and parents who did everything for their offspring.

This information came from Curtis in his testimony at the Mission.

He told us when they went downtown on a Friday evening to buy drugs; as a lark, the three of them stood in line and witnessed the Mission in action. They thought it was a gimmick to attract people to the Mission's way of thinking.

He told us that the second time they came to the Mission, they were greeted by Jack and a few young Christians.

"They invited us to become members of the Mission and go to Bible College.

We pretended we were interested, but when we left the Mission we were laughing and joking."

Curtis told us he goofed around by pretending he was a preacher and mocked the way preachers are so serious. He gave an imitation of a hell fire sermon which he had watched on TV. with his girlfriend. His friends laughed and made fun of the pastors at the Mission.

He told us they had no interest in being a member or going to Bible College.

He did tell us that his girlfriend is a Christian and goes to church and is in the choir and teaches Sunday School. "She does all the good things. I go to church with her at times. I keep finding myself falling asleep and needing prodding to stay awake during the service. Mostly it was caused by my coming down from drugs which I did on Friday night and sometimes on Saturday mornings."

Curtis went on to say, "I would tell Ruth I had to work, when really I was at my friends pad getting high," he confided.

"My parents have no connection with the church except when they need it for a baptism, wedding or a funeral.

When I told my girlfriend, Ruth, about our fun down on the street and how we went to the Mission, she was definitely interested. She asked me why I was down on skid row. I told her we were just playing around. Looking for something to laugh at."

Curtis told us,"The next time I came back to the Mission, I came with Ruth. She abhors the use of drugs but she loves me. I think she knows I have a bit of a habit as I've been with her after using. She gets upset but says nothing about drugs, only inferences as to what can happen to someone who is addicted. She's a registered nurse and hard to fool," he smiled

She insisted on my going to Bible College, "I will support you for three years. You can work at the dealership on weekends and at night."

"Here I am, enrolled in Bible College to my girlfriend's delight. But I'm not yet certain I've made the right decision. I need lots of prayer. It's all really new to me and I often wonder why I'm here."

Curtis enrolled and lived in the dormitory. He was one of the brightest students I've taught. Not the most knowledgeable in the scriptures, but very adroit and he has great writing and composition skills.

Curtis got along well with all the students and was happy all the time. He kept his job at the dealership and when he made a sale, he would treat everyone to pizza and pop.

Money was not a problem and he told everyone about his girl friend. He'd jokingly say he was sponging off of Ruth.

When Ruth had three days off work, she joined Curtis in the Bible College, auditing the class and helping Curtis with his homework and tutoring him in scriptural interpretation. They made a perfect couple.

She wanted to do more witnessing, so the two of them often went to the street after the Mission service to hand out goodies and to answer questions and share the gospel.

I was surprised at the spiritual growth Curtis displayed.

On the street, if he didn't have the answer to a question, he'd look to Ruth and she would answer or tell them she'd find the answer. A few times Curtis would run into the Mission and ask me questions about some topic. I had to be sharp in order to answer all his questions.

It was the ploy of some men from the street to go to the Old or New Testament and find the name of some remote person and ask what the students knew about that man or woman.

At times, I wasn't sure of the answer myself. I felt it wasn't necessary to search and find out that they were referring to the name of a person in a genealogy or in a crowd.

The students got onto this form of badgering, they told the person they would try to find the answer for them. That ended the game.

Curtis quickly learned to reverse the question and ask the street person what they knew about that particular person.

Curtis's biggest problem was that he had an incurable disease which at times laid him up with real pain and suffering for days and weeks at a time. We prayed for him and were happy when the pain subsided and he was once again active in the Mission and Bible College.

On week-ends he would travel to the suburbs to be with his girlfriend and visit his buddies. He'd also work at the dealership on Saturdays.

Fortunately, he never again joined with his friends on their weekend drug blasts.

At one time, upon returning from a weekend in the suburbs, he confided that he was really concerned about his friends. "They don't seem to get it," he said.

"I keep telling them they're on the path of destruction as the Bible says. What else can I do for them?"

I told Curtis we should pray for them and if possible bring them down to the Mission and let others witness to them. He told me he'd already asked them to come down, but they're too busy with their jobs, their drugs and getting high.

I advised him to take someone like Jack to visit them in the suburbs and between the two of you they might get the picture that what they're doing is dangerous to their health and well being. It could damage their career and their whole life. Curtis went back to the dorm feeling sad.

The Bible College goes on outreaches to give the students an idea of the types of ministry that are taking place in various parts of the country. We were planning an outreach to the small city where we met Ben and then continuing on to other small towns and cities in a fruit growing area of the country. It was harvest time and we felt it would be nice to have the students pick fruit and taste really fresh, ripe fruit from the trees in the orchards.

Ruth raised a red flag as far as Curtis was concerned. She told us if he had an attack when we were travelling, he would need to go to a hospital for a few days. Upon talking to Curtis he said he'd just have to go to a Motel or Hotel for a short time.

I felt it was necessary for Curtis to sign a release form so that the College would not be held responsible for any problems that might arise.

At a Counsel meeting it was agreed that all students should sign such a disclaimer.

Curtis was eager to go on the outreach. He told me his problem was controlled by drugs and he felt there was no need to worry. "I can feel an attack coming on for days before the big bang sets in," he informed me.

I have seen him laid up and holed up for days, in excruciating pain. I wasn't certain we should take him, but he insisted and almost broke into tears when I asked him if he thought he should stay home.

There were no other snags, so we set out on our seven day trip. At that time Ben and Becky were in their third year and this would be their final outreach. For some it was their first outreach and for others it was their fifth or sixth. Regardless, they were all having fun and looking forward to each stop over.

Christians are known for their hospitality and they displayed it when the bus pulled up in towns where we were spending the night and doing an arranged service. There were happy people wanting to feed the students and show their love. The students mingled and soon had the people laughing and joining in the fun.

We always had a program planned for each evening. The students put it together and everyone loved to listen to the worship in song. For many of the sponsors, the Gospel songs were new, but they listened to the words and were impressed.

The third night, Curtis was scheduled to give the sermon. I was interested to learn what his topic might be. He spoke on overcoming. I knew he was still concerned for his friends in the suburbs. It was a great sermon. He pulled it together telling how people in the Mission and Bible College had overcome great difficulties which made a major difference in their lives and the lives of others

He challenged all present to pray to God for the power to overcome and make a difference in the world. He told how the students had made a great sacrifice of time and resources in order to come to places like this and bring the good news of the gospel and show love and concern for God's people.

After the service, many came to him and to other students and thanked them for their commitment. One older man came to talk to me. He shook his head and asked me where we came up with such great young people. I told him on the skid row of a large city. He told me that was impossible. I then explained, telling him about the Mission and the Bible College. He told me we'd just made history. I told him God works in his town just as hard as He works on the streets of the big city.

We got back from the outreach without one problem. Curtis was fine and was ready to go on the next outreach. He asked me if Ruth could come on the next outreach. I told him we would have to take that request to the counsel.

Many times Ruth would come to the Mission and would go out on the street with Curtis to witness to the men and women who were wandering around lost in their sins and their addictions. Curtis and Ruth prayed for those who needed prayer and encouraged them to accept Jesus the Christ as their Lord and Saviour.

Curtis graduated and was commissioned after his first year. He became a pastor in training, which thrilled his girl friend. She came to the graduation with her family.

Curtis's school work was graded in the A to A+ range. All was going well. I felt he had great potential as a candidate for ministry. He was already talking about going to the more prestigious college, where our courses are transferrable for credits. His goal was the ministry. He understood addiction and wanted to minister to those in bondage to drugs. He talked about starting a rehabilitation centre, where he could show the love of Jesus to unfortunate souls and bring them into the kingdom of God through Bible studies based on what he had learned.

One Saturday night, Curtis, his girlfriend and two others were on the street praying and witnessing to lost souls. Crowds milled around them. When they were exhausted, Curtis invited his girlfriend to a Chinese dinner. He reached in his pocket to get his wallet and make sure he had enough money to splurge. To his horror, his wallet had been stolen by a pick-pocket. He went into a rant. " How could this happen? It's not fair!" He was beside himself.

I was getting ready to leave the Mission when he came in and told me what had happened. I knew he was upset and deflated. "How could any scumbag pull such a trick. Some of them are inhuman," he complained. He was filled with contempt.

I told him about my power saw and how it was stolen from the dormitory. I also told him how I loaned my bike to a student who said he needed it to get to work as he had no money for bus fare. The next week my students told me he had sold my bike to buy drugs.

The guy who stole my bike quit Bible College because he was too ashamed to come back and apologize. I wanted to tell him I forgave him. I wanted him to come back and repent. But he was gone. He did come to the Mission a few years later and we talked. The bicycle was never mentioned. Once again he disappeared."

I told Curtis, "I could have quit because of my power saw and bicycle."

I went on to tell him,"I would then have missed out teaching people like you. People who have great talent and are needed so badly in the ministry."

By now Ruth was with him and was holding his hand. She told him, "It was wrong, but we know what type of people we're ministering to. Please forgive him and hope he doesn't overdose on drugs bought with all that money. After all, it's just money," she stated.

"What about my credit cards and my other plastic?" Curtis asked.

"I'll help you cancel and get renewals," Ruth responded.

"How could anyone do such a thing when we're trying so hard to help them?"

I offered a twenty but Ruth said she had it covered. She told Curtis she was starved. "Let's go back to the place you like. It's really great food."

Curtis made it half way through the second year. He was the top student academically. His ministry was assured. He decided to go to the more prestigious Bible College and was talking about a master's degree. Ruth told him a Doctor of Divinity was not out of reach.

I'm in touch with this prestigious college which receives our best students and gives them credit for courses completed at our Bible College. I always bring up the names of students who excelled at our College. They thanked me for sending Curtis their way. They called him a very spiritual man and a real scholar with great potential.

Curtis was changed from a weekend addict who fell asleep during the church service to a scholar bent on getting his master's degree and then going to university to get his Doctorate of Divinity

Curtis has been radically changed He went from coming to skid row to buy drugs for his addiction, to using a College on skid row to start his journey as a student in seminar in order to prepare for ministry to lost souls and those in addiction.

CHAPTER FIVE

CINDY

Escaping Violence

1 Peter 1:18,19, "You were not redeemed by corruptible things but with the precious blood of Jesus the Christ."

CINDY came to the big city from another part of the country. The big city was her hope of a better life. She wandered around and did her best to stay out of trouble.

She went through some trials before she came to the Mission.

Two months after arriving in the big city she made it to the Mission.

Cindy was impressed by the testimonies of others. She gave her testimony and told how she came to be in the Mission.

She told us that when she arrived in the big city, she had no friends and was forced, by poverty, into the east end of the city, the skid row. She was in search of other members of her band. She counted on them to help her get established in this new setting.

She did find two older men from her reserve, who were hooked on rice wine and didn't have a dollar between them. She hung with them for two days and realized her life was going down hill

She told us that things happened on the downtown eastside which were as bad as those on her reserve. She informed us that on her reserve, gangs had been formed and there was rivalry which resulted in beatings and killings which scared her. "I had to leave that place or I might have been killed," she shook her head.

"Imagine, all over the country, drugs and other illegal activities are going on," she lamented.

"It was on the street right out there a pimp asked if I would work the streets for him. When I told him, "No!" He was going to beat me up. I ran into a store and told the owner what had happened. He told me to stay away from this end of town.

I couldn't stay away as I still had the hope of meeting someone from my home town who could help me.

I had to survive. I found this sleeping bag on a dumpster in the alley. It didn't smell too bad so I slept in it. At a thrift store I bought a big knife. Any pimp or dealer or whatever who came after me would feel the steel," she laughed.

Earlier, before Cindy came to the Mission, one of the members of the Mission, a first nations man, saw her sleeping on top of the dumpster in the alley.

Addicts shoot up their heroin and smoked their cocaine behind the dumpster where Cindy was sleeping.

Ricky, the mission member, took a cup of coffee and offered it to Cindy. He was startled when Cindy drew a large knife from under her sleeping bag and threatened to cut off his head.

Ricky knew what to expect the next time he visited her. He put coffee and some food at the end of the dumpster, spoke to her in his native language, which she didn't understand, and invited her to the Mission and departed.

This ritual went on for a week or more before she thanked him and asked if he would take her to the Mission.

When at the Mission, she met other First Nation persons and began to mellow. She told us she did meet a lady who came from her reserve. "She works at the Native Centre and invited me to come and visit. I'm going there next week. Perhaps they can help me," she stated happily.

Cindy observed everything that went on at the Mission. She took note of every person and how they fitted into the mosaic.

Later, she told me how impressed she was with the young students. They're not on drugs and they're not rebellious and arrogant. They don't belong to gangs.

She asked me why they were so happy. "You must pay them big money to do all that work and to be happy doing it," she suggested.

I told her they were volunteers and that they went to Bible College. I went on to explain about the Bible College and invited her to join in and make a difference in the world.

She told me her world was much different and she felt she didn't have the education needed to go to College.

I told her to think about it, "We'll help you as much as we can."

Soon Cindy was working in the kitchen and attending nearly every service. Ricky had arranged a place for her to stay.

Cindy began to adapt to the downtown eastside.

Not the sordid side of life on skid row, but a life which helped others and gave them encouragement.

Cindy was approached by a few young female students and asked to join the Bible College. Through the power of persuasion and the promise of success, Cindy came to the Bible College.

She told me not to expect too much as she went to a school on the reserve and didn't learn that much. She told me she was a brat and didn't do her homework or do all the assignments. "I really didn't care for school. The boys acted up and made it hard to hear and understand the teacher at times, so I gave up on it."

I told her she only had to do her best. "Others will give you all the help you need. I'll assign a tutor and you will work with her."

Cindy thought that was a good idea. She was soon absorbed in her studies. I heard her ask others, "Did that really happen or is it from some story book?"

The girls would laugh and tell her it was a miracle written about in the Bible and it really happened.

Cindy attended class as it was a diversion from the street and what she witnessed happening to her native men and women.

She kept asking me why we didn't do something to change the lives of these people who went from one problem to another, not realizing that they were wasting their lives.

I told her our government gives them money each month and the other government gives them more.

Her idea was to cut them off this tribute and make them go to work. I agreed and told her she could make that her goal in life. I told her, "Cut them off welfare, give them a shovel and tell them to go dig a big hole."

Cindy laughed and changed the subject.

Slowly, Cindy made progress in her reading and writing skills. Her essays were done on a computer as her handwriting needed practice.

People liked working in the kitchen with Cindy because she was a hard worker and a pleasant person. At times she would leave her shift in the kitchen and go talk to women who came into the Mission from off the street.

Prostitutes came later in the evening for a cup of coffee, a donut and most of all a place to get warm, as they wore skimpy outfits which gave no protection from the cold weather.

Cindy made it her ministry to talk to these young ladies, and older ones as well and try to get them to leave their profession and make a commitment to Jesus the Christ. She did it in a pleasant manner often laughing and bringing the ladies out of their misery into a happier state of mind.

In another testimony of Cindy's, she revealed some of the stories she had been told by these prostitutes. Things men wanted them to do. It was lurid and beyond what any normal person might imagine. Cindy cringed and told how she would never think of doing such a thing.

Cindy told these prostitutes to say, "NO! I don't do that."

They told her they needed the money for crack cocaine or for crystal meth. This gave Cindy something else to teach these women about getting off of drugs and getting into the Bible.

Cindy began to exhibit her true personality, smiling and being grateful for a new lease on life. She loved to give her testimony and now she used the Bible as her start for a testimony. Her testimony was no longer about her problems but related to her discovery of her Lord and Saviour.

Living and giving on the downtown eastside can be a drain on the pocket book. Cindy was an easy target for the pan-handlers. Their sad faces and emaciated looks got to her.

At times, Cindy ran short of cash. She was too proud to ask for money. She would rather do without.

At one point, Cindy got mixed up with a prostitute she knew from the street and was talked into making easy money.

Cindy later testified to some of the students, "It seemed so easy. I sometimes have the urge, now I could use it to make money. Rachael told me what I must do to protect myself and just pretend its not happening."

Cindy went on to tell the girls, "I thanked her but told Rachael no way. I knew it was against what I believed and what I was studying at the Bible College. The crazy thing is the thought of what Rachael told me kept coming back into my mind again and again. I mentally rehearsed what she told me to do and eventually I thought, just once won't matter.

I then remembered how I ministered to the prostitutes and told them to get out of that life and make something of themselves.

Here I was contemplating on doing the same thing. I rationalized and thought, "I'm not like them. I won't do those horrible things".

I learned about these testimonies from two of the students who asked me to intervene and help Cindy get back on the path to righteousness.

Cindy told two other girls, "After all a man is made for a woman and a woman for a man," she laughed.

"I met Rachael again and she asked me how I made out. I told her I had given it some thought but it wasn't for me. Deep down I knew somehow I was lying as I was harboring those thoughts. I walked the streets at night to see if any man would even look at me. I was dressed in my best clothes and wore high heels.

I nearly fell over when a really good looking young man asked me if I was for sale. I choked up, then remembered what to say. I blurted it out. We went to a hotel and I got prepared and I prepared him. It was over so quickly.

He left and I was alone. I thought I'd feel dirty, but I wished he would have stayed and talked. He was a real gentleman and he smelled really good."

Cindy looked up and asked the girls, "Why did I do it? I know it's wrong."

I told the girls that they should pray for Cindy and encourage her to keep close to her Lord and Saviour and not be tempted by her thoughts.

Her testimonies in the Mission became sessions of crying out to God for forgiveness. Promising God she'd never do anything wrong again.

In the Bible College, she was thrilled to find out what Jesus had done for her. His going to the cross so her sins could be forgiven.

I talked to Cindy and told her what the girls had revealed to me.

She broke down and cried. She asked me if God could forgive her sins. I told her, "If you ask from the bottom of your heart and know that you will not commit that sin again, you will be forgiven. Jesus said, "Go and sin no more."

She was confused and sat up straight.

"I can tell God it won't happen again, but what if I'm really tempted and fall?"

We had a long talk and we both prayed and prayed.

As far as I know, she gave up her life of sin.

Her testimony became how great her walk with Jesus had become. She kept giving that testimony for the two years she attended Bible College.

Although I did hear that she was friendly with some men,

I prayed that her knowledge of Jesus and her love for the gospel would keep her on the right path.

She didn't enrol in Bible College for the third year. She came to the Mission and gave her testimony a few times. She told me she was going home to her reserve for a visit. I didn't see her for a few months.

I later learned that she was not on the reserve, but rather she was working as an escort for a business man who travelled around the world. I talked to her when she came to the Mission. She told me all about her travels and assured me it was strictly business. Laughing, she told me, "He's too old to do it."

I believed her and I put an end to the malicious gossip which started among a few members of the Mission and was leaking into the College.

She once again attended Bible College and seemed to be settling in.

Her testimony was not a crying out to God, nor was it wonder at what Jesus had done or her. Rather it was from the scriptures and a type of preachamony. (Preaching the gospel in her own way.)

Cindy's walk became half and half. Half in the world and worldly and half in the church and spiritual. She had been told in the Bible study courses that a Christian's life cannot be partly for Jesus, but rather, "All for Jesus I surrender, all to Him I freely give."

She married but that only lasted a short time. Her husband is often in the Mission and he asks my help in reconciling their differences. At times, both her husband and Cindy are at the Mission.

Cindy told me she was enrolling in her final year and then she was going to plant a church. She told me she loved children and wanted to do a children's ministry in her village back home on the reserve which is plagued by violence.

"I want to tell them about Jesus and let Him keep them out of the gangs. Keep them from getting stabbed and killed and committing suicide."

I looked forward to her coming to class.

She came for three months and was totally absorbed in the teaching and agreed that what was being taught was just what she needed.

I gathered some information on doing a children's ministry and we went over it together.

Cindy told me she had been in touch with her mother and her sisters and told them she was graduating next spring and would then be doing a ministry on the reserve. She asked them to go to the band council and get permission for her to do this teaching ministry in order to stop the gang violence, the killings and acts of brutality.

Cindy and a few students took on the project of drafting a letter to the Band Counsel and also getting a years school program for children four and five years old ready to teach.

Cindy went from an abandoned person on top of a dumpster, wielding a big knife, to a person who was tempted and overcame temptation and is committing her life to a ministry with children on the reserve. A reserve which is wracked by violence and killings.

Amid her studies and the putting together of her Children's program, she still has time to come to the Mission and be filled through the music and the word.

In the Mission she smiles and is pleasant.

During an altar call, after I preached, she came forward and asked for prayer. I asked if there was anything specific to pray for. She replied, "I need direction." I prayed that the Holy Spirit would keep her on the path of righteousness, and give her direction in order to do her ministry.

At Bible College we often pray for her. She has issues and we all have issues. God has begun a great work in her and will not stop until it is finished. That is our prayer for Cindy.

Cindy has gone from a woman with a knife to a woman with the knowledge of God and the Sword of the Spirit the Word of God, for her weapon. We pray she will be led into a ministry where she can use her gifts, talents and the understanding of the scriptures to bring children and their parents to the Lord.

She has been radically changed by coming to Bible College and getting to know a loving Saviour.

CHAPTER SIX

DAN

Bent On Suicide

1 Corinthians 3:17, "If anyone destroys God's temple , God will destroy him; for God's temple is sacred, and you are that temple."

DAN came from the suburbs and was raised in a middle-class home. He completed high school and went to college. Had a career and a good job. His friends were from his school years as well as some from where he worked.

Three of his casual friends thought it cool to toke up on marihuana. Dan joined in and was soon addicted. He was wanting more highs so he started smoking weed in secret.

His friends from work invited him to a stag party, which turned out to be a binge on cocaine. Dan refused and said he'd stay with a toke of marijuana now and then. The pressure was on him to try one pipe. He finally complied.

Unfortunately, that was not his last. It escalated from there to heroin and crack cocaine. After two years of addiction, Dan had lost his job, lost all his savings and possessions and ended up on skid row.

When he went off drugs for a short time, from lack of funds, he was disgusted and angered at his dependency and wanted his old life back again. He visited some of his friends in the suburbs. They patronized him, but then turned their backs on him as he was an addict and they didn't want him around their families.

He felt their disgust. It was too much for him to bear.

Walking down the Eastside street on skid row, he looked in the window of the Mission and saw a pair of brown dress shoes, shiny and clean. He went in and picked up the shoes. "How much for these shoes?" he asked the pastor on duty.

"They're yours for free if they fit," the Pastor told him.

Dan said, "A man shouldn't end his life wearing a pair of worn out old sandals. There's no dignity in that is there?"

"What's your intention?" the Pastor asked.

Dan looked at his new shoes, smiled and answered, "That big old bridge has a fascination for me."

The Pastor realized he was suicidal. He told Dan he knew someone who would be his best friend and make his life worth living.

Dan was interested. He asked, "Who?"

"His name is Jesus and He loves you," the Pastor replied.

Dan flashed back to his days in Sunday School and at Church camps. He fell to his knees and wept. Amid tears he replied, "I want it all back. I want it so bad I can taste it."

The Pastor told Dan about the dormitory for those who can kick the habit.

" And there's also the Bible College when you're ready."

Dan didn't hesitate and told the Pastor he was ready.

Dan said, "I need what you've got, I really need a friend."

Dan entered the Mission as a volunteer rather than a recipient.

He never quit smiling. His smile was infectious and brought cheer to all he met.

Dan couldn't get enough of the Word of God and he fell in love with Jesus the Christ.

After a month of living in the dorm with other Christians, volunteering in the Mission and going to Bible College, he asked to be baptized.

For Dan, life took on new meaning. He no longer had thoughts of suicide, as life became too precious.

In his testimony, Dan confided,"I was brought up in a good home. My parents are Christians. As I got into my teens, I tried to evade going to Sunday School. It wasn't cool and I felt I could do without it. I did go to Sunday School when I was young, and had fun bugging the teacher and pulling jokes on the other kids. I remember how we would pull the chair away from those who went to the front to recite their Bible verse for the week. They would sit hard on the floor and everybody would laugh. We'd pull the hair of the good looking girls and some would turn and slap us. That's all I remember of the good times at Sunday School except for the names of some of the men who are in the Bible and what they did.

Every year my parents would send me and my sister to summer camp. I liked the swimming and the camp fires at night. I listened to the stories and could imagine myself doing some of the great things the men in the Bible did.

My Dad had the future planned for me. He planned that I would graduate with good marks, go to university and would live in suburbia in a big house, have a beautiful wife and lots of kids. Drive a big car or van and be somebody. Go camping in the summer and enjoy life to its fullest.

What's wrong with that dream? It doesn't include God and Jesus. That's what's wrong," Dan smiled and looked around.

"As I testified before, I became a once in a while junkie. Toking up on bud and getting a buzz. I wasn't aware that I have an addictive personality. When I tried cocaine, I felt so warm, so comforted."

As his teacher, I saw a problem in that part of the testimony. Dan looked too serene as he thought about drugs.

Dan concluded his testimony by telling everyone that he is a new creation and as such he is going to make a difference in people's lives. Dan told us he is going to go to university and become a suicide counsellor and a Christian counsellor.

I overheard a third year student tell another that Dan needed to counsel himself. I wondered what he meant. I surmised it had something to do with drugs, but I saw no real problem.

The next day I asked John what he meant by the statement, "He needs to counsel himself." John told me he had come through the same thing Dan is going through. "He looks great, but deep down inside there's a burning. If you don't put out the fire, it will burn you up," John concluded.

I thanked John for the insight. I put Dan on surveillance. I didn't tell him but I did let two others in on our suspicions and asked them to watch for signs of drug use and abuse.

They were to tell John, our lead guitarist, if they saw any signs.

Dan was now being carried away with the idea that he was going to become a counsellor and help people with drug and suicide problems. He likened it to the way the Mission and Bible College helped him.

He went so far as to go to his parent's home in the suburbs to retrieve his transcripts and have them ready for when he went to the university to enrol.

He gave a testimony telling what transpired when he called his father and asked if he could come home.

The testimony of Dan:

"I hadn't called my parents for months as I didn't want to have them worry about me. I also didn't want them to get their hopes built up knowing I was going to Bible College and then dropping out and going back to my addiction. It's a roller coaster for them and they've been on it before. This time I'm serious and I want that degree in Clinical Psychology so that I can have my own counselling clinic and make a difference for the Lord", Dan paused to reflect.

"When I started up the driveway, I could see my mother in the front window. I waved to her and she quickly opened the door. My father waited in the background. We talked about my sister's kids and about the friends I had and their families. That took what seemed like hours. I wanted to tell them that I was going back to university, but it had to wait.

Finally, I got my turn when my father asked what I was up to. I told him about the Mission and the College. He asked me, "Haven't you had enough of that end of town?"

I told him this was different. "They saved my life down there."

I didn't go into details about how I was going to commit suicide. I told them I needed my High School and College transcripts as I was going to be a counsellor after I finished university.

My dad just shook his head, he didn't believe I was serious. My mother was excited for me. She encouraged me and told me to hang in and not let anything get in my way."

Dan came back from his visit with his transcripts. I asked him how it went. He told me that his parents talked about family and friends. I told them I was going into Christian counselling. The only one negative was when I told them I was still on skid row but in a much different situation. My dad got in a little dig about my not getting off of skid row and the street. I let it go.

"By the way," Dan stated, "Some unfinished business. I heard John say, "You should counsel yourself." No offense taken. Maybe he's right. I want to learn how to counsel others after I counsel myself."

The guys at the dorm. told me how Dan had brought back a lot of pastries.

Freshly baked buns, cakes and pies. Dan was proud of his mother as she was a good cook.

Later, Dan told me he had once taken a few courses in Commerce and wondered if any credits would be transferable to his degree in Clinical Psychology. He mentioned that he was making an appointment with the university to learn what courses were mandatory for a degree.

I got caught up in the euphoria and forgot that there were possible signs of a relapse. From what I had observed everything was fine, but I often miss the little things that can go wrong with recovering addicts.

Two days later, John and Darryl came to my office. I knew this wasn't going to be good news. They had noticed that when Dan was not on his high about counselling, he was showing signs of mental fatigue and strain.

I told them," That's natural when you're planning a new career. One which will change your life."

John told me that Dan had missed curfew twice last week. "I heard him come home around two or three in the morning."

I agreed that this was a bad sign.

Darryl suggested a buddy be assigned to Dan and that we look at intervention.

I asked, "You mean rehabilitation?" Darryl nodded in the positive.

"It's best to err on the side of good judgement and prompt action, rather than procrastination and losing the guy to the streets."

I agreed and had Dan come to the office.

When I came to think about the matter, I remembered thinking, "He is the nice guy we all know, but I knew I had to look deeper."

Dan came and sat down. He asked, "Is it about my going to university?"

I asked how he was doing with his recovery from drugs.

He looked at the floor and knew I was onto something. He admitted to slipping back a little. He said, "My bones ache and my muscles are painful. I needed just one more hit of heroin, to ease the pain," he explained.

I suggested rehabilitation and told him I knew of a Christian run centre. "They have a good success rate in restoring Christians and street people in general to a better way of life."

He took a deep breath and forced himself to say, "Yes, I need it."

He asked, "How long will I be there?" I told him most stay at least six months and some up to two years. As long as it takes.

He asked, "What about my university?"

I told him the university would kick him out if he is caught using drugs.

He nodded, "When will I be going?"

I told him we would work at it together and get him in as soon as possible.

"One more request," he stated." Could I get some books on Psychology and study them while I'm recovering?"

I told him that there were probably many books on psychology at the rehabilitation centre.

I concluded by telling him I'd be in touch with the university and find out what texts are being used in the course. I made a note to remind myself.

I drove Dan to his new home away from home and wished him all the best. We prayed together and I left in peace.

I was in touch with the director and found out that Dan's one concern was that he goes to a church on Sundays. The director said he would take him to his church.

In summation, Dan went to the church with the director of the rehabilitation centre. Dan met and fell in love with a member of the choir. She had her own business and agreed to put Dan through university after they were married.

In turn, he would work at her business on weekends and when he had spare time.

We kept in touch. He made good progress in his rehabilitation.

Dan was in rehab. for a year and was released as he was deemed ready

As soon as he was released they were married.

After eight months of married life and working at his university career, he slipped. I caught him back on skid row.

"What are you doing?' I asked in horror. He told me lamely he had a doctor's appointment. I've heard that excuse before. I told him, "You have no doctor on skid row. Why are you lying to me?"

He broke down and cried. I told him not to throw away his life at this point.

I put him on the bus and sent him home. I phoned his wife and told her to get him some help.

Four years later, the Bible College had a reunion. Invitations went out to all former students. Dan brought his family to the reunion. We learned that he was the father of twins and all is well. He has finished his university course and is now in practice as a Christian counsellor. He gave me his business card. He told us he is also active in the church.

Upon talking to his wife, we learned that she is the choir leader and had taken a course in Christian Living. She explained that her business has boomed and she has another outlet.

Dan went from a man bent on suicide to a man with a life, wife and family. The time he spent at Bible College and in the Mission gave him a relationship with Jesus. He now has the Holy Spirit to guide him and a Heavenly Father to love him and a reason to live.

Dan has been radically changed.

CHAPTER SEVEN

SHANE

Blaming God

Matthew 20:26, "... whoever is great among you must be your servant... whoever wants to be first must be your slave."

Word got out that a new student would be enrolling in the Bible College in the near future.

I asked the Assistant Pastor where this guy was coming from. He answered, "He's coming right off the street."

"What's his name?" The pastor shrugged and told me he hadn't met him as yet.

"I know he's coming as I had this vision, this message from the Spirit of God," the Pastor informed me.

Two weeks went by and no mystery student surfaced.

On the next Tuesday, the Pastor came to my class smiling. He told me excitedly, "He came into the Mission last night. I was greeting at the door and the Holy Spirit whispered, 'He's the one,' " he said excitedly. "Not only that but the Spirit told me he's going to make a difference in the church."

"When will this mystery man be enrolling?"

"He'll be coming to class on Thursday. He's already enrolled."

I was teaching that class so I was looking forward to meeting this person who would make a difference in the church.

I told my class on Wednesday, that they were going to have to shape up and work hard as this new student is special.

I arrive at class early every day in order to have time for anyone who needs help and to receive assignments. Our class, on that Thursday, was in the Mission as we were doing a research project. I had to set it up for research.

During the class, a man with a full beard, dressed in shabby and worn clothes came into the Mission.

Two of the students told him this was a Bible College class and he should come back later for the church service and the meal.

The bearded man told them, "A guy in charge asked me to come and be part of the College." I overheard the conversation with the girls and this man from the street.

I had been given his name as he was registered. I asked, "Are you Shane?" The man nodded.

"We 're expecting you," I encouraged.

I pointed to a chair near the front of the class, but Shane shook his head and pulled up a chair near the back of the room. That is where Shane sat for the next four weeks. He kept to himself and wouldn't engage in any socializing.

I wondered what he looked like under his full, curly beard which hid all but his two beady eyes.

After a few days he confided in me that the reason he sat so far away from the other students was that he smelled. I nodded my agreement as I had detected a repugnant odour the first day.

I wanted to tell him about the dormitory, but I thought, "Not yet."

He badly needed to shower and to put on some clean clothes.

Two of the girls, in a round-about way, made that suggestion. They offered to take him to the Thrift Shop and pick out some used but clean clothes for him. He pretended not to hear their offer.

What surprised me was that he did his assignments in a very legible handwriting. The content of the essays and projects were not at a college level, but he had room to improve. He took pride in his assignments.

All of us were pleasantly surprised when Shane came to class cleanly shaven and with second hand but clean clothes. He finally loosened up and talked to some of his classmates. He moved his chair ten feet closer to the rest of the class.

Through testimonies on his part and through his essays and class work, we pieced together some of his past and where he was at the present.

He made friends with Ben and Chris. I learned from them that trauma kept Shane from seeking the Lord as his Redeemer and Saviour.

Shane revealed the trauma in a testimony.

He told us that he was a twin and both of them were put into a foster home at six years of age after the death of their mother who they dearly loved. There was no father in their life as he had abdicated when the twins were born.

If that wasn't enough, he and his brother were in a bad car accident. He held his brother in his arms as his life ebbed away.

He blamed God and vowed he would never trust Him again.

Shane said that he was giving God another chance to show His love and mercy. He told us he was tired of life on the street and taking drugs to blow his mind. He also told us that he did read his Bible. "The Bible in one hand and a can of beer in the other," he laughingly told the class.

I learned that he was on disability from the government because of the trauma he suffered. He told us he couldn't keep a job as he would fly off the handle too easily.

Shane moved into the dormitory and thought it was great at first, but people got on his nerves and he blew up a few times over petty issues. People in the dorm and in the College kept their distance, not wanting to set him off on a tangent.

It became evident to Shane that he should move out of the dorm and he did.

He found a room in a hotel nearby where the Salvation Army has warriors staying.

These are young Salvation Army warriors for the Lord who minister in the downtown east side, skid row as part of their training.

They had a prayer room which intrigued Shane. He spent a lot of time with these young people from the Salvation Army. At one point he told me he was going to quit the College and join the army. I kidded him and asked him if he would become a general or a Sargent major. He responded, "Don't bother me."

At the Mission, Shane started stacking and unstacking chairs and mopping the floor. He was never too happy with that job, but he persevered.

From there, he worked in the kitchen. He enjoyed that much more than the janitorial work. He then worked his way up the ladder of jobs which demanded more responsibility.

After a year he was on the counsel and making a difference. He put forward some good ideas. Some were acted upon and some were tabled for further consideration.

Shane graduated after his first year at the College and was commissioned.

He liked to tell people that now he could go out and preach, teach and lay hands on the sick and they will receive healing. He thought it a joke that he could drive out demons, speak in new tongues, pick up poisonous snakes and drink deadly poison. (Mark 16:15-18)

Most people look forward to graduation with all the pomp and ceremony. Shane was different, he told me he wouldn't be attending the graduation ceremony.

Knowing that he was grandstanding, I didn't get sucked into a pity party or ask him why he wasn't going to attend the ceremonies. I ignored him.

He came back and asked if I had heard what he said. I told him I heard that he wasn't coming to the graduation ceremony and it was OK with me.

On graduation day, all the girls were fixing their hair, putting on their makeup and sporting their best dresses. The guys were spiking their hair, shining their shoes and looking great in their Thrift Store suits.

I was told that there was a run on suits at the thrift stores.

For graduation, we borrow caps and gowns from the prestigious College.

Everyone was trying them on and getting ready.

One of the girls asked, "Where is Shane?"

I told her he said he wasn't interested in graduation and wouldn't attend.

"He has to attend!" she exclaimed and headed out the door with a friend to bring Shane to the Mission, where graduation was being celebrated.

Shane was dragged in. He arrived but wouldn't wear a gown or a toga. I had had about all I could take from him and his childish antics.

By now a few people were trying to coax him into getting ready.

I went and told, him, "Don't listen to them Shane. You can sit at the back of the room, with the guests, and you'll fit in just fine "

Everyone dispersed and left Shane alone to mull over the matter.

He sheepishly went and got a gown and a cap. Humiliated, he sat in his designated chair with the rest of the class.

The first half of the second year was not that eventful for Shane.

People were getting to know him and didn't fall for his sometimes childish behaviour and attitude.

He told me that he would be the senior pastor of the Mission some day.

He said, that when he has graduated and is ordained, he will be a contender for the job. "If the Senior Pastor moves to another ministry," he acknowledged.

I knew this was an effort to see if I had my sights set on being the Senior Pastor at some point in the future. I was the Dean of the College which was enough for me.

I told him there was no chance that the Senior Pastor would move on. After all, he and his wife are the founders of the Mission.

"And for your information, I'm not interested in being the Senior pastor."

Another person in line for the job was the Assistant Pastor who had been with the Mission for six years. John went so far as to tell him, "You shouldn't be in the Mission on skid row. You're too well educated and too refined."

The Assistant Pastor and I got together and laughed at this guy, who is only in his second year and already trying to push his way to the top of the ladder.

It was two and a half years after the problems we had with the all night shelter for people from the street. It was the middle of December and frost was forming at night. We had had one snow fall which still left snow on the side streets.

Only a few third year students remembered the fiasco we had with the shelter for the homeless. Now we had another group of students who wanted to give shelter to the homeless in the Mission on wintery nights.

I told the students we had been there and done that. I explained that it ended in a fiasco.

I went on to tell them that I'm not against helping people, but there must be controls and equipment in place. I told the students that we have to make rules and regulations in order to protect the volunteers and the people who come off the street.

People from the street must register. There must be strict rules as to times of entry and times of departure. A log book must be available to record any instances of behaviour, either good or bad.

If coffee and sweets are served, we must decide when and to whom.

Shane argued for the shelter and volunteered to head up this venture. I asked if anyone else was interested in taking on this commitment. No hand went up.

I wondered if Shane was up to such a responsibility. A motion was passed to have Shane head up the midnight shelter.

Shane proved himself and recruited volunteers to help. He had established a sign up sheet and had the times of duty posted.

I was involved as supervisor, as it was a student sponsored project.

I dropped in around one in the morning once a week to make certain the set rules were being obeyed and to field any problems and make suggestions.

The fifth week, I went to the Mission on my one o'clock inspection and realized that rules were being broken and there was utter confusion. Doors were supposed to be locked at 12:30 with no exit or entry. If they left the Mission there was no getting back in. I watched from the car and saw people coming out, smoking a cigarette drinking their coffee and going back into the Mission.

In the meantime, the door was not locked and people walking by were entering the premises. I went and checked the nightly registry and found only nineteen signatures and I counted thirty-two residents.

I was going to bring this to the attention of Shane, but he was too busy handing out coffee as his assistants didn't show up. I also learned that the person who was to sing and lead worship didn't come that night.

As I was leaving, I said good-bye to Shane and told him he'd better lock the door as uninvited guests were entering.

Shane looked at me as if to say, "Are you crazy. How can I do the job of three people."

I detected that Shane was shouldering too much responsibility. His fatigue affected his studies as he was not able to do his homework and be at the Mission all night, almost every night.

I wrote my evaluation of the program and what I had observed. I handed it to the Counsel Chairman, a third year student. He called an emergency meeting of the Council. It took them three minutes of discussion to decide to shut down the shelter.

I was happy now that I didn't have to go out at one in the morning to watch people smoke, drink coffee and break the rules.

Shane protested the decision rather weakly, but in the end he knew it was the right decision.

Shane was given new responsibilities taking over the scheduling of preachers and recruiting leaders to do worship in song.

In his quest for a greater role in the Mission and in the church, he enrolled in an upgrading skills program at a nearby Mission. It was a program whereby he could earn a grade twelve equivalent degree. He needed his grade twelve as he only had grade nine and part of grade ten. He told me that grade twelve in one year was his goal.

I helped him with his homework as did others who were high school graduates. It was tough at first, but after a few good report cards, he knew he had the mental capacity to succeed. He asked for less help and strived to do the courses on his own.

We celebrated his grade twelve equivalent graduation.

This was the first step toward his goal as an ordained pastor and the Senior Pastor of the Mission.

Shane completed his three years at Bible College and made it known that he was going to pastor a church.

Coincidentally, the Senior Pastor moved on as he had a family and they needed more support than he could derive from the Mission where all are volunteers. I was asked to replace the Senior Pastor but I declined. I was asked a second time and I was tempted. I asked my wife what she thought. She told me I would be crazy to give up teaching at the Bible College to take over the Mission.

She reminded me of the time the Senior Pastor went to India on a mission trip for three months and left me in charge. I remembered all the running around and the organization. The many times I was called to the Mission as well as the times I was called out at two in the morning to buy diapers for a baby, to settle a marriage dispute and to drive an ailing person to the hospital.

Needless to say, I declined the offer to be the Senior Pastor.

Shane felt he was ready to step in and take over the Mission. He made it known that he was the man for the job. He kept asking the pastor who else was bidding for the job. He told me that he was going to get it for sure as no one else was in line.

To his dismay, the Church Board of the denomination, assigned another couple. Shane was disappointed, but he quickly introduced himself to this couple and tried his hardest to get into their good books. He ran the Mission and worked every job and every angle in order to get to be the assistant pastor. He also belittled the previous assistant pastor to the point where he stepped aside and became the treasurer.

On his way to the top, Shane applied for ordination and licencing. He was accepted and was ordained. There was a celebration, which he told me he would not attend. I told him he needed to grow up if he ever hoped to lead a congregation.

"People look to the leader to arrange such events where people can show appreciation for another's advancement," I informed him.

He thought about it and thanked me.

He came and was the centre of attention and thanked people for coming and sharing in his good fortune.

When he received his licence, he told me he was looking for a couple to marry. He asked me if I knew of anyone who wanted to get married. Six months later he got the chance to conduct a marriage ceremony for a couple who were part of the Mission. They had worked together and knew each other. The young man was a plumber and did our repairs at the Mission and College. His wife to be played the guitar and led worship at the Mission and at other churches.

I was invited, but the wedding was out of town and I couldn't take the time away from the Bible College.

Shane also enrolled in the Prestigious Bible College and took courses by correspondence.

The couple who were appointed as Senior Pastors, lasted only a year and a half. They weren't called to skid row and the challenges they encountered were too stressful. They opted to go back to the quiet solitude of a ministry in suburbia.

Upon the resignation of this couple, Sean applied to take over the Mission as the Senior Pastor. It was the answer to his prayers. He soon found that it was a bigger job than he had imagined. He ran the Mission for two years and realized it was not going to pay the bills.

He had met a beautiful girl who was part of a group which came to do ministry on skid row as part of their outreach summer program. I met her and she is a lovely young lady. I also met her parents who came to see the Mission and the Bible College to check it out. They were not impressed with the skid row. She went home with her parents. He kept in touch and often told me about her. He kept telling me that he loved her and he knew she loved him.

He applied for a job and asked me to give a good recommendation, which I did. He worked at his new job as well as running the Mission. He tried to get me to take over the Mission but I had no intention of becoming the Senior Pastor.

The Assistant Pastor was right in telling us that this man was called by God to do a ministry in the body of Christ.

I laugh when I remember his first day at the Mission, with his full beard and stinky street clothes. Too smelly to sit with the other students. He was discovered by the assistant Pastor after a vision of one who would make a difference in the church.

Shane has been radically changed and is still making his mark in the church. He has moved to another city and has a paid position in a large downtown church. It is the same city where his girl friend lives. He calls me and tells me how things are going in his relationship with his girl friend and in his position in the church. We keep praying for Shane.

CHAPTER EIGHT

STACEY

Prostitution to Prestige

Psalm 106:47, "Save us, O Lord our God, and gather us from the nations, that we may give thanks to your holy name and glory in Your presence."

STACEY gave her testimony a number of times in the Mission and at the College. She is a First Nations lady; proud of her heritage, but ashamed of her treatment on the Native Reserve.

She came to the Mission two years after arriving in the city. It was a Wednesday night. According to her she was tired of drinking and doing drugs to cover her shame and disgust at the fact that she was now a prostitute and an addict.

Her prostitution was a way of making money and getting even for what some men did to her as a child. She told how men from a drinking house on the reserve would grab her lunch as she was on her way to school. It started in grade one and continued for six years.

As she got older, they would touch her sexually and make fun of her.

Fortunately, a school bus took her to a Junior High School in a nearby town.

She didn't have to walk by the drinking house. But the damage was done, she was traumatized and hated men.

Now she used men for her own advantage by making them care for her and telling them how much she loved them. When they were in her trap, she'd turn on them and tell them how she hated them and despised them.

She smiled as she told us, "Some even cried and begged me to marry them after I told them I hated them. It's really weird."

She continued her testimony, "I have a room right over there." She pointed to the hotel across the street from the Mission.

She was clean and sober that Wednesday night and she wanted something different from her sordid life on the street hustling men and getting drunk or stoned.

She got in the line up and came into the Mission. She knew some people and they welcomed her. She got carried away with the singing, testimonies and the message which convicted her.

She remembered the times her mother took her to revival meetings on her reserve and on neighbouring reserves. This first visit triggered the feeling of freedom from drugs, drinking and drudgery.

Stacey became a regular and her second testimony was a ground breaker.

She testified, "I've been clean for two days. No drugs, booze or prostituting. Man does it ever hurt, but I'm winning with the help of my Lord Jesus."

Stacey started coming to the Bible College. She wasn't a great student, but she persevered. Often she'd come and be ready to study, but somebody would tick her off and she'd leave in a huff, often scattering her notes and books onto the floor.

Some of her friends would pick them up and put them in their locker for when she returned to class.

However, there were days when she'd make it through the whole lesson.

Her testimonies continued. "It's been a month and I'm hanging in. Pray for me. I'm so scared I'll fall," she'd cry. Sobbing tears and wiping them with a tissue someone offered. As she left the microphone, she would force a smile which made everyone feel better.

Stacey went onto the streets and talked to the prostitutes and to women who were hooked on drugs. She wanted to help them like Jesus was helping her. She didn't force her religion on others, but she gave her testimony. Telling how traumatized she was over her treatment at the hands of the men in the drinking house.

She would then tell how Jesus set her free. "And he'll set you free if you'll allow him to come into your life," she would encourage.

We had a hard time getting Stacey to take her studies seriously. She had so many excuses as to why she didn't do her homework or why she didn't have an assignment handed in.

Stacey was a strong, self willed person who needed a bit more self discipline and a desire to achieve academically. On her registration form she stated that she had completed high school. From the essays she did write and other written work, I doubted that she completed more than grade six or seven.

These matters didn't phase Stacey. She relied on her verbosity and on her ability to out talk and out yell her opponent. These skills were honed as she gave her testimonies and became involved in social issues that affected her people; the homeless and the disadvantaged.

She did not consider herself as the underdog, but rather as the spokesperson for those who cannot speak out for themselves.

Stacey did just enough work at the College to qualify for a certificate. She earned the right to be commissioned. The right to go out and preach, teach and lay hands on the sick and heal them through the blood and beaten body of Jesus her Saviour.

When I explained what the significance of being commissioned was, Stacey decided that she would preach more often and teach those on the street to change their ways and get their life in order.

It was a great celebration when Stacey was one year without falling. She bought herself a big cake and shared it with the people from the street. After her testimony the men cheered and yelled, "Keep it up babe." and "You can do it."

As a result of her testimonies, a number of men quit their drugs and drinking and went back to their homes. Before they went, they gave their testimonies of how her life changing testimony had affected their lives. They were great testimonies and people were changed.

We all celebrated this one year achievement and looked forward to the two years celebration.

At the one year graduation ceremony, Stacey was ready to celebrate. She told the class that she missed graduating in her home town, so now she's going to make up for it and really make it a day to remember. When she ran up to receive her certificate, everyone laughed and clapped. Stacey bowed and did a little native dance step.

Nobody knew that she was a native dancer. She had never danced before.

She told us dancing reminded her of her village and that reminded her of the men's drinking house. I knew then that she needed inner divine healing in order to free herself from that trauma.

I made a mental note to bring this to her attention at a more appropriate time. Being a one year graduate, Stacey was given the chance to preach and she loved it. Her first sermon was an enhanced testimony, but it touched many hearts.

After she took courses in sermon preparation with emphasis on topical and expository sermons, she became quite proficient and delivered some really meaningful and touching sermons. The best thing is, she put her heart into what she was preaching.

At the time she was developing her preaching skills, a first nations travelling evangelist came to the Mission and delivered a series of three sermons over four nights. These sermons really touched Stacey and she asked for his notes so that she could develop a similar style. She had fun delivering her evangelical sermons, using some of the sayings and scriptures used by the travelling evangelist.

For a while there were lots of 'Halleluiahs' and, 'I'll say amen to that.' when Stacey preached in the Mission. I got into the mood and we all had some fun.

Two weeks after her graduation, I had Stacey in my office and we discussed the issue of the drinking men's house. I told her she should face that issue and put it to rest. She agreed and we went through some pretty intense sessions where she and Jesus walked by that house and she forgave those men. She knew them by name and forgave each one. There was a lot of crying and she went through a lot of tissues, but in the end she felt relieved and set free.

As a result of our letting her speak and preach, it gave her confidence to speak out on issues she championed in the community. She decided she would make a difference in people's lives. She joined a group of women who wanted their problems and rights addressed to the government.

Stacey was chosen to be the spokesperson as she was loud and eloquent and not afraid to be behind a microphone.

When she spoke, at a forum, to the representatives from the three levels of government, they listened and agreed to make some changes.

They arranged to sit down with her and a couple of other educated First Nations women and hammer out some measures that would be beneficial to the first nations and to all others in society.

This meant that they had to go to the capital city and put forward their views on issues that had been festering for many years.

The one issue that was foremost at the time was the disappearance of more than twenty nine women of the night, prostitutes, from off the streets of the downtown eastside skid row. They had disappeared without a trace.

What added fuel to the fire for Stacey was that a couple of the missing women had been saved at the Mission. One young lady of the night, came and listened to the gospel music and the word of God in the message. She was also touched by the testimonies of Stacey and some other students.

She became a regular, opting to come to the church rather than working the streets. Having felt a great love for Jesus the Christ, she asked to be baptised. Her wish was granted and a number of people came to witness her baptism in the cold waters of the ocean.

After her baptism, she came to the Mission regularly for some months. Without any explanation, she quit coming to the Mission. She was not seen on the street. We learned that she had become one of the twenty nine missing persons from the street.

This fuelled the cause for Stacey and she spent many hours with victim's families. Many were First nations ladies who were missing.

It ended up with Stacey being hired by the government to speak for the disadvantaged and bring forth issues from the community.

Stacey continued to come to the Mission, but her testimonies were geared to her job. She loved the fact that she could fight for the rights of women on the Down town east side and those on the reserves and get paid for it. She didn't think of it as a job but rather as a form of ministry.

In one of her testimonies she challenged everyone who had a cause, to fight for that cause as long as it would benefit others in society and bring glory to God.

Stacey was transferred to a better position in another part of the country. She let us know where she was and invited us to send an outreach to that small city as they needed the Holy Spirit at work in their community.

At a Bible College counsel meeting it was decided to go to that city and let Stacey speak and reach out to the lost souls.

It took a days drive, twelve hours, to get there and everyone was tired when we arrived. I had done my share of driving and it was tiring as the road had lots of curves and steep hills.

When Stacey came out to greet us, she was the spark we needed to keep us going. She hadn't changed a bit. Talking a mile a minute and hugging everyone. She had a great meal prepared with the help of her neighbours.

All week end the food never stopped coming. There was great hospitality.

That night we did a service. The music was great. People were moved. Stacey danced to a lively song and a few native women joined in. One of the third year students gave a great message. Stacey gave her testimony which amazed people.

I looked around and saw that people were touched and strengthened in their faith and their walk with the Lord Jesus.

The greatest surprise was that Stacey had a boy friend and informed us that she was getting married. He was a tall handsome young man with a great smile. I remembered how she hated men because of the drinking house, and now she is getting married. I thanked God for the inner healing of the Lord who walked with Stacey and healed her trauma.

The outreach was a success. Stacey preached the final message. I heard people tell her she must take over the church. One man told her, "We need some life in this place. You young people are the ones we need in order to bring to life the moving of the Holy Spirit."

Coming to the Mission and the Bible College had a profound effect on Stacey. She grew in so many ways. The trauma that haunted her was gradually replaced by a love for the Lord.

I see her occasionally, when she comes to the big city. She's still outspoken, but in a more refined manner. So different from the loud young lady who came into the Mission that Wednesday night. She has been changed profoundly.

The same lady whose testimony was, "It's been two days and I'm still clean. It's so hard, but Jesus is with me all the way." And Jesus is still with her.

She's been radically changed from a prostitute and addict to a fighter for human rights.

CHAPTER NINE

HENRY

Fetal Alcohol Syndrome

Psalm 14:2, "The Lord looks down from heaven on the sons of men to see if there are any who understand and any who seek God.

HENRY appeared in the Mission on a Saturday night.

He came with three friends and they disrupted the service. They were happy, but for the wrong reason. Our bouncer kept telling them to be quiet and respect the house of the Lord.

Henry argued that he had the right to laugh and be happy.

The bouncer on duty was a big First Nations man who tolerated no foolishness. He often told how righteous indignation for the sanctity of the house of the Lord made him keep order.

He got into the face of Henry and started moving him toward the door. This sobering action caused Henry to back down and promise to behave.

The next night he came back and apologized once again to the bouncer, who introduced Henry to the staff and the students.

Henry learned to enjoy the music at the Mission. He listened to the testimonies and was convicted by the sermons.

He took a liking to those living in the dormitory and two weeks later asked if he could move in. It was agreed he could live in the dormitory but he was told that he must follow the rules. No drinking, drugs, smoking, no women and you must attend Bible College.

Henry agreed and came to classes. I soon discovered that Henry could not read at a level higher than grade two. He was unable to write little more than his name and very simple words.

Henry told me he was taught to read, but he forgot how.

He was given a tutor who taught him to read and do simple mathematics. The first tutor gathered together some easy books at his level, but Henry insisted on only reading the Bible.

This disagreement resulted in his getting a second tutor, who was more patient and lenient. Ryan, his new tutor, taught him until he felt he could read on his own.

Not only did Henry want to learn to read, but he also wanted to learn to play the guitar.

John was a professional guitarist, who was overcoming a drug problem. He agreed to teach Henry to play the guitar.

The guitar playing became acceptable, but Henry could not sing in tune. It was irritating listening to him sing. He ruined every gospel song he attempted to sing as he sang so off key.

Henry was given voice lessons by a couple of the better singers, but it did very little good.

There were a couple of songs no one else sang which became his saving grace. People had never heard the new songs he sang so they couldn't criticize.

Henry turned from the guitar and singing to playing the drums.

Soon worship leaders were asking him to accompany them during the service.

I took lessons from him and other drummers. I thought I was doing quite well. I accompanied one of the singers. Henry laughed and told me I was doing it backwards. That was the end of my drumming career.

Not long after the beginning of Henry's career as a drummer, he learned the bass guitar and was in demand in other churches as well as at the Mission.

After six months, Henry could read his Bible, which was written in simple English.

His essays and written sermons were now at a grade six level or perhaps a higher level. His handwriting was still not great so he relied on the computer in order to make the essays and sermons legible so that we could read and evaluate them

All did not run smoothly for Henry. One day the captain of the house had an argument with him. When in an argument, Henry would quote scripture to back up his opinions and to put forward his point of view. Such as, "Christ set me free." Using this favourite scripture, he would ask. "Why are you trying to make me obey the laws and man made rules when I'm a free man?"

This argument riled those who were trying to make Henry conform to the rules and regulations of the dorm and the Mission.

If anyone said something that was a bit worldly, Henry took him or her to task. This caused frayed nerves and often arguments would break out.

Henry was in a world of his own.

We determined that he had, 'Fetal Alcohol Syndrome.'

This syndrome is caused by the mother drinking alcohol when the fetus is developing. When this happens, the baby is born with developmental problems. These problems cause irrational behaviour and the inability of the person to make informed and rational decisions throughout their life.

These are the very problems Henry faces on a daily basis as the result of this syndrome.

On one occasion, the head of the dorm and Henry did not see eye to eye. There was a difference of opinion. The head of the house had put up with enough from Henry and things came to the boiling point. Henry invited the dorm leader to come outside and he'd finish the argument. They ended up wrestling on the front lawn.

Others from the dorm had to break up the scuffle.

Henry was evicted for that and other reasons. But he remained loyal to the Mission and never missed a day of Bible College.

After three months, Henry asked to move back into the dormitory.

Permission to move back into the dormitory was conditional. There was a new dorm captain who felt he could handle Henry.

We had to keep reminding him not to cause any problems or he'd be out again. The new dorm captain gave Henry many chances to reform himself.

Henry also had a few problems at the Mission. He set himself up as the enforcer and the final authority, in cases of persons from the street causing trouble at the Mission.

He would talk gruffly and in a demanding and demeaning manner to the offenders who were disrupting the service. If they would not stop their bad behaviour he would demand that they leave the Mission.

This often erupted into cursing and swearing from those being evicted.

When a person would not cooperate and do what he demanded, Henry would use brute force. Pushing and shoving them towards the door. This manhandling often broke out in fist fights and chairs being knocked over.

As well, innocent people were being pushed around

An emergency counsel meeting was called to deal with Henry and his enforcement of the law.

He was told again and again not to use this method of dealing with people from the street. He wouldn't listen, so now he was confronted at a counsel meeting.

Rules were put in place so that everyone would know how to deal with those disrupting the service.

Henry thought we were picking on him and making it appear that he was the culprit, the one causing the trouble. He defended his actions. He told us he was getting to the root of the problem and resolving the issue promptly.

Henry was handed a copy of the rules as laid out by the students and by the staff.

He promptly crushed the list of rules and threw his copy into the garbage can.

Henry lost his job as enforcer. He kept arguing that it was the quickest way of getting rid of trouble makers.

We told him it might work on the street, but we had a higher calling.

He thought about it in that light and somewhat agreed.

He told us that Jesus enforced the law by taking a rope and chasing the animals out of the temple and overturning the money changers tables to get rid of those abusing the temple. He tried to make the comparison. He said he was imitating Jesus in getting rid of the people abusing the Mission and causing trouble.

We didn't buy the argument and the comparison.

More than once he told myself and the other Pastors that we were not doing things according to the rules and regulations. He was big into rules, if they were in his favour.

Henry liked to work in the kitchen. At times he would cause trouble and have to be corrected.

At one point, the head of the kitchen had received a shipment of fruit cocktails in small cups left over from a banquet at a five star hotel. The kitchen supervisor told Henry to give one to each patron who came to be served. There were enough cups of fruit to last for two days.

Henry, didn't listen to the supervisor and he decided he'd be generous. He started giving two and sometimes three to each person he served.

I heard a loud shout coming from the kitchen. I wondered what Henry had done this time.

The supervisor ushered Henry to the door of the kitchen and told him not to come back. Henry was not happy with being evicted from the kitchen.

I spoke to Henry regarding that issue. He told me the supervisor was stingy. I asked him if he had heard the instructions to give one to each person.

Henry told me he did things his way. I told him that's what gets you into trouble. Henry told me, "I know what I'm doing."

At times I wondered.

The next day I greeted him warmly. He had a grudge, but shook his head and laughed it off. Telling me, "You're lucky I'm a Christian."

Henry did not want to give his testimony. He told me he'd have to tell all his secrets. I informed him it was telling what you have been through in life and what happened when you came to the Lord. He was still reluctant. I asked him if he was ashamed of something he had done. He told me it wasn't what he had done but what others had done to him.

I left it at that and let him form his own testimony.

One night, a month later, at the Mission, he got up and testified.

He told how his mother was an alcoholic. A bad alcoholic. When he was born his aunt adopted him as she knew his mother would abandon and abuse him.

He told us, "I don't know which of the men my mom slept with in her drunken stupor, who became my father." He went on to tell that his father was killed in a hunting accident.

He verified that he had Fetal Alcohol Syndrome by saying, "School was difficult for me as I couldn't remember from one day to the next what I had learned. I stayed in grade one for two years and in grade two for two years. It didn't do much good as I wasn't learning much. By grade six I was three years older than the other kids To me they were young brats. I dropped out of school," he gathered his thoughts.

"I helped my uncle on his farm. We fenced and did chores. My uncle loved to hunt and fish. He had a boat and we both enjoyed getting out on the lake. My life was good," Henry stopped to remember the good times.

"One day the truant officer, the big authority, came to the farm and told my uncle I must go back to school. My uncle explained that I had a hard time learning. I told them I didn't need any more embarrassment at being in a class with much younger kids.

He told me and my uncle that I could go to grade nine in a special class. It was either go to that class or be taken away from my uncle and aunt and placed in foster care.

Henry said he was in those classes for three years. I learned how to cook and how to do some woodwork and how to do art. Also some reading and writing. He was proud to say he had graduated.

"My uncle sold the farm and went to the big city as my aunt needed to be near a doctor and a hospital.

I didn't come with them but went to a small city a hundred miles from our farm. I had a girlfriend and we got married. I was married for three years and we had a baby boy who is now eight years old.

I guess I got on my wife's nerves once too often and she kicked me out. It really hurt me as I love my son. I went back and she got a restraining order.

When I got drunk and came to visit my son, I guess I broke the order and ended up in jail.

I didn't like jail. It took away my freedom. No fishing or hunting.

When I was released, I came to the big city to stay with my aunt and uncle. They live in a complex where no overnight visitors are allowed.

My uncle died but my aunt still lives in the city and I visit her quite often.

The greatest part of my testimony is that I am learning to read and I can read the Bible and write much better, especially on the computer. I love to play gospel songs on the bass guitar and I love to play the drums and sing. I've been told I have great rhythm which makes me a good drummer.

I really love what I'm learning at Bible College. We've got the best teachers in the world. When I graduate from Bible College, I'm going to go back to my home town and plant a church. The only thing is, I need a Christian lady to be my partner in the church. Someone who can play the piano and sing beautifully."

Henry paused to look around at all the ladies in the Mission. He smiled and made people laugh.

"By the way, if anyone here in the Mission wants to change their life and become a new creation, come to Bible College. You don't have to be smart, you just have to have a desire to serve the Lord and be blessed."

Henry left the podium amid a round of applause. As the result of his testimony, two students were added to the College.

It is our policy to take an outreach into the area from which the students come from. At a counsel meeting it was decided to go to Henry's home town. When Henry learned of this decision, he had his cousin get in touch with the elders and the band council and set up a welcoming committee.

It was a two day trip. We stopped in the small city where Henry had lived with his wife. We looked forward to meeting his ex wife and son. We were disappointed to learn that she remarried and her husband took her to live on his reserve a few hundred miles to the North East.

We had arranged to do a service in the church where Henry was married. He met a few of his friends who still lived in the city and they talked about old times.

The College students did the service which was well accepted. As they switched into gospel rock, the place started to come alive. People were singing and dancing in the aisles.

On our way to the village and the farm on which Henry had lived, we passed cars on the highway coming from the opposite direction. Henry watched every car that passed us and proclaimed that the driver and passengers were his cousins. It soon became a joke as the students would ask him. "Whose in that car?" As it passed Henry changed and said, "They're my friends and my cousins."

We had to get off the highway and travel a gravel road which had some sharp turns. Henry navigated and we arrived at his reserve. He pointed out the school and the gymnasium, the band office and the house his mother used to lived in.

Henry was welcomed and our students stayed in the church hall.

We spent three very pleasant days in the mountains. There was the lake where Henry and his uncle fished and the hills where he hunted. It was so serene, so quiet and peaceful that the students fell in love with the place.

We had our first service in an old church with a peddle organ and beautiful wood grain interior. The church overflowed with people so we had the next service in the large gymnasium.

To our surprise, people came from neighbouring first nations villages to take part in the services and the festivities. They brought their guitars and fiddles and we shared the stage with them. They also brought enough food to feed an army.

We decided to stay an extra two days and have another four services, two a day as the people encouraged us and begged us to stay and worship with them.

On the way home, Henry told us that ministering in his native village was his choice of ministry. Some of the students volunteered to help him set up a ministry in his village. Some had never seen and experienced the pristine beauty of the mountains, valleys and lakes. It overwhelmed them.

Henry graduated after the first year of studies and was commissioned. That proved to be an incentive. He started to preach regularly.

He had witnessed many evangelists who came to the Mission and brought new life to the congregation. He adopted their style and their methods.

I heard him practice in the dormitory. He would stand in front of the mirror and deliver his sermon with hands waving and calling for amens and hallelujahs.

The guys in the dormitory laughed and called out amen and hallelujah.

After studying the course on Divine Healing, Henry was intrigued with the gift of healing. He wanted to heal everyone who came into the Mission. He would go around and ask the regulars if he could pray and ask God to heal them. Many had no physical infirmities and nothing to pray for.

I took him aside and told him to pray for the gift of 'knowing'. I explained that he could then know what to pray for and it would be more effective. We prayed together and he told me he had received that gift.

After that, if Henry would see someone limping he would tell them he would pray for the healing of their legs. If they seemed to be favouring a sore shoulder or a bad back, Henry used his gift of knowing and prayed for them.

It wasn't exactly what I had taught, but it worked for him.

Henry came for the second year. For him it was too much. He got behind with his essays and term papers. Half way through the term, he told me he would like to take some of the courses over again. I agreed it would be a good idea.

He didn't graduate the second year. He had to take extra courses to gain his second year certificate.

It took Henry four event filled years to graduate and be considered for ordination and licensing.

In the fourth year, Henry applied for ordination. He had some of the third year students help him with the paperwork. I heard one of the students tell Henry he could omit that comment. Henry insisted on reporting the whole truth even when it wasn't part of the application.

Three months later, Henry told me that there was a problem with his ordination. Henry was advised of the problem, but he did not make it public.

This didn't stop Henry. He appealed and reapplied, omitting some of the damaging remarks. He was told that his ordination was up for review and it would take a few months as the review panel would not meet again for three months.

Henry is a symbol of what God can do in our lives if we persevere in his love. Henry went from an illiterate to a Bible College graduate in four short years. It took Henry an extra year to complete the program but it was worth it.

Henry was scheduled to preach at the graduation service. I was surprised to listen to an evangelistic message with great use of the scriptures.

My wife keeps telling him he should go on the road and preach the gospel in Native communities.

Since then, I have heard him preach many times at the Mission. I am impressed each time at his knowledge and understanding of God's word.

Henry still plays the drums and the Bass guitar in various Churches and Missions.

One day, not long ago, I was in the kitchen of the Mission and I heard someone singing after the service. It was so out of tune, I hurriedly ran out to stop this cat calling. I shook my head when I saw it was Henry.

He looked at me and smiled.

Two weeks later, I heard a drummer who was better than average. I looked around the corner from the kitchen to see Henry accompanying the worship leader.

Another day I watched as Henry and others carried in heavy boxes of supplies for the kitchen.

Everything Henry does, he does it with a smile and a love for the Lord. He just keeps on doing what he can for the Lord. Always at home in the Body of Christ.

He told me one day he would have his own church, "But I've got to have a wife like yours who supports my ministry. It's got to be a team ministry."

Henry has had a few lady friends but so far not the right one.

He is still going from one Mission to another looking for the right lady to share his dream of going back home to the mountains and the lakes and bringing the gospel to his people.

Henry has been radically changed from an illiterate to a College graduate. From someone who didn't know the Lord to a lover of his precious Jesus.

CHAPTER TEN

HILDA

Possessed and Controlling

Colossians 3:17, "And whatever you do , whether in word or deed, do it all in the name of the Lord Jesus, giving thanks to God the Father through Him.

HILDA came to the Mission on her own. She did not know anyone as she was from a city far from this setting.

After three or four visits to the Mission and enrolling in the Bible College, Hilda gave her testimony.

She told that she was from a reserve on the prairies.

"I didn't know until I was six years old that I had been taken from my parents when I was born."

She said her foster parents let her know that she was from a reserve not far from the city in which they lived.

"They drove me to the reserve and talked to some of my relatives. I didn't want to stay there. I didn't visit the reserve again until I was sixteen years old.

My foster parents are really nice and I can go home anytime I like.

I have a sister who was placed in the same home and we are the best of friends.

We went to school together and we went to Sunday School every Sunday. We had a great life as our foster mother is really kind and gentle.

I used to get into trouble because I was bossy with my sister. I wanted the biggest piece of pie and the best toys. I wanted to control the games we played. If I didn't get my way I'd pout and go to my room and put my face in a pillow. If that didn't work, I'd quit eating and go on a hunger strike. I was a bit of a brat always wanting my own way.

My sister still lives in the city close to our foster parent's place.

I decided I would be on my own and make my way in life. I worked and saved my money. I had a good job in an Auto Parts supply company. They wanted me to stay and they gave me a raise, but I decided to come to the big city.

I was always in the church and have a desire to have my own church some day. I was told never to abandon my dreams and that is why I am going to Bible College."

I was interested to learn that this First Nations young lady was raised in a Christian home by Caucasian foster parents who love her and raised her as their own. The other thing is that she feels little affinity to the native culture.

From the beginning, Hilda chose her friends carefully. At first some people thought she was stuck-up as she wouldn't mingle with just anyone.

She enrolled in the Bible College after hearing the invitation at the Mission. Hilda kept to herself until she formed a group of friends.

She had a goal and that was to have her own church.

In order to make this dream come true she had to have a husband. I watched how she systematically selected the man she wanted and how she manipulated him.

Hilda was not blessed with outer beauty, but she did know how to use make-up to enhance her outer appearance. What she lacked in outer beauty she made up in projecting an image of innocence and loving kindness; helplessness and needing someone to lean on.

She didn't aspire to leadership and did as little serving and helping in the Mission and Bible College as possible.

When a position that was to be filled by a student came available in the Mission, the kitchen or Dormitory, Hilda looked the other way, never volunteering.

It did surprise me when John, the lead guitarist, volunteered to teach music and take over the signing up of worship leaders. Hilda immediately volunteered to be his assistant.

When John said he didn't need an assistant she was crushed. After the council meeting, she cornered John and I heard her ask him why he was being so cruel to her. She came onto him with all her charm. He recanted and said she could do the phoning, after he gave her the list of names and times.

That led to a relationship which saw them sit together during class and go around hand in hand, in and out of the Mission and the Bible College.

On an outreach to a smaller town, John said something to her that ticked her off. She came storming out of the church hall, where we were staying and sat in the van, hiding her face in a pillow.

I watched as John went over and talked to her. She played the broken hearted lover to a tee. Soon they were together in the van, soothing her hurt pride and making everything better again.

The next week, Hilda and John attended the prayer meeting held every Friday night after the service at midnight. It would often last until two in the morning or later.

John sat at the back of the Mission; but Hilda joined the prayer circle. There was a time of praying for the Mission, for the Bible College and for all the Missions and churches in the city. A time of praying for finances and situations that had arisen during the week.

Then came a time of silent prayer and meditation. After ten of twelve minutes of silent prayer a demon manifested. From the mouth of Hilda came a man's deep voice saying, "You can't have her, she's ours."

Hilda, under the demon's spell, ran across the prayer circle and started choking the leader.

Others, including John, pulled her away and sat her down. The two leaders prayed against the demons in the name of Jesus Christ of Nazareth. Demanding that they identify themselves and come out of her.

One of the leaders, bound the demons and six obeyed and came out of Hilda. They knew that the Name of Jesus had the power to defeat them and make them leave.

The problem was, the demons were not given directions as to where to go. They should have been told to go to Jesus the Christ so He could deal with them.

The demons roamed freely and who they entered no one immediately knew.

The next day, I was asked to pray for the removal of one spirit that refused to come out of Hilda. I did so and determined that it was a controlling spirit that could only be exorcised by prayer and fasting. I told

Hilda that she too must pray and fast. I asked her to let me know two days in advance of our getting together to have the spirit exorcised.

I figured that incident would scare John and he'd turn and run, but he hung in and they got engaged. He told me he felt sorry for Hilda.

The worst thing is, John's demeanor and character changed a week or so after that Friday night prayer meeting. He went back to drinking and doing drugs. His personality changed and he lost his connection to the Holy Spirit and to Jesus the Christ. He stopped playing the guitar and became lethargic.

I had a conversation with him and he started coming against the teachings of the Bible College and against my role as a teacher.

I tried to convince him to go for therapy in order to get rid of his craving for drugs and drink. He complied and went into rehabilitation for a short time.

Hilda came to Bible College and completed her first year. Their relationship never did get back on track. Hilda became pregnant with John's baby.

I could tell John was not into the relationship. He abandoned the Mission and went so far as to tell me the Bible College was a form of brain washing.

I was convinced that my perception was correct. A demon, set loose from Hilda, had entered him. I suggested that we pray for deliverance from any spirit that might be present and harming him. He would not let me pray for deliverance.

For some reason he still hung around the Mission and at times came to the Bible College. There were a number of us praying for John as we knew he was being led astray by an evil spirit or a demon.

Unknown to me, three of the third year students confronted John and told him he needed to let them pray and lay hands on him. At first John told them he was alright. No problem. They told him it was for his benefit.

Finally, John consented and the three laid hands on John and in the name of Jesus the Christ, they prayed for deliverance from any demon or evil spirit.

First of all they prayed for their own protection and for the protection of everyone. They then prayed that any spirit or demon, released, would go directly to Jesus and he would deal with them.

These students had taken the course in Divine Healing and they were putting into practice what they had learned.

The next day they reported to me that the demon was bound and exorcised. I was happy because I knew this was a burden for John and for Hilda

I was especially pleased when John picked up the electric guitar and started making beautiful music as he accompanied the worship leader. Some of the students complimented him and he enjoyed the accolades.

When Hilda saw what was happening, she demanded that John come with her. John asked to play just one more number. Hilda started for the door in a huff. John put down the guitar and followed her.

In one course I teach, I talk about witchcraft. Most students thought I was teaching about witches and goblins.

They were surprised to learn that witchcraft is used by someone to control another person.

Some people commit witchcraft through shedding tears, playing the role of the jilted or ignored partner. They want to get their own way.

Others withhold showing love and concern. They might tell their husband that they are not feeling well, when asked to make love.

Both Hilda and John were in the class when I taught this lesson as a result of watching Hilda commit witchcraft with John.

She was not happy and told me , "You're trying to break up our relationship, but its not going to work." I didn't deny the accusation as it was my intention to let John know that he had a problem on his hands.

A week later, John told me that he was out of the relationship. I asked if it was something I had said. He told me that he was tired of being a door mat.

For three months, John was out of the picture all together. He went to his parent's place in a small town where his father owns a grocery and dry goods store.

I heard that Hilda was going to follow him and bring him home. I wanted to tell her to leave him alone, but it was out of my jurisdiction.

Hilda was talking to some of the girls and told them she didn't want his baby and she wasn't going to let him run away and make her take care of his child.

This was the first I knew about a baby out of wedlock. It had just been conceived as there were no signs to indicate she was pregnant.

I reported this circumstance to the board in order that a decision might be made regarding their status in the Bible College. It was agreed that they would speak to Hilda.

Hilda didn't go to John's home town. She had been in touch by phone with his father and learned that John was in a detox centre and doing very well. She also learned that his parents had talked him into going for treatment as they didn't know he was still dependent on drugs.

She confided that she didn't tell them that she was pregnant with John's baby. I told Hilda that we had prayed that John wouldn't come back until he had kicked his drug habit. I didn't tell her that we had prayed that she wouldn't go to his town, as she was too controlling and she might destroy him and disrupt his family.

Hilda came before the board with regard to her being pregnant with a child from another student. She told them a wedding had been planned but that John needed treatment and was in a rehabilitation centre. She advised them that as soon as he was released, they would be married.

This seemed to satisfy the board of directors of the College.

I hadn't heard of any wedding plans. I realized that I was out of the loop.

Hilda came to the College and became involved in her studies and she started hanging out with the girls in her class.

The class decided that they would start a home study group. It was brought up at the counsel meeting. It was Hilda's idea. It proved to be quite popular with the students. They put forward some very good and well thought out ideas. The problem was, some of their ideas conflicted with Hilda's plans.

I wondered how they were going to get around the problem of making a go of this home study group when it didn't incorporate all of Hilda's suggestions I couldn't see any compromise on her part. She was adamant that her methods were the only ones that would work.

They struck a committee to study the proposals.

They were to bring a report back to counsel for its approval.

This was the way many controversies are resolved. However, it was not the way Hilda wanted this one to be resolved.

She made a motion to let her start the group and resolve conflicts as they arose. This got the backing of a small group who decided to start the home study and let the committee do whatever it wanted to do, which in the end would not be binding.

Score one for Hilda. She got her way again.

The study group was a success and went on for a few months.

Twice I brought the need for prayer and fasting to the attention of Hilda. She told me she was too busy but would let me know when she had time.

It was graduation and everyone was busy preparing their clothes and getting their hair done and handing in last minute assignments.

The big day arrived. The Mission was decorated and the chairs arranged for each level of graduation. The back row was for first year students, the middle section for the second year students and the front row for the third and final year students.

To everyone's surprise, John walked in two hours prior to the start of the program. A group of students welcomed him and made certain that he sat with the graduates as he had only missed a few months of study.

John had come with his parents as they knew how much this meant to him.

I had to get the approval of at least one member of the board to award John with a certificate. It was a rush job. She agreed to graduate him for his second year providing he came back the next year to make up the two courses he missed.

I was not in on presenting this ultimatum to John and his parents.

John agreed to the proposal providing his relationship with Hilda was resolved. He had some doubts as to whether they could overcome their differences.

The graduation took place. Caps and gowns were fitted and the ceremony started a few minutes late as John had to suit up.

John sat with his buddies. Hilda had a seat reserved for him but it remained vacant. I felt a chill in the air.

Hilda was showing signs of pregnancy at the time of her graduation. She was receiving her second year certificate. She went to the stage and made a short address. There were some who thought she shouldn't accept her certificate as she was pregnant with John's child and he had abandoned her.

After the ceremony, Hilda made it a point of talking to the parents of John. I could tell that they were totally surprised when she told them she was carrying John's baby.

At first the mother was shocked, but her maternal instincts came through. After all this would make her a grandmother.

While Hilda was talking to John's parents, John cornered me and asked what I thought they should do about getting back together again.

This put me in an awkward position as I didn't want to lie. To tell him that I felt there would be bliss and everything would be rosy would be a lie. To hedge my bets and say you should give it a try, would also be misleading.

I told John, "You know her character and her motivations, don't you?"

He agreed that she needed control at all times and she was domineering.

"So how are you going to change these characteristics and have a relationship that works?" I asked.

"There must be a way."

I told him counselling was the only option. If it works you will be happy together.

The two months holidays after graduation proved to be eventful for Hilda and John.

A baby boy was born to Hilda, six weeks after graduation. John was present at the birth.

I learned that they had had three weeks of marriage counselling prior to the birth of their baby boy.

My wife and I were invited to the baptism.

During the reception, after the ceremony, John came over and told me things were much better between them. He told me, "This counsellor really lit into Hilda. She got angry and stormed out. I was going to get her and talk her into coming back. The counsellor told me to sit down and we'd have a long talk. After half an hour, Hilda came and demanded I leave and come with her. The counsellor told her to sit down and listen to him. He lit into her. He told her she needed the therapy more than me."

John said he laughed at the way the therapist handled Hilda.

He told me that she needed a good talking to. The counsellor asked her if she wanted this relationship to work. She said she did. He told her point blank how she would have to change. No more controlling and demanding her own way.

John told me, "The counsellor didn't call it witchcraft like you did, but he convinced her she had to stop being controlling and so bossy. So far so good," John smiled.

John then told me a wedding was being planned. He hinted that Hilda was going to ask a favour of me. I tried to pry it out of him but he only laughed.

Two days later Hilda came up to me at the Mission. I could tell she was now for real. No pretense and no wanting to control the conversation. She asked me if I would give her away. I told her I'd be honoured to take part in the ceremony.

The wedding took place a week before College resumed. Most of the students were already living in the dormitory or they had other accommodation. They were showing up at the Mission, eager to start work and to start studying.

The wedding was a simple one at the Mission on a Saturday afternoon. Decorations turned the otherwise drab Mission into an array of colour.

Being summer, the dress was informal. Girls in bright summer dresses and the guys in short sleeved shirts and some in shorts. The wedding party was more formal with suits and long dresses.

I had never seen John in a suit and well groomed. I didn't realize how really handsome he was. Tall and well muscled.

Hilda wore a beautiful wedding gown and carried a bouquet of summer flowers picked from the garden of one of the board members.

John's parents and his sister came to the wedding along with his uncles, aunts cousins and friends.

Hilda had no family present as her foster parents were not informed as she was too embarrassed to let them know she had given birth out of wedlock.

Bible College started a week later. I felt there would be a problem with baby sitting while Hilda and John came to the College.

I soon learned that there was no problem They brought John Junior with them to classes. I wondered what would happen if the baby got cranky and started to cry and make a fuss. That didn't happen because as soon as the baby fussed, one of the girls in the class would pick him up and rock him.

Hilda soon knew when he was hungry and she would sit at the back of the room and breast feed him, while listening to the lecture.

Thanksgiving takes place every day, but as a celebrated holiday it takes place once a year. Hilda and John went to his parents for Thanksgiving and stayed for the week end plus two days.

The counsellor had given Hilda a list of signs to be aware of which might trigger her controlling and rebellious disposition. He had also given John a list of things to be aware of which might help him put a stop to any destructive behaviour.

On Saturday night, John's parents offered to take care of the baby and allow Hilda and John to go to a movie or do something without worrying about their son.

They left the house without deciding where they should go and what they should do. The options were limited as they were in a small town.

John gave a list of suggestions like a movie, a restaurant or a walk in the park. Hilda suggested the movie. "We can have popcorn and a pop. Pretend we're teenagers," she laughed. When they got to the theatre it was playing an old movie which they had already seen and didn't particularly enjoy.

Hilda asked if there was another movie theatre. John told her, "No luck. We're fortunate to have this one movie house as everybody watches TV."

Hilda got upset and started to take it out on John. It was all his fault for bringing her here to this remote village At first he tried to defend himself, but then he remembered what the counsellor had told him was a sign of regression.

John pointed out to Hilda that she was regressing into a catatonic state. Hilda became aware of what she was doing and stopped her ranting.

She folded herself into the arms of John and apologized.

When they returned to the big city, John felt that he had some control. He told Hilda neither of them had to be in control, but both were able to share responsibilities.

I had a chance to talk to Hilda. I told her she should have someone pray against the controlling spirit which causes her problems. She agreed. I asked a person I knew to pray with me and the controlling spirit, having lost most of it s power, was released and sent to Jesus to deal with it.

Christmas was great with a baby in the house. So many friends dropped by with gifts for John Jr.

John spent more time playing his guitar. He also played the piano. He was writing music once again, now that he felt free from drugs from a demon and a controlling wife in his life. He composed a gospel song. He played and sang the song at the Mission. It got him a big round of applause. The students who heard it wanted to learn the words and the tune so that they could sing it when they led worship.

Both Hilda and John completed their third year at the College.

By the time they graduated, they had a son and a daughter on the way.

I had them come separately for a session to go over the history of their time at the College and find out where they are going from here and how we can be of help.

When I interviewed John, he told me that he was going to learn his father's business and become his partner. Later, he would take over his father's business in the small town. I asked him what Hilda thought of this move.

He told me they had discussed it from a financial point of view and from a church plant possibility. He explained to me that Hilda still wants a church of her own. He said that God is good because the old pastor of the Evangelical Free Church is retiring and selling his church to the highest bidder. "So far there are no bidders. My dad is willing to put up one tenth and co-sign at the bank for the remainder. It's already a certainty we will get the church. When we get there we will really rock the place. We will bring in the young people and let them have a relationship with Jesus our Lord and Saviour."

I could hear the joy in his voice. I congratulated him on his wise decision and wished him all the best

When I talked with Hilda she had the same story. She did add that she thought it a great idea to get established in a community rather than be a nonentity in the big city.

John came to the Mission a drug addict with the great gift of making music to the Lord. He is now leaving the College completely clean of drugs and with a heart to plant a church and lead worship which will rock that small town and bring the young people into a relationship with the Lord.

Hilda came to the Mission and to the Bible College with six demons and a controlling spirit all of which were cast out of her.

With Christian counselling and an understanding husband, she is going to a small town to plant a church, which is her dream come true.

Both John and Hilda have been radically changed for the better.

CHAPTER ELEVEN

RYAN

Running from Life

1 Corinthians 2:10, "The Spirit searches all things, even the deep things of God. For who among men knows the thoughts of a man except the man's spirit within him?"

I went to the dormitory in order to check on the health of Curtis who had a bout with his incurable ailment. He was comfortable and told me he would be in class the next day. I gave him the notes on what we had studied the last few days. I knew he would have no problem understanding the concepts.

As I was leaving the dorm, I noticed RYAN a well-dressed, handsome young man. Totally different from most who are on the streets of the Downtown, eastside. I wondered where he came from and why he was coming to the dormitory and why he was speaking to the guys.

He looked at me as I approached the group. He probably wondered why I spent time in that area.

From the conversation with the students, I realized he didn't know any of them.

Ryan smiled a lot and was personable. Soon the guys from the house were laughing with him and welcoming him into the fellowship. He told them that he was looking for a place to live as he had just left his residence in the suburbs.

By now I was part of the group. They asked me if Ryan could live with them in the dormitory.

I looked Ryan over and felt good vibes. I told him we have rules and regulations and indicated that if he read these rules and agreed to obey them and keep a good rapport with the residents, he could move in. I asked him when he wanted to begin residency.

He told me, "Right now."

"I've got my bags in the back of a friend's car which is parked around the corner."

I wondered where he came from and who told him about the dormitory and about the Mission. I left those questions to be answered later.

I thought more about it on my way home. People who come to the downtown east side usually do so for a reason. Many come to buy drugs, although I didn't detect any signs of Ryan's being a drug addict. I can usually tell by the eyes and by the mannerisms.

Another reason many come down here is to meet people as they are lonely and don't have any friends. Others have just been released from jail and they hope to meet former inmates. I didn't determine any of these as the reason for Ryan's being on skid row as he was driven downtown by a friend. It was a puzzle.

Ryan seemed to fit in well. He was soon pulling his weight at the Mission. As well he was pushing weights in our makeshift weight room.

The guys from the first class and the first residents of the dorm had filled paint cans with metal washers, bolts and nuts mixed with cement to make barbells. They also did the same to make weights. They had bicycle inner tubes to do stretching exercises and a few skipping ropes for cardio-vascular training. We were near the sea wall which was great for running and power walking.

Ryan joined the gym team and worked out every day except Sunday which is the Sabbath, a day of rest.

We encourage all students to be physically active as they have to sit in class for four hours a day.

The next week, Ryan enrolled in the Bible College.

He was one of the brighter ones and was a pleasure to have in the class. I kept wondering what brought him to this end of town. He didn't do drugs, drink or smoke. He was clean cut and educated.

Ryan talked to the girls but he preferred to keep company with the guys. He kept the discussions lively and there was a lot of laughing and joking when he was present.

With the girls, he talked about class assignments and topics related to the Mission and his hopes for the future.

Ryan gave his testimony two weeks after arriving on the scene and at the Mission.

"I have two sisters and one brother. My family comes from a city about two hundred and some miles from here. You all know where Central City is.

My father is a teacher and my mother is a stay at home mom.

I have lots of cousins, aunts and uncles. We are a close knit family. None of my family has come to live in the big city. They prefer to live in a smaller city where everyone knows each other. Some day I'll return home."

His voice cracked as he told how he wished he could return home.

Ryan continued, "I'm enrolled in Bible College as I need College skills in order to prepare for my becoming a lawyer. I also need a lot of cash for tuition fees to university. Right now, I'm having a great time living with my Christian brothers and sisters. I love the atmosphere and I'm getting my thoughts together. I'm still struggling with issues which have not been resolved. With Jesus in my life and the Holy Spirit guiding me, my walk is more meaningful and more fulfilling. I know most here are going into ministry. As I learned in class, there are many types of ministries. I know I will fit into one of these categories. Right now, I'm discovering who I am and what I need to do in order to change my life and make myself worthy to be with the Lord."

Everyone clapped and some went and hugged Ryan and told him."Well done."

The next day in class some wanted to discuss where we are going and how we are to get there. I put my lesson on hold and the students started to unload some of their baggage. They referred to the testimony of Ryan.

The question came up, "Can a person be a lawyer and still be a practising Christian?" Ryan answered that question by telling them that there are many types of lawyers. He told them all lawyers don't defend criminals and try to get them pardoned. "I want to help those who are wrongly convicted and those who can't afford a high class lawyer," Ryan stated.

I read between the lines and wondered if Ryan had been wrongfully convicted or if he had spent a lot of money on his defence. I sometimes wonder if my mind isn't working overtime thinking such thoughts Reading between the lines can at times lead me on the wrong path and in the wrong direction.

John asked Ryan how he intended to make enough money for tuition and still go to Bible College.

I had wondered the same thing. I did notice that Ryan spent a great deal of time in his room. I thought it was spent on his studies. He revealed what he was doing and why he spent the weekends away from the dorm.

The next day, Ryan brought his collection of hand made jewellery to the class. It was really stunning. He explained that he had taken a course on making this jewellery and he had an outlet in a mall, sharing a booth with another person.

The girls were all over his display asking the price and at times two of them wanting the same set of earrings or the same pendants. Ryan explained that he was taking orders and would deliver the merchandise in a day or two.

I got into the action and ordered two pairs of earrings for my wife and my daughter.

One of the girls suggested that Ryan set up his display in the Mission at least one day a week. She was told it would have to be approved by the board.

At the board meeting that week the suggestion was approved. They also recommended that other locations be opened to Ryan to sell his collection of jewellery as the proceeds were going towards his becoming a Christian lawyer.

A few weeks later, Irene enrolled in the Bible College. She is a middle aged woman. She asked Ryan in a sarcastic tone, "What are you doing here?"

Ryan ignored her. It appeared that they knew each other and that there was probably a relationship gone sour, or a friendship which ended on a bad note.

Ryan evaded her and would walk the opposite direction when she was around. They both kept away from each other.

At first it affected Ryan and I knew he'd rather not be in the same room as her.

Irene is an outgoing, outspoken, gregarious somewhat overweight blond haired lady who filled the room when she arrived. She wanted everyone to notice her and she kept things stirred up.

She was a smothering type who wanted to know everyone's business. She tried to look and act young.

During the worship with song, she puts everything she has into the music. She raises her arms and dances to the gospel rock. It brought a bit of gusto to the group and soon others were following her lead.

All except Ryan and a few of his friends who were too reserved and too macho.

Irene would grab some of them and swing them around, but she never touched Ryan.

I often wondered what the link was between these two.

Ryan did everything asked of him and volunteered to do extra duties.

The girls in the class wondered which one he would be more than friendly with. He talked to them all but kept his distance. Hilda tried to pull him into her trap, but Ryan wasn't buying her charm and seduction.

For the class, his testimony was simple.

He grew up in a good family and still retained ties with his family in a different city. He has two sisters and a brother who were still living with his parents.

He'd come to our city with a friend who went back to his home town and Ryan stayed. He had a good job, but there was a misunderstanding and he got fired. He was falsely accused of a misdemeanour, which got him into trouble. He never admitted to jail time, but reading between the lines; and rumour had it, this was the case.

Our policy is that no one will be judged by what they have done, but rather by who they are now and what they are doing for the Kingdom of God.

I watched the reaction of Irene when Ryan was giving his testimony. She was agitated and could hardly keep from interrupting.

During a conference session with Irene and one of her friends, she told all she knew about Ryan. It revealed why the two of them were not able to get along.

I cannot reveal the information divulged in the room as it is privileged information.

I did recommend that they come together and work out forgiveness. She said she wasn't ready to forgive him.

At a later date, I had a conference with Ryan. I told him what had been divulged when in conference with Irene. He admitted to some of the allegations but added his problems started as the result of her jumping to conclusions.

I wondered how the two of them could come together in the same room, let alone in the Mission and the College.

One day it blew wide open at a council meeting, when Ryan put down Irene and she spilled out a portion of her anger.

She asked me to intervene and have Ryan arrested.

Ryan then insisted that I have Irene arrested for false allegations.

This incident, terrible as it seemed at the time, brought to a head the animosity each held for the other.

Curtis took over as referee and called for a truce. He gave a short sermon on forgiveness and prayer.

We prayed for each in turn and asked them to forgive each other.

It was a tearful time but a time of release. I told them that what is bound on earth will be bound in heaven. You must break the bond, seek forgiveness for the past events, which keep you filled with anger and resentment. Otherwise the things of the past will destroy you and keep you from the peace Jesus has promised.

Irene wanted more time to think about it. Ryan agreed that he had had enough, and it was time to move on. He asked Irene to forgive him and move on.

Irene wouldn't let go of her past anger and hurt. She left the Mission and the Bible College. She went to another Bible School in a different part of the city where she graduated two years later using the credits received at our College. She became a missionary and went on mission trips to various third world countries. Spreading the gospel and making a difference in people's lives.

She occasionally visits the Mission and feels like she is still part of our family.

I had a session with her and she agreed to forgive Ryan and bring peace to herself and to those he had affected.

Ryan continued his studies and at one point became the Assistant Pastor in the Mission.

He has been present when Irene comes to dance to the gospel rock played by John our lead guitarist. She is especially friendly with Becky and Stacey.

When Ryan and Irene cross paths at the Mission or at times in the dormitory, they make eye contact and nod to each other. They don't talk or converse. There is still some distance between them.

Ryan told me he had to go home to visit his parents and make things right with the family.

"I can't keep hiding from my past. I need to get it out in the open and ask forgiveness for what I did as an adolescent. I hurt some people and I want them to know that I was responsible and am remorseful. I want back in the family as a person who needs their love and support."

Ryan took two weeks off of Bible College to get his life straightened out.

He gave a testimony at the graduation ceremony. Each student who graduates tells where they are going and what they are doing with the knowledge they have gained at Bible College and by preaching and being part of the service at the Mission

Ryan told that his dream of becoming a Christian lawyer is being fulfilled.

He informed us that he had enrolled in a University which would accept some of the credits he has earned at the Bible College.

He told us that the president of the university is a born again Christian. He explained that one of the board members of our College was a friend of the president of the University and is working on Ryan's behalf.

Ryan exuded, "Isn't it great what God can do for those who love him. Not only will I receive first year credits, but I have my name in for a bursary controlled by the president of the university. He informed me that I was on the list of recipients."

Everyone clapped and were elated at the news.

Ryan went from a person in trouble with the law, and running from problems with his family and others, to a law abiding born again spirit filled Christian who is going to serve the Lord as a lawyer with the purpose of bringing justice to all who need his services.

He has been radically changed and his life will radically affect others.

CHAPTER TWELVE

MATTHEW

Suicidal Drunk

Matthew 16:27,"For the Son of Man is going to come in His Father's glory with his angels, and then he will reward each person according to what he has done."

MATTHEW came to the Mission for the wrong reasons and with the wrong attitude

He is a First Nations man who tried to forget his past by tipping the bottle and getting stinking drunk. Not a nice introduction, but it fit the man who first came to the Mission at that time.

For months he came in various stages of intoxication. A few times he caused trouble and was asked not to yell and curse when the service was in progress.

The bouncer, another First Nations man who loves the church and loves God, confronted him. The bouncer is a big man, Matthew is a grasshopper in comparison. Matthew backed down, took a seat and was quiet.

The next day, Matthew came relatively sober. He apologized to the bouncer and told him he was sorry for his bad behaviour. Rather than stagger out of the Mission, Matthew stayed for the service.

I observed that he was genuinely interested in what was being sang and what was being preached and the testimony that was given by one of the students.

I made it a point to talk to him before he left for home.

Upon speaking to him, I found out that he was married and had children, but he had left his family in a village far away. He let his wife raise their children.

"They're better off without me," he contended.

He had left the reserve more than ten years before and was on the streets for most of that time.

The rest of the time he told me he was in jail for stealing, assault and various drug and alcohol related offences. "I'm not really sure if that's all the offenses but its enough," he laughed.

"I'm not proud for sure," he said, with his head bowed.

Matthew went on to tell that he'd tried to commit suicide a few times. "I just wanted to put myself out of my misery."

I told him about my best friend Jesus ,and how He could be his best friend.

"I ain't got no best friends," he confided. "When I got money, I got lots of friends," he laughed.

I felt that he was getting to the end of his rope. I invited him to keep coming to the Mission.

He asked, "Can I do anything to help?" I told him he could help set up the chairs and tables any morning or night and clean up after the service.

"Sounds good to me," he said as he departed.

That intervention put Matthew on the road to recovery.

The next night he was waiting when I opened the door. I took him through the steps we take to make the operation of the Mission run smoothly. He was a quick learner. I watched as he prepared the Mission for the service. He prepared the coffee and juice, put on the hot dogs to cook and readied the condiments.

When the other volunteers arrived, they wondered who is this man was who is putting us out of a job.

I introduced Matthew and he was soon accepted as one of the team.

He didn't feel he was smart enough to go to our College. He told me if it was grade three he'd consider enrolling. "My kids never went to college and they're a lot smarter than I am. They finished high school and I only finished the eighth grade," he said sadly. "I finished but I still can't read and I haven't written more than my name on my government cheque for ten or more years," he shook his head,

"The only label I read is the one on a wine bottle or on rice wine," Matthew laughed and laughed, "Me in College, what a dream."

I didn't ask him again. I did tell Stacey, a first nations lady with clout, to talk to him and see if she could get him to give the College a try.

Two days later, I was at the Mission and I observed Matthew in the kitchen working away. I wanted to ask him if Stacey had talked to him. I thought better of it and went about my business.

After the service and the clean up was taking place, I turned around and Matthew was standing beside me. I greeted him and told him he was doing a good job in the kitchen and cleaning the place.

He looked at me and smiled. I felt there was more than just his coming to the front of the Mission to stand beside me.

Matthew shook his head and said, "That lady sure is something. She could talk a man into doing anything she wants."

I knew who 'she' was and what she had told him.

"Don't be coy with me," Matthew said with a smile, "I know you put her up to trying to get me into that College."

I admitted that I did talk to her.

"Now she has me registered and all ready to go."

I laughed and told Matthew that was the best news I'd heard all day.

Matthew was not quite as dysfunctional as Henry. They were both from the same part of the country.

Matthew shook his head and told me, "Henry keeps telling people I'm his cousin. I really might be but I'm not proud of it."

I told him, "With Henry anyone born within one hundred miles of his village is his cousin."

Matthew laughed and said, "That's for sure."

Matthew gave his testimony.

He told everyone that he had great parents and had a good upbringing He said he wasn't that good in school, "I kept thinking about my dog and my horse and the fun I'd have after school. If it wasn't with my animals it was fun playing soccer and baseball with my friends

School was a bit of a blur. I was there in body but my mind was somewhere else. The teacher got tired of asking me for the answers and getting no reply. When the report card came home, I'd get a lickin' for not paying attention and getting failing grades. I didn't like the licking that my mom made my dad apply.

As soon as I reached fourteen, I quit school.

The problem was I couldn't get a decent job. Day labour and sometimes I'd work for a week or a few months.

I got a girl pregnant and I was forced by her brothers and uncles to marry her and take care of her. I really didn't like her as she was a slut and had slept with too many guys before we were married. She wasn't just second hand she had too many hands on her.

I divorced her and got me a better wife.

Unfortunately, my new wife chose the wrong man. I wasn't rich and I wasn't a high school graduate. I was nothing and had no value in the community. I love my wife, but as the kids started to come, I was over my head. I got tired of begging for food to feed my family. I was ready to work at anything to put food on the table and dress them properly for school.

I thought I'd come to the big city and get a good job. I'd send money home and in that way I would know they were eating and having a good life. I was willing to be a slave and sacrifice my life for my wife and kids.

It's pretty obvious that I didn't get that good job and make that big money. It drove me crazy to know that I was such a failure. I drowned my grief in a bottle and later in a fix.

The great thing is that they have accepted me in Bible College. Every time I think about it I have to pinch myself to make sure I'm not dreaming," he laughed.

"I'll check back in a few months and tell you how it's going.

Another thing. You guys who are wasting your time and your life drinking and doing drugs, being a parasite; get yourself in gear and get some schooling and make a difference in your life. Come to Bible College with me and the gang," Matthew encouraged.

Matthew did need help learning to read and he needed lots of practice with writing skills.

When we started on the Downtown east side, skid row, we knew there would be those who needed skills upgrading. It is part of the program. We match second and third year students with those needing help in reading and writing.

Matthew was motivated. He got a good tutor and applied himself.

Like others who come into the program, he wanted to learn how to play the guitar. We had a number of guitar teachers. We have a couple of musicians who are professionals but had drug problems that they were overcoming. They came to the mission and volunteered their time to sing worship to the Lord and teach others how to play the guitar. We also have those who have been taught by the professionals and have become proficient on the guitar. They too helped anyone who wanted to learn.

At the Mission ,everyone starts as floor cleaners and chair stackers and chair setter uppers. From there they go to work in the kitchen Matthew had already done his share of chairs and tables. There was an opening in the kitchen and Matthew was happy to pitch in and do the job.

Because he was eager and available, after six months he was promoted to assistant and then be the head of the kitchen.

Matthew ran a tight ship and all who worked with him knew they must be on time and not shirk their duties. He made changes to the system which riled a few of the regulars, who had been with the Mission for years.

We were soon soothing shattered egos and making changes back to the old system. We told Matthew that changes can only be made with the consent of the staff of the Mission.

Soon after that, Matthew made more changes. He was reprimanded and asked nicely to keep to the posted required duties schedule.

He argued that if he was in charge, he should have people do things the right way.

He was told that there are many ways but there is only one way the Mission carries out its duties. He was told, "You've read the procedures manual. Now follow it."

Matthew stormed out of the kitchen and out of the Mission. We thought we'd lost him.

I was not in the Mission when it happened. The next day I was informed about the cause and was also told he'd said he was quitting everything.

This has happened before but not too often. I wondered where he was and also wondered if he had tied one on.

In such cases I feel like we have lost one who has potential. I really thought we'd rescued one from the street. "Over a minor incident, the street claimed him back again," I thought.

Two days later he appeared in class. He acted as if nothing had happened

The students didn't ask any questions. He went with his tutor to the dormitory and did his studying.

Matthew did not want to live in the dorm. He had a room of his own in a rundown hotel. He had lived there for ten years and didn't want to give up what he considered was the best room in the hotel.

As I was leaving, I passed Matthew's desk and nonchalantly said, "I'll see you at the Mission." Matthew replied, "I'm finished with the Mission. They're a bunch of jerks. They boss everybody around."

I was not shocked as I had heard about the confrontation. I told Matthew that they really needed his help. "They have a promotion in store for you," I whispered.

After two more days, Matthew returned to the Mission and apologized to the staff and the kitchen volunteers.

He was reinstated and took on new responsibilities. No more kitchen for him. He was put in charge of arranging pastors for two services a day which he carried out for two years.

In both of the two years, Matthew graduated with good marks. Students are also marked on their work habits in the college and at the Mission. They are marked on their participation in class and in other settings.

Matthew marked quite high on his work habits, but not so well on his ability to get along with others in all situations.

At graduation the first year, Matthew had been sought out by two of his sons. They heard from others on the reserve who had visited the Mission, that their father was working in the Mission and going to Bible College.

Two weeks before graduation, they contacted Matthew. He told me about the reunion. I thought he would be elated. The problem was he didn't know how to relate to the responsibility of entertaining his sons. "I don't know how to handle my own boys. I try to say the right thing, but I feel ashamed having deserted them and wasted all those years in a drunken and drug filled stupor."

I could only tell him to convey love to his boys. "They have finally found the father they needed all these years. Let them love you for what you have become."

At the graduation, Matthew introduced everyone to his two sons. He was so proud when others made a fuss over his protege.

Matthew visits with his boys quite often. The boys are both working at a restaurant. They like to take Matthew out for a meal and tell him about their mother and all the relatives back home.

The second year at the college and Mission slipped by quickly for Matthew. He was now preaching on a regular basis and was leading worship with his new guitar and singing the worship songs he had mastered.

He was part of the outreach that went to Henry's village. Matthew took them to his village only eighteen miles further along the highway.

He had a reunion with his family and his friends. He had time to visit with his wife and apologize for treating her with disrespect.

The group had a good time in his village.

They then went to a ranch owned by an uncle of Matthew. The students rode horses and fed chickens and played with the kid goats. Some took pleasure playing with and petting the dogs and cats.

At the second year graduation ceremony, Matthew sang a gospel song that had been written by John. He told how he loved that song as it touched his heart.

When he went up to receive his certificate, his sons were there again and were all smiles.

His sons had retained their jobs in the restaurant. They kept Matthew informed as to what was happening in their village back home.

They also phoned and passed on word to the relatives in his village telling them that their father had completed two years of college. "He graduated second year in College Isn't that great!"

The family was getting along really well. Matthew started to laugh with them and enjoy their company.

In his third year, Matthew appointed himself as overseer of the whole Mission. Everyone was affected. For three months, he was the policeman. He was the final authority. If anyone had an issue, he would deal with it.

He went so far as to tell the volunteers and the students that he had authority over the staff and they were under his jurisdiction.

I received a phone call at home from a distraught volunteer telling me what was going on at the Mission. "He's told people that they shouldn't listen to the assistant pastor on issues that were related to discipline in the Mission.

Matthew tells everyone, 'Come to me and I will resolve all your problems.' He's getting really pushy," the volunteer told me.

The truth is, I saw this coming. I had told the Senior Pastor of the Mission that he had a problem on his hands. He told me he'd keep an eye on Matthew.

At a staff meeting we had to clip his wings. We pointed out that we operated as facilitators not as dictators and policemen. His authoritarian style was completely opposed to our more relaxed, loving and caring approach.

He realized his mistake and opted to complete his studies and step down from all other responsibilities.

Peace once again came to the Mission. People who quit because of the badgering and pushing around, by his heavy handed approach, were contacted and came back to the Mission. A few didn't come back as they thought his badgering and bullying had gone too far.

Matthew loved to play the guitar and sing, which he did until the end of his studies at the Bible College.

At this time, Alice, a First Nations young lady, came to the Mission with her sister. I knew the sister as she would come to the Sunday morning service. When it was testimonies time, she would come to the microphone and ask if she could sing a song. It was always the same song with eight verses and nine choruses. No one else sings that song as it has too many verses. Alice enjoyed the service and started coming regularly to the evening service at the Mission. She then enrolled in Bible College. She needed some upgrading in math and English. According to our formula, Matthew was to do the tutoring.

For the first four sessions they went to the dormitory study room or they stayed at the Mission for his teaching.

One morning soon after that, Matthew met me at the door before class. I knew something was not right with him. He explained how Alice had asked him to come to her apartment for the tutoring session as she had made some chocolate chip cookies and she would make a cup of tea. "I sat in the living room and she excused herself and went to the other room. She came back dressed in a skimpy dressing gown, above her knees. I knew what she wanted. It made me ill to think that she thought I would stoop so low.

I left in a hurry I told her what I thought of her.I knew I had to forgive her and I did."

Alice came to class the next day as if nothing had happened. I had the lady teacher talk to her. I learned that she was not well and was on medication.

A few weeks later she came to the Mission with a tall, well built, handsome young man. He was all smiles and she was proud of her catch. She brought him to Bible College and he was really interested. He came to class for two months.

One day he was distraught. He was angry. He claimed that he had become infected with HIV and Aids. He blamed those at the Mission for not warning him of this danger. He left the College with a lot of cursing and swearing.

I felt I might know who infected him. I always warn the students to stay away from sexual contact with all women on skid row. He had heard my warning, but it was too late as he was already infected.

Three months later, Alice was confined to a wheelchair. A year or so later Alice died. I attended her funeral as I knew her family.

Matthew took it upon himself to mentor others and counsel people from the Mission and those in the College who needed help with their studies or with their problems.

He assisted in the Mission and initiated some repairs which he completed along with some volunteers.

He made it known that he desired to be ordained when he graduated. He became a candidate for ordination which pleased everyone.

Imagine an addict and drunk who wanted to commit suicide; was radically changed in three short years.

Now he is becoming a candidate for ordination in the hopes of becoming the pastor of a Church.

Unfortunately, something in his past life became a stumbling block and his ordination was denied.

We, at the Bible College, have no recourse in regards to a denial. It is up to the review board of the denomination.

They told Matthew why they had to reject his application. He accepted the consequences. They told him he could plant a church and do what he was trained to do, but he had to do it without being ordained.

Lack of ordination did not deter Matthew. He figured it was God's will.

He told me he prayed and the Holy Spirit is now guiding him along the path he should go.

He has become an avid reader and student. He took what he has learned in Bible College and went on to upgrade his skills in order to enter university.

I have kept in touch with him over the years. He did his upgrading and entered a prestigious university.

During his last year at the College, he was going around with a lady who was very active in a mainline church in a trendy area of the city. She was teaching a course at our College. She really liked him and I guess he really liked her. They were married and are living happily ever after

She has a high paying job and has been supporting Matthew in his studies.

The last I heard, not too long ago, is that he is completing a degree in Psychology in his quest to become a Christian counsellor.

He still comes to the Mission and the College occasionally and we have a chat.

Matthew went from a drunk and rebellious first nations man bent on suicide to a university student going in for Christian counselling. He has been radically changed over the period of a few years.

CHAPTER THIRTEEN

ROY

Worshipping Creation

Proverbs 3:27, "Do not withhold good from those who deserve it when it is in your power to act.

ROY is a young First Nations man who came to the Mission to check it out. He partook of the food and coffee and analysed the set up. He was approached by two members and welcomed. They asked him if he would like to be part of the Mission as a volunteer. He nodded and shrugged but was non-committal, preferring to remain on the outside looking in.

He left without saying goodbye or acknowledging the fact that he was welcomed.

Two days later, he returned and displayed the same nonchalant attitude.

I spoke to him briefly but received no indication that he had any interest in the Mission or the Bible College.

"I'm just hanging around. Any problem with that?" was his response.

I felt there was more to his visits, but I couldn't pinpoint his motivation. There are so many people coming into the Mission each night that one more didn't really make a big difference.

The thing about Roy was that he did a lot of staring and observing. It was as if he was making mental notes of all the staff, volunteers and students. As Cindy put it, "He gives me the creeps. Staring at me all the time."

This on and off attendance and scrutiny ended when he came to the Bible College and enrolled. A surprise to everyone. I waited for his testimony before speaking to him other than to welcome him to the College.

He testified that he was in no hurry to get involved."I was looking to see if the Great Spirit was in this place. I discern it could be. But there are a couple of people who need more knowledge of the Spirit and how it works in their lives."

This started some students questioning what he saw in them. It also started some finger pointing and set a few back on their heels.

He concluded that part of his testimony by stating, "If I didn't discern the Great Spirit and the possibility of each person rising to their potential, I wouldn't darken the doors of the College or the Mission."

He went on to tell us that he is from a native band on the prairies. "We're different from those in other parts of the country. We are a proud people and we have a great history. My father is a chief and some day I too will be a chief if my older brother doesn't take on the responsibility.

Our Indian way states that I must make myself ready. I still believe in the ways of my forefathers. They have much wisdom and worship the Great creator. I too worship this spirit. That is why we take such good care of the earth. It is our heritage.

You might ask why I came to your College. Perhaps we can find some mutual understanding. My father learned from a travelling evangelist about your Mission and your Bible College. He told me it allowed first nations people to learn what the missionaries taught our people many years ago.

If I am to be chief, I must complete my spiritual preparations.

We have the physical to develop, the mental and the spiritual.

Physically I am a prime specimen. I can run for miles in my mocassins and I can lift weights. Mentally, I have been trained by my elders and I have completed high school. After I complete my spiritual training, I will go to university in a city near my reserve. Some people ask me why I worship the gods of my ancestors. I tell them there is only one god in the universe and it is the Great creator.

I was defending my god when I was struck in the face for my insolence. I struck back and it ended in a fight. I was charged with assault and battery as I am too strong. The charges were dropped. I don't believe in fighting, but I had to defend the god of my mother and father and my many aunts and uncles.

There is more I can tell you, but it will wait for another time. After I have learned much about your God and His Son."

I heard a few comments in the next week ranging from, "He's real spiritual." To the other extreme, "He really thinks he's great."

After this testimony, Roy had to prove himself. I didn't intervene except to ask a few dissenters to see if they could find a fault in his testimony.

Roy opted to live in the dormitory. Although he wasn't aware of the scriptures, he lived out the command to, 'be joyful always'.

I learned he had been to a church service when he was young. He had also been to weddings. That was the extent of his going to church.

He had very little knowledge of Christian thinking.

His essays were different as he viewed everything from a spiritual perspective according to his native spirituality.

Because of his aptitude and his training in spiritual matters he was given credit for his way of thinking. He came a month late but was able to do a correspondence course and set himself up for graduation.

I observed his fellowshipping in the dormitory, College and Mission. He moved easily between the students from the college and the men on the street.

Many from the street came to the Mission primarily for the food we serve twice a day. They are also given spiritual food in the form of worship in song and in the word of God, in testimonies and fellowship with the believers.

On outreaches, Roy participated and was helpful in setting up and getting everything ready for the services. He played the guitar and sang contemporary songs. He quickly learned gospel songs and took delight in singing to the Lord and praising God Almighty. I often wondered which god he sang praises to.

He was always the first to get up in the morning and put on the coffee and cook breakfast. His pleasant demeanor set the tone for the day and everyone was happy and having fun.

He was all business when it came to witnessing to a community during the outreaches. He went onto the street and talked to strangers as if he had known them for years. He took a group of students with him and went knocking on doors and inviting people to our worship services.

He was great with First Nations persons as some of them are shy, but they opened up to his personality and smiling countenance. Not only his own people, but all he encountered and spoke with recognized the Spirit in him and responded positively.

Roy never once criticized or faulted our Christian teachings. He had a Bible and decided he would read every word.

Out in the yard he would perform his native ceremonies. He would light a fire and take some special dried grass and wipe smoke over his body as a cleansing. He would often sit cross legged and meditate.

No one bothered him as he has the right to his way of praying and meditating.

After two months of Bible College, he started asking questions about what he had read in the Bible and what he learned in class. He tried to make comparisons with native teachings and native spirituality and that of the Christian belief.

His remarks led me to believe that his native spirit was being replaced with the Holy Spirit who was beginning to work in his life

I heard him tell one of the guys from the dormitory , "Your Lord Jesus is a miracle man. It is no wonder you give your life to Him and want to become like Him."

Another time I heard him tell one of the lady students, "My ancestors were great warriors and were judged on their prowess in battle. Your Jesus is judged by his love and compassion. I am trying to understand the difference."

The student's response was, "Our Jesus Christ is a warrior for the faith as he voluntarily was beaten, nailed to the cross and died so that we could have our sins forgiven, overcome death and we could be friends with God our Father."

I watched as Roy digested the great things Jesus did for us. Suddenly his face lit up. He looked at Cindy and exclaimed, "I think he did it for me and my parents, my aunts and uncles."

Roy came to my office for a visit. In the first three months I have a visit with every new student. I asked him how things were going.

He shook his head, "Can I tell you the truth?" I told him he could tell me anything and it would not be repeated to anyone

Roy told me that he was in a state of confusion. "I know I should keep my native beliefs and keep them as my priority Yet I know people on my reserve who are Christians. They stay on the reserve as natives, but they worship your God and his Son Jesus. They come to the potlatches and wipe smoke for cleansing as it is our custom. My question is, can I take parts of each belief and become half and half."

I asked him, "Why would you want to do that?

He said he wants to be a good chief to all his people, the Christians and the worshippers of the creator and of creation.

I told him we worship the one who created the universe. He did not tell us to worship his creation. He created the beauty for all to enjoy and care for.

I explained, "You must make the decision to have creation as part of your mental process, understanding the way God put the earth together and keeps it together. This you will learn at university when you study the sciences."

I went on to tell him, "You must treat the spiritual as a separate part which brings us into the presence of God Almighty and into His Kingdom. As you testified, there is the physical, the mental and the spiritual."

I waited for Roy to form an understanding in his mind. He told me, "I do know some chiefs who are Christians. I used to think they were traitors. Now that I think about it, they are the best chiefs. They do not cheat and lie. They don't take the money that must go to the people." Roy looked at me and smiled. "You have the right answers, thank you. Now I am set free and I will be free indeed."

We laughed together as Roy began using verses from the scriptures.

Roy had a bounce to his step as he left the office. I knew the light of Jesus was beginning to shine in his life.

Two weeks later, I watched as he walked down the street. Regulars from the Mission stopped him as he walked along and asked that he pray for them.

First nations people offered him a drink from their brown paper bag, but he gently refused and started telling them about Jesus.

One man broke down and started crying. Roy took him back to the Mission and witnessed Christ Jesus to him.

At counsel meetings, Roy put forward some good ideas which were acted upon. We now have a new door on the kitchen and the fridge has been moved to make more room for the servers.

Roy did his stint in the kitchen. He was a good worker and got along well with the volunteers, staff and the people from the street. Most people are in the kitchen at the beginning of their stay in the dorm, but Roy opted to wait until he understood where he was going and how he was to get there before committing himself to tasks.

He testified that he had now made the decision to follow Jesus. "I will be a Christian chief and if not a chief, I will be a Christian church leader in my community."

The people from the street did not understand what Roy had gone through in order to make this decision. The students did understand and gave Roy a standing ovation.

By now, the term was ending as graduation was about to take place. There was a great deal of activity as some had outstanding essays to complete and all had final tests to write.

Roy did not get caught up in all the preparations. He went into the back yard, lit a fire, took some grass and wiped the smoke over his body. He sat cross legged and meditated.

I wanted desperately to know what he prayed for and to whom he prayed.

No one commented on his practise as it is personal.

At graduation, Roy was dressed in his native apparel. Wearing his moccasins and a beautiful beaded buckskin jacket.

I smiled but wondered if his native spirituality had really been replaced by the love of Jesus and a commitment to follow the commands and obey what is written in the scriptures.

It was graduation and Roy proudly accepted his certificate as a commissioned Christian.

We had discussed in class the meaning behind each of the three certificates and diplomas. When each person accepted theirs, they knew the were committing their life to Jesus the Christ and His Father.

Before leaving for the summer, I had a brief chat with Roy.

He told me he was taking this time to go back to be with his family, a trip of over 1200 miles.

"I've a few cousins who need the Lord in their lives," he told me.

"Now that I know the true Lord and Saviour, I can witness not only to my parents but also to my brother who is a borderline alcoholic. Every time I go to visit, it's always, "Lets party." If he wants to become the chief, he has to smarten up. His standing in the community is not that great. I will spend the summer bringing him to the Lord.

We said our good-byes and he was on his way by bus.

When Bible College convened in the fall, Roy was not there. We sometimes lose one or two who get a job or get interested in other ventures.

I felt that perhaps Roy would come back in his own time. Maybe a week or so late but it didn't happen.

I did get a call from him telling me he was working with the band.

"When I showed them my graduation certificate from the Bible College they told me I must prepare to be the chief. I must go to university and take courses.

I told them I was enrolled in Bible College for two more years. They told me, that I must spend six months at a Native College learning the ways of the band and their relationship with the government.

The leaders of the band told me, " After that you will go to university and then you are free to complete Bible College."

"They have my life planned for the next five years," he laughed.

I assured him we would be waiting and happy to greet him when he returned to the Bible College.

He thanked us for bringing Christ Jesus into his life.

He told me, "When I showed them my diploma and I told them I was going to graduate some day, at the Bible College, they talked me into preparing myself to be the chief. I didn't know a diploma had that much influence," he laughed.

"My father is old and wants to retire. My brother stepped down as a candidate for chief as he is too sick to carry such a load of responsibility."

Roy explained, "God does such great things in my life. Now I can help my people as a Christian leader. I have many plans to make my reserve the most prosperous and the most spiritually guided."

"I shared my ideas with the band elders and they are very happy."

Roy went from being a worshipper of creation to being a worshipper of the Great God Almighty the Creator of heaven and the earth.

He has been radically changed by coming to Bible College.

As a result of his coming to Bible College he is becoming a Christian chief and band leader in his nation.

One year later, Roy got in touch with the College by e-mail.

Roy assured us he was doing well and doing his own ministry among his people on the reserve. He bragged that he had brought over twenty converts to the Lord that year.

In my reply by email I asked if we could take an outreach to his reserve when he becomes chief.

In our exchange of e-mails, he said he would be honoured to have the students visit his reserve.

The students were sad when told Roy wouldn't come back to the College for a few years.

They were happy to know that he was doing the ministry that God had sent him to do.

We pray for Roy on many occasions, asking God to keep him strong in the faith and make His will for Roy's people known to Roy.

The counsel agreed to have an outreach in the future go to the reserve where Roy is becoming the chief and leading his people into worshipping and honouring the Lord.

CHAPTER FOURTEEN

JOYCE

Last Chance

Psalm 113:2,3 "Let the name of the Lord be praised, both now and forevermore. From the rising of the sun to the place where it set, the name of the Lord is to be praised."

JOYCE came from the suburbs to the Downtown eastside for one reason only and that was to go to Bible College. Upon registration she told the registrar, "I have been to church a few times, like Christmas and Easter, but I feel I haven't learned anything. I need to have something more in my life."

I learned that she had just been divorced from her husband as she had become too domineering and argumentative. She told one of the staff, "I need something and I think it's the Lord."

She told the students, "My life is really a mess. I can't go on this way. I messed up our marriage and have ruined the life of my husband and my daughter. I need help. I went to a Psychiatrist but he only told me what I already knew. He prescribed pills that made me hallucinate. It was really scary and weird. I was in a different world when on those pills I threw them in the garbage.

I'm going to try religion as a last resort. If that doesn't work I'm going to commit suicide. It's that serious."

The students hugged her and told her she must pray and let the Lord Jesus bring her peace and fill her with joy.

Later, I asked her why she had selected our College on skid row?

She told me our College was the least expensive and because it was affiliated with a more prestigious college and the courses are recognized and transferrable, to the prestigious college, it is what she could afford at this time . She added that our College has a good reputation. It is also great in that it gives a person practical job training at the Mission.

I realized that she had done her homework and knew all about our Bible College and the benefits it affords.

It turned out that she knew Dan's wife and she had told her about the Mission and the Bible College.

Joyce never missed a class and she did her best in every course. She tried to get top marks in every subject. She was a late bloomer in that she was in her mid forties.

She dressed in the latest fashion and was immaculately groomed and coiffured. She always smelled like roses.

The other girls were in jeans and t-shirts, shorts and halters in the summer.

There is no dress code except people had to wear shirts and pants or shorts and t-shirts. Shoes or sandals are also mandatory.

Every beginner has to start sweeping and mopping the floors.

The men have to stack and set up the chairs for the services.

From there they work in the kitchen and work their way into the more challenging positions.

First year students took a back seat to second and third year students.

Everyone takes pride in their position on the podium and in the front facing the congregation at the Mission on Sunday mornings.

Students are given these promotions when it was determined they have earned the right to move up and when they will benefit by the place of honour. It was also based on what year they were enrolled in.

JOYCE, on her first Sunday, moved herself into a position reserved for those with seniority. It was my duty to inform her of the ranking and ask her to move back.

She was embarrassed. After the service she asked me why I didn't inform her before she made such a fool of herself. I apologized and brought her attention to the 'MISSION MANUAL'.

She admitted she hadn't read the manual, which is one of the priorities with all new students. She thumbed through the manual and felt better knowing what was expected of her.

I observed her working in the kitchen and was happy to see that she was not condescending but rather she was very accommodating to the men and women from the street. On the whole, she got along quite well with the students.

On one occasion she got upset when Stacey made a disparaging remark. They got into a shouting match after class. Joyce was in the right, but Stacey, being the outgoing person she was and having a short fuse, came at Joyce with a vengeance.

I let it go its course. A couple of guys and girls put a stop to it. Stacey threw her books down on the floor, with papers flying and stomped out. Joyce felt sorry that she had lost her cool. She picked up Stacey's books and papers and put them in her locker.

"I can't believe I did such a thing," she stated in disbelief.

A student asked what happened? Joyce told her side of the story which made sense.

As time went by, Joyce was given more and more responsibility.

When Joyce left the College each day, she went directly to work as a clerk in a ladies fashion shop in an upscale mall.

This kept her busy and didn't give her too much time for study and doing her assignments.

She had to drive twenty minutes to her work, as her job was closer to her home than it was to the College.

She would leave the class after only a short time to socialize.

She worked some mornings when her classes started at one o'clock. This gave her time after class to socialize and work on her assignments.

Three outreaches each year are mandatory for all students and necessary for graduation. This put Joyce in a tenuous situation. It meant that she had to take time off work.

We made arrangements on her behalf.

She only had to go on outreaches that would last for no more than one or two days on weekends. Joyce thanked us. She looked forward to these outreaches.

The first outreach was to a village where they were just starting a Mission. They asked us to bring some students in order to let young people know that it was cool to go to church and volunteer. They also asked us to bring a young worship team and an on fire evangelical preacher.

We fulfilled all the criteria. It was an overnight weekend trip returning Sunday evening.

Everyone brought their sleeping bags, foams and a pillow. A back pack with spare clothes and toiletries.

Joyce arrived at the van with two big suitcases and an overnight bag. She was prepared for a weeks stay. She didn't have a sleeping bag, only a pair of sheets and a thin quilt. No pillow and no foam or air mattress.

All night, she let people know how cold she was. She kept telling different people to turn up the heat. She didn't know that the heat was controlled by a thermostat in the office below the Mission.

The girls covered her with their jackets and one young man gave her an extra blanket to help keep her warm.

She was the first one up and put on the coffee. Roy helped her with the eggs, toast and bacon. Joyce kept telling him how cold it was. He told her she'd get used to it.

At the Sunday service, Joyce was asked to join the singers on the stage. It was the first time she was asked to do worship. She was really nervous. I told her to turn her microphone low and if she made a mistake no one would know the difference.

She looked at me as if I were crazy. She told me, "I won't sing unless people can hear me. I've got a good voice."

On the trip home, Joyce joined in the singing and the joking. When we arrived home she thanked me and told me she enjoyed everything except the cold nights.

"I'm going to buy the best down-filled sleeping bag money can buy and an air mattress," she exclaimed.

On Monday, she asked when we were going on the next over nighter. I told her we hadn't planned one, but I'd let her know in lots of time.

We were signing up people for an international two week outreach. to Mexico in two months time.

We warned the students that it would be in a slum area of a large city. They would be working with children and their parents in some unsanitary conditions..

I was surprised to see that Joyce had signed up for herself and her nineteen year old daughter, Evelyn, who was graduating from high school that year.

Joyce told Becky that she was taking her two weeks holiday to go on the mission trip and Evelyn was taking two weeks off of school.

Evelyn was well known to the students as she would come to class with her mother, when she had a day off school.

She is a very attractive young lady. The guys gave her a second look and sometimes another look as she is totally different from most of the girls in the College.

Joyce gave her testimony at the Mission on a Sunday.

She told us that she was raised in a good family but not a religious family. "My father told my sister and I that religion was a crutch for those not able to get along on their own.

My mother sent us to Sunday school but she never came to the church. She didn't want to cause trouble with my father.

I had one aunt and uncle who were regular church goers. My father told me they were a little odd. I believed him and laughed behind their backs.

When I was old enough, I quit Sunday School and never went to church again.

My sister moved away and I rarely see her. We do phone once a month and I hear about her children and her husband. She keeps telling me that they are living a great life.

I didn't tell her that I had to kick my husband out of the house as he wasn't listening to me and he was always arguing. We had a big disagreement and I told him he could leave. I didn't think he had the backbone to pack up and go. I was wrong. I pleaded with him to come back, but he's a stubborn Irishman," she confided.

"My life has gone downhill from there. I had to take a job, which I find very difficult. The owner of the store is very nice which makes it somewhat pleasant.

Also, I had to sell our second car as I couldn't afford the insurance. My daughter sides with my husband and the two of them pick on me at times.

Not so much Evelyn. She is only upset that this all happened before she graduated and left home.

I don't want to work for anyone else, so I thought the ministry would be right for me. I don't know only what I learned at Sunday School, but our neighbour is a minister and he seems to keep pretty good hours and he lives in a nice house.

That's about all I can tell you. Thanks."

I wanted to tell Joyce about the broken hours we Pastors keep. A phone call at two in the morning asking us to settle a domestic dispute.

Someone else asking us to come to the hospital and pray or the police station for support. There are often long and broken hours. Not eight hours and its finished.

Joyce was promoted and given the task of greeting at the door. She was a really great greeter. She asked people their names and she remembered those names and greeted each person the next time they came to the mission.

I didn't go on the trip to Mexico. I wondered how this prim and proper lady would manage in a slum setting. She disliked the downtown eastside slums, now she was going to an even filthier area.

This trip, Joyce had a sleeping bag and everything she needed.

Evelyn had taken tips from Joyce and was well equipped for the trip.

I got a call on the evening of the second day.

I was told that Joyce had a difference of opinion with Stacey. There was a shouting match and Stacey started throwing things around. Joyce wanted to take a bus back home. The leader told me, "I had to be the referee."

He went on to explain, "We had to stop for a few hours and pray. Things calmed down.

During that prayer, the students held hands in a circle.

The Holy Spirit came down in power on all the group and they were all filled with the Spirit of God. Some were crying, others fell on their backs, some kept praising the Lord."

"I have never witnessed such an event," he proclaimed, "It was unbelievable!"

When they returned I learned that Joyce and Stacey were now the best of friends. They told me that Joyce took on the role of mother to the younger students and to some of the older students as well.

One of the guys told me that Joyce actually glowed in the power of the Spirit.

I had the leader of the trip give his testimony of the trip at the Mission and to the College.

Evelyn, the daughter of Joyce ,noticed the difference in her mother and started to come with her more often to class and stay for the lesson.

A month after the trip was graduation. Joyce really looked forward to being commissioned. She told me she knew what commissioned meant to the followers of Jesus.

"Just to think that I am being commissioned to go out and do a ministry."

The mother and father of Joyce came to the graduation. He was proud of his daughter. He told me she was never happier. I didn't get into the topic of religion as I knew his views on the subject. I wondered if he still thought that religion was a crutch, now that his daughter was filled with the Spirit.

I was surprised to see Evelyn arrive with her father. He was a big handsome Irishman. I knew why Joyce wanted him back again.

I prayed that they would get together as they made a stunning couple.

That summer went by quickly and soon we were enrolling new students as well as those returning. Our students did the enrolling. At times I'd come and greet those who were returning and introduce myself to the new students.

Joyce and Evelyn came in together. I was surprised to see Evelyn go to the table where new students enrolled. I told Joyce, "That's a pleasant surprise."

Joyce told me that Evelyn, upon graduating, was not certain what career to pursue. "She is trying out ministry as one of her options."

She told me that Evelyn was appalled at what she saw on the streets when she first came to the Mission. Men and women shooting up drugs in plain view. Prostitutes on street corners and drunks drinking from a brown paper bag sitting at the bus stop near the Mission.

Homeless men and women sleeping in doorways and on the steps of a church where they were fed and given clean clothes.

So many just hanging around, lost souls with no direction in their life.

Evelyn asked her mother what could be done for them. Joyce told her, "We can love those who come into the Mission and give them the word of God. Give them something to eat. Listen to their story comfort and counsel them."

Evelyn was still very new to the streets, she asked Stacey, "Can you give them money. They look so sad."

Stacey told her, "Money buys drugs or alcohol. We need a long term solution."

"What is the solution?" Evelyn asked eagerly.

"For many it's been a walk with Jesus; they need His love and our love."

Evelyn nodded in agreement. "Perhaps this is the answer to my career goal."

Stacey agreed

Evelyn looked at the people, who came into the Mission, with new eyes and a different attitude. She told the class that she wants to study for at least one year at the College and then go into Social work. She wants to help those in need.

Evelyn was a cut above most of the students when it came to writing essays and sermons. She loved to read the texts and the books in the library.

I wasn't sure our College was the answer. It is geared as a starting point for further studies. Some of our courses are recognized for credit at the more prestigious college.

I asked Joyce if she thought Evelyn would be better off enrolling in the four year fully accredited program.

Evelyn took my advice. She asked her father if he would support her in her studies and he agreed.

A week later we got the news that Evelyn had been accepted. She moved closer to the new College and was happy in her dormitory setting.

She would come down to meet with her mother at the Mission and they would go out for a meal now and then.

They were very close and enjoyed each others company.

Joyce came to the Mission and the College as a last resort. She tried to be happy making money, but that only brought her problems. Her authoritarian attitude drove her husband away. With everything she worshipped in the dust, she turned to Jesus.

Joyce worked hard for three years and graduated with honours.

When she was powerfully transformed by the Holy Spirit on the way to Mexico, her life took on new meaning. She was radically changed and commissioned for service to the Lord..

She is now an assistant pastor in a newly formed church in the suburbs near her home. It's an evangelical church.

Joyce had the phone number of some of the worship leaders that came to the Mission. She chose the best ones for their new church.

Evelyn told us that her father has dated her mother a few times. "Things are looking up," she smiled.

CHAPTER FIFTEEN

EDGAR

Atheist

Psalm 145:8,9 "The Lord is gracious and compassionate, slow to anger and rich in love. The Lord is good to all; He has compassion on all that He has made."

Curtis started going on the street and doing ministry after each service.

He and his girl friend, Ruth, witnessed to hundreds of people over a period of two and a half years. They would gather from two to twenty people at a time and have them listen to their message of hope in the Lord Jesus Christ.

One night, they witnessed to a small group and were heckled by Edgar. Some street people wanted to shut this atheist up forcefully. Curtis and Ruth calmed them down and brought Edgar into the Mission.

He was young and handsome, dressed neatly and was well groomed, light brown skin which led me to believe he was from either Central American or the Philippines or another South Asian country.

Curtis sat at a table with Edgar and served him coffee and a sweet roll.

They talked for about twenty minutes, then Edgar got up and left.

Curtis came over to tell me about his latest hope of bringing a lost soul to Christ. He told me that Edgar claimed to be an atheist.

I told Curtis that atheists are sometimes difficult to bring to the Lord.

Curtis told me he didn't think Edgar would come back to the Mission as they had had a very intense session. Lots of friction.

The next night, I was evaluating a sermon for one of the students who was preaching for the first time. The music was still playing so I had some time to think about my next days lesson.

I was enjoying the music as a former student was leading the worship.

I was aware that someone had pulled up a chair and was sitting beside me. I looked over and saw it was Edgar. I acknowledged him and greeted him warmly.

"Is Curtis coming tonight?" he asked

I told him Curtis has a test tomorrow and is studying.

"Is he going to university?"

"No, he's going to Bible College," I informed him.

Edgar looked at me and asked why I was down on skid row.

I was going to ask him the same question, but I asked, "Why shouldn't I be on skid row?"

"You look like you should be in some ivory tower at a big university."

I thanked him for the complement and told him I was the dean of the College down here on skid row.

Edgar was eager to tell me he was an atheist. "I don't believe in anything related to the Bible and all that. I believe that someone was high on drugs and made up the whole story."

I told him, "If you believe something doesn't exist, it must exist in order for you to refute its existence."

Edgar smiled. He knew I was not going to agree with him. He changed the subject. "So what exactly do you teach at the College?" he asked.

I told him I taught the books of scripture and the doctrines of God.

"Do you believe everything you teach?"

I told Edgar I had been studying the Bible for forty years and I believe every word, as it is God inspired.

"You mean its taken you forty years to read one book?" he exclaimed.

I told him that with the Bible and related books of doctrine it's a life-time study.

That ended our conversation. The preacher was introduced and I told Edgar I had to listen as I was evaluating the sermon. He was very polite; he stayed and listened to the sermon.

Edgar wanted to know more. After the sermon he asked me what the doctrines were.

I told him to come to the College and he would find out.

Edgar told me he had to get going. "Tell Curtis I'll see him tomorrow."

I wondered what made Edgar tick.

I learned from Curtis that Edgar was from the Honduras. His parents were very rich land owners. I also found out that he was living with his aunt in an upscale neighbourhood in the city. He wanted to go to university, but his transcripts had not arrived and he was classified in the country as a tourist, which didn't qualify him to study. He told Curtis it was all under review. He couldn't work and he couldn't go to university.

Edgar regarded Curtis as his best friend. He kept hanging around the Mission and the dormitory.

One night, I was at the Mission and asked Edgar if he would like to enroll in the Bible College. He looked at me as if I were nuts.

"Me, come to Bible College! I don't think so"

Curtis was with him and told him if he didn't like it he could walk out at any time. "It's better than hanging around the streets doing nothing all day."

It took a few days for Edgar to build up the courage to even attend one class.

I heard Curtis ask him, "What have you got to lose?"

Monday, Curtis was all smiles as he escorted Edgar to class.

We were studying the Book of Colossians. We were going over Chapter two where Paul was saying:

Colossians 2:2-4, My purpose is that they may be encouraged in heart and united in love, so that they may know the mystery of God, namely, Christ in whom are hidden all treasures of wisdom and knowledge. I tell you this so that no one may deceive you by fine-sounding arguments."

These scriptures opened the door to a great deal of discussion. I had asked Edgar to listen and learn as I knew it was all new to him and he would have a multitude of questions. I told him I would be available after class to go over some areas of concern with him.

Edgar did have questions which Curtis and I answered to the best of our ability. I knew that he was interested but he felt he was in spiritual kindergarten trying to be a Bible College student.

I loaned him a book which gave a very simple understanding of the scriptures.

To my surprise, Edgar kept coming back again and again. I kept encouraging him and answering his many questions. He never again mentioned the word atheist.

At the College, Edgar gave his testimony.

He told why he was in this end of town. He'd met some other Hondurans who made their living on the street. "I'd never do what they're doing, but I like my countrymen.

I'm applying for landed immigrant status. If not I'll be deported," he stated.

"In the Honduras my family is highly respected in the community. My father owns a large ranch, a sugar cane plantation and processing facility. My life is easy, but I must be educated as I will be the governor of my province some day," he smiled.

"Money talks in my country," he laughed.

"My aunt talked my father into having me be educated in this great country as credentials from these universities are highly regarded in my land.

Wish me luck that I will be successful in my review and will be allowed to go to university in this great city."

He went on to tell us, "I received some bad information when I applied to the government and it has hindered the chances of my living in this country and going to university."

He ended his testimony by saying, "I love this country and the people are so very kind, thank you."

Edgar was beginning to show his humble side.

I watched him as he made friends, wondering which group he would associate with. It was sometimes an indicator of where he would end up.

He floated between groups and used his charm to receive invitations to be part of their cliques. By the way, we do not endorse cliques.

He attended classes regularly and carried out his assignments. We completed our study of Colossians and the Doctrine of Anthropology, which is the study of how man fits into the spiritual mosaic with regard to sin.

Edgar was beginning to become engrossed in the studies. He had fewer questions and his essays were well written. They conveyed to us that he was becoming more familiar with the scriptures and the doctrines.

Our next topic was, 'The Book of Revelation'.

He took a keen interest in this Book as it grabbed his attention.

On the third day of classes, he blurted out, "Hey!"

I asked if he had a problem with my teaching.

"On the contrary, this is great stuff."

I smiled thinking this guy is for real. I realized he was understanding the Book of Revelation, which many Christians steer clear of as there is imagery and symbols they don't understand.

I wrote a booklet on the Book of Revelation, so that the students didn't have to make copious notes. They just had to follow along as I taught.

Edgar kept the booklet with him wherever he went. He'd pull it from his pocket and check the information with the Bible and nod his agreement.

Bible College was a sort of diversion for Edgar. I heard him tell a student that the Bible was a great book and also coming to College was a good way to learn better English.

I didn't mind his wanting to learn better English. I only hoped some knowledge and understanding of the scriptures would give him a spiritual foundation.

When Evelyn, the daughter of Joyce enrolled as a student, I noticed that Edgar paid close attention to her. It was not long until their friendship blossomed. I wanted to tell her to go slow, but I was not in a position to do so.

Joyce was now in her third year and coming up to graduation

Joyce liked Edgar and the two of them got along quite well. She was still filled with the Holy Spirit and this intrigued Edgar.

I noticed when they were at the Mission, Edgar had Evelyn's hand clasped in his.

After class the two of them waited for Joyce to set up the kitchen then all three left the College together. They were laughing and joking.

I thought perhaps I was wrong in thinking Edgar and Evelyn might be getting too chummy.

I watched the relationship develop. There were times of great joy and times where Evelyn was upset with Edgar.

One day after class when Edgar was waiting for Evelyn, I had a talk with him. He assured me everything was O.K.. He told me, "Evelyn gets uptight and demands her way. She's definitely spoiled. But I can manage her. She's coming around."

This disturbed me. Edgar, from my observation, was prone to manipulate and control women. Many swooned and wanted to be near him and be his friend for life.

He was extra nice to me, as he was taught to respect his elders and especially his teachers.

When something happened on a week-end, I heard the news early Monday morning.

Everyone was in a state of shock. The word had it that Edgar had knocked Evelyn unconscious and she was taken away in an ambulance.

I found it hard to believe that Edgar would do such a thing. I told the members of the class not to jump to conclusions without solid evidence.

Edgar didn't come to the Mission or to Bible College that day. I tried to contact him at his home, but he was not available. I asked Curtis what he knew about the situation.

Curtis told me he wasn't with Edgar at the time and knew only what people from the street had told him.

I asked what the street people had seen. He told me there were conflicting reports. Some said it was an accident others said it was intentional.

After class, on Monday, Edgar came from behind me on the street and said, "I'm sorry. It wasn't as bad as they make it out to be. It was an accident."

He told me how Evelyn was in a bad mood. It was after class on Friday. She wanted to go to a movie. "I had already seen that movie and it was boring. I wanted to go to the Mission to meet Curtis. I had his watch and wanted to give it back to him. She gets jealous when I go with Curtis or even talk with him and ignore her.

She started ranting and told me I could go meet Curtis but she was going home. She turned quickly. I saw she was off balance, I reached out to keep her from falling, she spun and hit her head on the metal post of the bus stop and got knocked out."

Somebody called the ambulance, the police came and I was arrested, which is bad for my immigration application. I told the police what happened, but a witness gave a different story. He said I pushed her against the metal post. I just pray that Evelyn will tell the truth."

Edgar looked over and said, "Guess I'm in your black book."

I replied, "I don't have a black book but I do have a prayer journal, I'll pray for you."

"Does this mean I'll miss Rapture?" he asked innocently.

I motioned him to come with me to the restaurant.

During our conversation, Edgar broke down and cried.

"I really do like her, but I guess we're not meant for each other," he mumbled.

I thought how wrong I was not warning Evelyn about Edgar. I should have been warning Edgar about Evelyn.

It all got sorted out before going to the courts. Edgar was exonerated.

Edgar asked if he could return to Bible College. I told him he must tell the Bible Class students exactly what happened and what he had learned from the whole affair.

"I want you to tell them how this has affected you spiritually."

"All that?" Edgar asked, as he went to the dormitory to meet Curtis and ask for help in getting his papers for immigration filled out.

Evelyn stopped coming to the Mission. She came to her mother's graduation.

The unfortunate trauma soured both of them on the Downtown Eastside.

Evelyn continued with her studies at the more prestigious Bible College.

Joyce continued on and graduated with honours.

I had a talk with Joyce after she graduated. She told me she was given a promotion where she works. She was happy to be going to an 'alive' church in suburbia and has taken an active role in the ministry of the church.

"It's a new church plant. Because I graduated from Bible College, they made me the Assistant Pastor. It's my job to advertise and bring people into the church."

She was very proud that they asked her to give her testimony at her new church.

She started by telling them, "I'm not ashamed of my diploma. I worked hard for it. God has given me a ministry in which I can excel. What more can I ask?

By the way if anyone wants to better their life, go to Bible College and let God fill you with a love for Jesus. It will change your life."

Edgar completed his first year and was commissioned. He told how he would always treasure this certificate which meant he is now ready to go home and preach and teach, lay hands on the sick and they will be healed. He told how spiritual healing is necessary in his country.

Edgar was more than half way through his second year at the Bible College when he was given permission to enter university. His review was successful and he is now a landed immigrant.

Jokingly he told the class, "Money talks in this country as well as in mine."

He explained that he plans to be the first born again Christian governor in his province in the Honduras. He thanked us for praying for his review which was successful.

Edgar went from being an atheist to becoming a born again young man with a dream, The dream of becoming a governor who will promote Christian morals and ethics in his country. Possibly the president of the Honduras, who knows?

He was radically changed from being an atheist to being a child of God.

CHAPTER SIXTEEN

SHARON

Confused

Colossians 1:25 "God gave me to present to you the word of God in its fullness-the mystery that has been kept hidden for ages and generations, but is now disclosed to the saints 'Christ in you, the hope of glory."

Becky and Cindy liked to keep busy. They both lived in the co-ed dormitory. They not only come to the Mission but they also attended other church services, conferences and events at other churches and missions.

They meet young ladies and young men and ask them to come to our Bible College.

It was at a conference that they met Sharon. They told her about our Mission and Bible College.

Sharon was sceptical and wanted time to think about it. She had Cindy write down her phone number and told Cindy she could phone in three days or maybe more.

Cindy phoned and Sharon told her she had decided, to give it a try. She also told Cindy that she wasn't really sure if she would come to the Mission and meet her."It's a bad part of town."

Sharon did come to the Mission and Cindy was there to greet her. Sharon looked around at the people from the street and they made her nervous. She went to the front and sat in a side chair.

Cindy asked her why she sat there with the old folks. Sharon told her, "So no one can come from behind and hurt me."

She was wringing here hands and she had a nervous twitch which made her blink too often.

Sharon is an oriental young lady. She is big boned and carries a bit of extra weight. She wears glasses which she keeps adjusting. Her black hair is straight and she has bangs which makes her round face even rounder. Her clothes are not designer and they are not coordinated, but they suited her personality

I heard Cindy ask her if she wanted to come to the Bible College. "It's a lot of fun and you're with some great people," Cindy explained.

Sharon asked, "Where is this College? You know I have to ride the bus. I don't want to have to walk too far in this end of town."

Cindy told her it was only half a block from the bus stop. "I walk it every day and I'm still here. I've never had any problems."

By now, the two were joined by Becky and Stacey.

Sharon asked Becky, "Do you think it's a good idea for me to go to Bible College? I'm really not too sure I should."

Becky told her what the Bible College had done for her. By now Becky's speech had improved considerably and she had a very slight limp.

Stacey knew she was going to be next to give advice. Before being asked she told Sharon it was her decision. "Pray about it and let the Holy Spirit guide you."

Sharon told Stacey she wasn't sure the Holy Spirit was doing much of anything in her life.

Stacey told her she needed what the College could offer her. "You must come and get straightened out."

I overheard the conversations and I shook my head. As the four walked away I wondered how Sharon would make out at the College. If she couldn't make a simple decision without the help of four others, how could she possibly succeed in her studies?

The next night Sharon came back to the Mission. She approached me and asked what I thought the College could do for her. I was going to tell her a great deal, but I asked her, "What are your goals in life. What do you feel called to do for the Lord?"

Her answer to both was, "I don't know. I don't think about those things."

In a round about way she asked me, "What are the options?"

I told her,"There are no options but rather there are opportunities. God has a plan and a purpose for your life and the life of all he has created. At the Bible College you will learn how to access God's plan and purpose and change your life.".

This was way too much information for Sharon. She told me she would have to think about it and maybe get some advice and help somewhere else.

The next week she came to the Mission and told me she wanted to become a missionary like Mother Theresa.

I realized she had done some research or someone had planted the idea in her head.

I told her she could do anything God called her to do.

I also told her that being a missionary was a noble calling and we would do everything in our power to help her fulfill her plan and goal.

She told me she thought of that all by herself. "It's my secret plan," she confided.

I was going to tell her that God might have had something to do with her getting that message but I didn't want to confuse her.

She enrolled in Bible College. After a few days, I could tell that she didn't have much of a spiritual background as everything was new to her.

At our meeting in my office, she told me about all the churches and conferences she'd been to.

I asked her what she had learned from these sermons and conferences.

"I learned that there are a lot of good speakers. I can't tell you what I learned because I forget. If you tell me something, maybe I could remember," she answered.

I told her I'd be telling her a great deal and I'd expect her to remember all of what was taught.

"I'll try, but I can't promise," she said walking away.

She wouldn't give a testimony at the Mission, but she did give a testimony in front of the class.

She started by telling us that she wasn't very good at speaking in front of others, so she wrote it down and would read it.

"My mother is a Buddhist. She wants me to follow her religion. I went to the temple with her and did what others did. They never teach you anything except how to light candles and be quiet. I met some nice people but they didn't have anything to say to me. I got tired of smiling at everyone.

My mother tries to control me. She always wants me to lose weight.

She gets upset as I have a body that is similar to my father's. She told me she wants me to be slim and petite. I've tried to please her, but she looks at me, shakes her head and walks away.

She tried to stop me from coming to the Mission and the Bible College. I had to lie to her and tell her it is an upgrading course for university. It might be the truth.

My father is a bit different. He has no interest in religion. He says my mother can do the religious stuff for the both of them.

He likes to keep in touch with his homeland. He'd rather live there but my mother refuses to go with him. In our homeland we have beautiful properties which have lots of produce. We can live very nicely."

Sharon told the class that in her father's land most are Buddhists. "They need to get to know Jesus The thing is, I have to get to know Him first so I can tell them everything I learn.

My mother wanted me to be cute and slim. I'm a big disappointment to her. My father wanted a boy. That is the custom in his land.

My mother wouldn't give him a son, so he wanted me to be his son. He would take me out and throw the ball for me to catch. Most of the time it hit me and made me cry.

I tried skating in the hope I might be a figure skater. I spent most of the skating session laying on the ice. I'd get up, take a few glides and fall down again and again."

The students laughed as it was really funny the way Sharon presented it.

"I had to learn to play chess because my father plays chess in his country. I never won a game except when my father cheated and let me win.

My father and my mother have given up on me.

My mother tells me I will never amount to anything. My father just lets me do what I want to," she stopped to think.

"A lot of people have given up on me, but I know that Jesus will never give up on me, I hope."

A few in the class assured her that Jesus loves her just as she is and so do we.

Sharon said, "That's not all, I know about myself, but I guess its enough."

Sharon was not that dumb. She put in a lot of effort into completing her assignments and essays.

She was assigned a tutor from the third year class, who helped her and kept her assignments current.

She wanted to sit up near the front as she has an eye problem and needed more than glasses. I learned from her that she has a form of macular degeneration and at times she has only peripheral vision.

With all her handicaps, she did acceptable work. I noticed that she is now much more relaxed and laughs a lot. Happy to be accepted for who she is.

She kept telling everyone that she was going to be a missionary in her father's land. "They've got to get to know Jesus and give up the candle lighting and the meditation while thinking of Buddha and other things," she told the class.

I got in touch with a missionary from the far east, who worked at a mission in a country near to her father's land. He was on leave and was speaking in our city. I invited him to come to the College and tell the class what is needed in order to be a missionary in a foreign country.

Sharon was really pleased to find out that a missionary was coming to speak to her. She gathered pictures of famous missionaries and had put them in an album. When Reg Watson came to the College he was impressed to learn that we had a student who was interested in doing missionary work in a land close to where he is ministering

Sharon had a multitude of questions. Reg answered them all.

When Sharon completed her first year, she really looked forward to graduation. She told the class that she graduated from high school with a conditional pass. "Now I'm getting a real pass. I'm going to be commissioned."

Many of the students had parents come to their graduation. Others had friends and relatives Sharon had only one friend. An older lady who kept calling her Shannon. That didn't bother Sharon, as this was her night and she was happy.

She came and enrolled for her second year. When she gave her testimony it shocked the class.

She started by telling the class that her problem was not that unusual but it was a real problem for her.

She told the class, "I really don't know if I'm a man or a woman. I couldn't tell my mother or she'd have me sent to the funny farm.

Some people think I'm weird when I tell them.

I've been a woman all these years but I keep thinking I'm a man. The thing is, I'm not plumbed like a man. It's so confusing. It really bothers me. Can I be both? I've got to resolve this some day. I need help and that's why I'm here because I believe Jesus can help me. I need your prayers. Thanks."

You could hear a pin drop. I know my jaw dropped.

I thanked Sharon and told her she was brave to give that testimony. "We certainly will pray and ask God to take away the wrong feelings and enhance the right feelings and make you into whatever he created you to be."

It took a few weeks for the students to come to grips with the conundrum.

The best thing is, people were treating Sharon normally and encouraging her.

Sharon completed her third year with a great deal more understanding of the scriptures and the doctrines as well as the promises and spiritual gifts of God.

For her final graduation ceremony, Sharon's father turned up. He was a short, well built man with a ready smile. His appearance was that of a well to do farmer.

I had a short talk with him. He thanked us for giving his daughter courage and a change in personality. I asked him if he supported her vision of becoming a missionary in his land.

He told me that many times Sharon had told him that he should go to Bible College.

"She wants me to become a Christian and give my life to Christ. I find that peculiar. My wife wants me to be a Buddhist and my daughter wants me to be a Christian. I find it strange, but I suppose I can learn from my daughter," he laughed.

Sharon went on to do Missionary work in the province where her father has his farm and his other properties. She has a lady friend who is a Christian and they work together. Her friend is a relative of her father.

Sharon explained that there are about one hundred Christians in the village of over ten thousand where her father has some properties.

"I can speak their language, as we speak this language at home. I needed some refreshing in things that pertain to the language of the Christian religion. If I can't understand a word or phrase, I can turn to my relative for an interpretation. I'm learning all the time. "

Sharon comes to the Mission for a visit when she returns to our city. She tells the students what it is like to be a missionary in a foreign land and she shows pictures of the members of her Bible study groups.

Sharon does her ministry in a town near her father's farm.

The last time Sharon came to the Mission and to the College, she told us that her father had built a church for her in his town on land he owns. She showed us pictures of her church.

She also told us she has an opening for a student to learn the language and then preach in her church and do Bible Studies in different towns.

Sharon has been radically changed from being a shy introverted, insecure person into being a soldier for Christ Jesus. She now has a ministry in two provinces and a church plant in her father's town.

CHAPTER SEVENTEEN

EDUARDO AND JUAN

Refugees

Mark 4:20, "Others like seed sown on good soil, hear the word, accept it, and produce a crop thirty, sixty or even a hundred times what they have sown."

EDUARDO and his friend Juan came to the mission looking for food. Eduardo spoke broken English but Juan struggled with the language. Eduardo asked one of the men in the line how he could get some food.

The man told him to wait until the serving started.

Juan waited in line but Eduardo elected to go to one of the staff and ask for food.

I heard him tell her, "We haven't eaten for three days, please, even a slice of bread."

She beckoned me over to talk to him. I told him to sit at a table and I would see what I could do. There were frozen sausages and left over fried rice in the fridge. Our meal that night was soup and a sandwich. I had a volunteer fry the sausages and prepare the rice.

To satisfy their immediate hunger, I took them some sandwiches and poured glasses of milk. A staff member brought the boys into the staff room and set food before them.

I watched as they stuffed the food down. They were starved.

I sat with them and Eduardo told me how they had come from a country many hundred of miles from our city. He told me about the hardships they had gone through to get to this country.

"I will become an immigrant and work hard," Eduardo said with a smile.

I knew this might not be the case as they had no identification papers. Eduardo told me his papers were stolen along with their money.

Juan, in his limited English said, "We are refugees."

I asked if there was a war in their country. They looked at each other and didn't reply. I asked where they were staying. They told me on the street or under the bridge.

I took them to the dormitory. They thanked me and promised to pay when they received some money.

The next day one of the staff took them to Human Resources and to the immigration office. They were classified as refugees and given money to live on until their claims were processed.

Eduardo and Juan fitted in well with the people in the Mission and as students in the Bible College.

Juan stayed close to Eduardo as his English was limited and he didn't understand when he was spoken to. He looked to Eduardo for interpretations.

I noticed that in class he was puzzled and confused. I knew that if I were in his country I'd be terribly confused as I don't speak much Spanish.

Eduardo was well educated and found the studies at the College enlightening and fascinating.

There were times he didn't completely agree with everything taught, as he had been brought up in a church with different interpretations and beliefs. But he listened attentively and didn't question the teachings.

He was brought up in a church that did not encourage reading the Bible but rather there was an emphasis on liturgy and rituals.

He told the class, "In my mother's church, we are told by the priest that if we read the Bible we are prone to make grievous errors in interpretation of the word of God and that is a venial sin."

Matthew told him that we have the Holy Spirit who guides us as we read and interprets what we read. Matthew pointed out that there are symbols that we must understand. That is why we study and learn.

Eduardo thanked him and told him, "I will learn many new things."

Another time Eduardo told the class that music in his church was hymns and chants. "There are no words to learn. We must sit and let the music speak to us."

He went on to say, "In this Mission church, young people sing gospel songs, gospel rock and country gospel which has a beat and a rhythm. The word s are meaningful and uplifting. I like it very much."

Both Eduardo and Juan agreed that our music was uplifting and inspiring.

A few times Juan danced to the beat of the music. He did a quick step and people clapped to the beat of the drums and guitars.

We were pleased to have both boys in the Mission and Bible College.

They pulled their weight in the Mission wanting to do more than their share of the work.

Eduardo worked in the kitchen and Juan assisted the janitor in setting up for services and in the cleaning of the Mission and College.

The ladies in the kitchen took a shine to Eduardo who was very well mannered and often flattered the ladies. He insisted on doing all the heavy work and the lifting.

He liked to make whatever he served look appetizing and appealing. He would put a leaf of lettuce or a slice of red pepper on the side of the plate.

The people who came into the Mission thought it was great.

Juan was not quite as eager as Eduardo. After a few months, he became lethargic and wanted to be alone most of the time.

I spoke to him and asked about this change of mood.

He confided in me that he was home-sick. "This is the best country, but my people are on my mind. My people are always happy. Here people do not honour me. Here I am just another person on skid row. I am looked down on. People on the street look at me and frown. It is difficult for me."

He went on to tell me, " I have a girl friend who I wish to marry. Here I have friends but not true friends."

I asked him about Eduardo as a friend.

"He is good, but he comes from the city. I come from a poor family in the Bario. We like each other but we are not the same. At home we will not speak very much to each other."

I asked, "So what is your plan?"

"I will work hard and make money. As a refugee I cannot work. I cannot get a job. The government says no. It makes me sad. I have energy but it is wasted."

Juan stayed in the dormitory and did some work around the Mission. He liked to dig in the garden, use the hammer and do manual labour. "I must keep in shape." he laughed. He did some landscaping at both dorms and built a cabinet for the musical instruments.

Eduardo was not inclined to do hard labour. He did lift weights and ran with others on the seawall. He also played soccer and made the Mission soccer team.

I watched a tournament the students had arranged between another church team. Both Juan and Eduardo carried the College team as their footwork and their moves were far superior to the other players. It was great to watch them head the ball and dazzle with footwork and passing.

They were equally as good at baseball. Juan was a really good pitcher and Eduardo played first base.

Juan grew spiritually as he began to understand what was being taught. He had many questions at first. Eduardo explained many concepts to him.

Giving his testimony, Juan told the class:

"At home I go to church. My mother is very good in the church. She knows all the responses. I know some responses. If I miss saying one, my mother looks at me."

He thought for a moment and smiled. "I like it with responses, but that is not your way. Sometimes I still make a proper response to the Word of God in my mind. Is that wrong?" He looked to me for an answer.

I told him that we can worship God in many ways. Your response is between you and God.

Juan went on to tell about his girlfriend:

"My Maria is very beautiful. She comes from a big family. They are a proud family. Her father is on the council of the Bario. Maria comes to church with me and sits beside my mother She is waiting for me to return as we love each other. I will make money and then go home and build a house so we can get married. I like very much your country, but I love my country. There I have many friends and cousins. Here I have noone."

Juan was homesick. He wanted to work and make money to send home to his mother and Maria.

A year of waiting went by rather quickly. Both Juan and Eduardo were scheduled to graduate in one month. Juan was able to write essays with the help of his tutor and he had a firmer grasp of the Bible and the doctrines.

Juan learned the English language and worked hard at his studies.

The waiting for official status became too much for Juan. He went to the Immigration office. He told the clerk, "I am young. I am wasting my energy, please help me so I can get a job and make some money."

The clerk agreed to check his file and determine whether he could work. She told him to come back in three days.

Those three days weighed heavily on Juan. He asked that we pray for a good outcome.

Matthew went with Juan for moral support when he returned to the immigration office.

Juan spoke to a different clerk. She took some time and finally handed Juan a document which stated that his application for refugee status had been denied.

Matthew put his arm around Juan to comfort him as he was in shock.

Juan asked the clerk, "Why?" She told him he could look it up on the internet.

Juan explained that he didn't have internet. The clerk went into the files and brought out another paper which stated the day and time of his departure as he was being deported.

Juan came back to the dormitory and stayed in his room for the rest of the day. He was given six weeks before his departure date.

Eduardo knew that there was something more to Juan's secluding himself than being homesick.

The next day Juan gave his testimony at the Mission:

"I am in shock. I had very bad news yesterday. I will be deported."

Those who heard the news were saying, "Oh no. That can't happen."

Juan continued, "This is a great country and I thank you God for the time I have spent here. I have become a real Christian. What more can I ask. I have found God who lives in my heart. I never knew that personal

God. In this country I have also found my best friend, Jesus the Christ. I am now filled with the Holy Spirit. In my town I never knew the Holy Spirit. He cannot come into our life as my people still worship statues and idols. They do not know that Jesus is God. So much they have to learn. I can now tell them what I have learned," Juan paused.

"Yes, I wanted your money as we are poor. I dreamed of being rich in this country and then going home as a hero. God said no. He told me you go home and teach what you have learned at the Bible College and in the Mission.

Do not cry for me but send me with your prayers. Maybe you will come to my Bario on an International outreach. I like your outreaches, they are fun and meaningful.

I still have some time with you. I must learn much more in that time as I don't know everything. Thank you and God bless you all."

Juan was respected and he would be missed.

Eduardo was rocked by this announcement as he knew he too would be served papers for deportation. He talked to the men in the dormitory and in the Mission.

Someone told him that if he got married, the government wouldn't be able to deport him.

When he told me that he was going to marry a lady so he could stay in the country, I told him that was the worst possible solution.

He told me his back was against the wall. "I've got to do something quick. It's my only chance."

Eduardo asked some of the College girls if they would do him a favour. They were shocked at the proposal. He looked around the Mission for a quick fix, but there were no positive responses to his proposal to get married.

News got around that Eduardo was offering money to any lady who would marry him but not consummate the marriage. In other words there would be no living together.

A young girl, who at times came to the Mission, heard of his plight. No one else would give her the time of day. She was a prostitute, but didn't have many admirers as she was not dressed nicely and had open sores on her face. Her hair was stringy and needed washing.

She came to the dormitory and asked to be introduced to Eduardo. Curtis asked, "Why?" She told him that she heard at the Mission that a man was looking for a wife.

Curtis told her to go away, but Eduardo overheard the conversation and thanked Curtis. He asked the girl to come into the living room.

When she met him she smiled, as Eduardo is handsome and impeccably dressed and groomed.

Curtis overheard the conversation and told me that Eduardo told her this was a business arrangement, nothing more.

She asked him how much he was going to pay up front.

Eduardo told her, "When I'm a citizen, I will work and pay you one thousand dollars. If you agree to the wedding and I am not deported, I will pay you one hundred dollars up front after the wedding."

She said it was no deal unless he gave her at least two hundred up front. She put out her hand. Eduardo told her he would give her two hundred dollars after the wedding ceremony and the signatures were recognized.

She thought Eduardo wanted her body. She made sexual advances but he backed away and told her, "This is business not pleasure." She pouted and left the dormitory.

Eduardo told me the complete story not knowing that I had heard it from Curtis. He added that in their country if a marriage is not consummated it can be annulled. "Is that the way in this country?" he asked.

I told him I'd have to get more information on that angle. I told him I had heard about it in other countries but not in our country.

"This marriage must be annulled. I cannot keep her for a wife," Eduardo stated emphatically.

Eduardo was pleased with the arrangement, as he felt he would soon be a citizen of the country and able to work and get his education at a university.

The next day, I did my warning lecture on sexually transmitted diseases on the Downtown eastside. We were most concerned about HIV and Aids as well as Hepatitis C, Syphilis and other sexually transmitted diseases.

The students were told that prostitutes were often the carriers. It was out of concern for Eduardo that I gave the lecture. Eduardo bowed his head as he knew we were afraid that he might be tempted and fall into her clutches.

Eduardo thanked me for my concern he told the class, "I have high regard for my body as a temple of God. I will never desecrate this temple."

The next day, Eduardo told me more about their arrangement. He asked if I had found out anything about marriages being annulled if they are not consummated.

I told him I had asked a person who knew about such things. He told me there was a process, but it might take time and be costly.

Eduardo told me more about his situation, I told him we would pray for him and her.

Tammy, his prostitute wife to be, started coming to the Mission on a regular basis. I also heard that she was contemplating enrolling in the College.

She took every opportunity to get close to Eduardo.

He took every opportunity to avoid her without ending their business arrangement.

When Tammy came to class, I noticed that the girls did not invite her to join them.

She was numb to their snubs and pulled up a chair to the front table and started talking to Stacey and Becky.

They informed her that there was to be no talking when I was teaching.

That night, Eduardo and Tammy appeared at the Mission and asked me to marry them this coming Saturday. I looked in my day planner and found I was unavailable.

They were married by a Justice of the Peace.

Along with the wedding reception, we had a going away party for Juan.

He had finished enough course work and attended enough days in order to graduate the first year and be commissioned. By now he was well liked and known by all of the regulars at the Mission.

He was really pleased when we presented him with his first year certificate.

Juan told us he knew what commissioned meant and assured us that he would go out and teach and preach when he got home.

In class the next Monday, he asked if he could preach one sermon at the Mission.

He had preached a couple of practice sermons at the College, now he wanted to preach at the Mission.

The last night before he was deported, he preached a sermon on 'Assurances of God'. He told how he was now assured of the blessings of God. Assured of the promises of God and assured a place in heaven at the rapture, when Jesus was coming for those who were eagerly awaiting His return.

He told us that in his country he had no assurance." Now I have the assurance of eternal life with my Lord Jesus," he preached with a smile.

We were all sorry to see him leave. The girls made a big fuss over him. The guys each shook his hand and gave him a friendly hug.

On the way to the airport the next day, Juan told me he had mixed feelings.

"I like this country, it has been good to me. Yet I am looking forward to going home. I miss my Maria, my mother and father and everyone that I love.

Now that I can speak English and read English, I will get a good job. I have a diploma to present which is worth much gold in my country.

I will be respected. by those in power and by those in authority.

I hope to save my people from their idolatry and pagan worship. All is not bad. Do not weep for me, just pray that I will have strong faith and I will have courage in the Lord."

We had an hour to talk before he had to board his plane.

Juan told me, "My love for money has been replaced with a love for the Lord Jesus."

We said our goodbyes. Juan reminded me about an outreach to his village.

A week after the wedding ceremony, which gave Eduardo new hope to stay in the country, an order of deportation came in the mail.

Before the Mission was opened, Eduardo was waiting at the door.

I smiled as I greeted him, but he was not smiling. "They can't do this to me," he complained.

I reminded him that I had warned him that marriage was not the solution.

He hung his head and asked. "Is there any other way?"

I explained that he could go home and apply for immigration status.

I told him that another thing he could do was to apply as a student. But that will only get you into the country, but with no right to work.

My only other suggestion was that he go to legal aide and speak to an immigration lawyer.

Eduardo's eyes lit up and he thanked me.

The news came that the lawyer had told Eduardo that the order of deportation was irrevocable.

Eduardo came to the Bible College after being to the lawyer. One of the girls asked where his wife was. Eduardo told her that the wedding was being annulled.

I had Eduardo explain the meaning of annulment to the class.

He told them that the marriage was never consummated, That is, there was no joining together in sex which makes a couple one body.

Eduardo explained that in his country it is legal. "Now that I am going home I have the right to annul the wedding in my country."

This caused some to shake their heads. Others asked about the legality of such a right. I turned it into a research project. I found that was the easiest way out. If I didn't know the answer, I turned it into a research assignment.

Eduardo told the class that he had no ties with Tammy. "I have paid her off and she is satisfied"

Eduardo gave his last testimony before the class.

"I am very fortunate in coming to know so many Christians. You are a great bunch of people. I now have enough knowledge and understanding to bring me into the presence of God and to walk with my Lord and Saviour guided by the Holy Spirit.

In my land I could never find a College like this and a Mission to let me get practical experience in preaching and working for those who are in need.

Added to that, I can now play the guitar and the drums. Another first for me.

Hopefully, you will visit my city some day. You are all welcome. My father will honour you as you are my best friends and you are true believers in God and His Son Jesus the Christ.

More than money, I wanted to go to university in your country as a degree from your universities is highly honoured in my country. When I go home, I will apply for immigrant status and enter your country legally and pursue higher education in your universities.

I took Eduardo to the airport and we had a long talk. We had to wait over an hour for the plane to take on passengers.

Eduardo told me that there was a born-again church in his village.

He explained, "I thought they were far out and really loud. Too carried away in their religion. Now I know that they are genuine. I will go to that church," he laughed,

"My parents will disown me as they are staunch believers in their faith."

He shook his head and said, "I will have to convert them and bring the real Jesus who loves us and died for us, into their lives."

He took the text book that we are using and told me there was enough information in the text book for him to use in the transformation of his people.

"I also have the Holy Spirit to teach me and guide me in my bringing them to the Lord. All I need is to know the will of the Father for my life."

He took out his certificate and proudly exclaimed, "Now that I am commissioned, I can teach and preach and lay hands on the sick and they will be healed."

I laughed along with Eduardo and gave him a blessing as he went to board his plane.

I watched as the immigration officer accompanied Eduardo to the exit.

Both Juan and Eduardo came as refugees. They told me of the hardships they had suffered in getting into our country. Being beaten and robbed, but they put that all behind and are now on fire for the Lord.

Both were radically changed from a religion which gave them no hope, into a relationship with Jesus the Christ and His Father, God Almighty. Both are filled with the Holy Spirit and bent on bringing others into the Kingdom of God.

CHAPTER EIGHTEEN

ALEX

Chronic Alcoholic

Romans 10:9&13, "That if you confess with your mouth, "Jesus is Lord," and believe in your heart that God raised him from the dead, you will be saved. Everyone who calls on the name of the Lord will be saved."

ALEX became a regular nuisance as he came to the Mission drunk on rice wine, wanting to talk and be loud. Behaviour he exhibited in the bars he frequented.

The members of the Mission kept telling him to be quiet and respect the house of God. It didn't seem to register. A few times he was ushered to the door as the service was compromised by his unruly and rude behaviour.

Everyone became irritated with his loud cursing and total disregard for the Word of God and the sanctity of the house of God.

This went on for weeks. At times he lost control of his bladder and the urine smell was overpowering.

We had to give him an ultimatum, "Come sober or stay away."

The next time he came to the Mission, he was almost sober and we had a talk. He told me, "I'm an alcoholic and I can't help myself."

I told him, "Jesus is your only hope. He will help you if you ask in prayer."

He told me, "I don't know Jesus but I've heard about God." Whereupon he cursed using God's name in vain and laughed.

I told him, "Come back another day when you haven't been drinking."

I went on to say, "If you've been drinking heavy, please don't come to the service."

"Is this forever?" he asked.

"Yes, if you're drunk it's forever."

He thought about it and shook his head. "I'll try, but it'll be hard."

The greeter at the door was told to determine if Alex was sober enough to participate in the service. If he comes drunk, tell him, we would love for him to come back another day.

To my surprise, Alex came reasonably sober and actually listened to the music and to the complete sermon, without one outburst.

For this behaviour, he was welcomed by a few of his First Nations people. They talked to him and treated him with respect.

Alex preferred this show of affection and respect more than the stigma of being a drunk.

He came quite regularly after that and was accepted. He made new friends in the Mission.

The occasional time he missed coming to the Mission,we knew he had tied one on and was respecting our wishes.

Easter Sunday, he came to the eleven o'clock morning service at the Mission. He was dressed in clean, presentable clothes and wore a big smile.

He listened attentively to the music and the sermon. I noticed he had a puzzled look during the singing of one of the gospel songs.

After the sermon he cornered me and challenged me.

He told me, "It says in that song, 'My king would die for me'. There's no way a king would die for me. No one would die for me."

I spent some time telling him about Jesus; His love, death and resurrection. The Holy Spirit came upon Alex. He went to the altar and got on his knees. He wept and wept.

A Pastor went and put her arms around his shoulder. He came out of the huddle with two other believers who joined in praying for him.

I watched and saw a look of joy and peace in his eyes and on his countenance. The three who prayed for him asked Jesus to come into his life.

"Come in and take away his sins, and fill him with the power to do the will of God, and fill him with the Holy Spirit."

It was a total transformation in his life. He was a changed man.

Alex came to every service for the next three weeks filled with the Spirit. His testimony was that he had no desire to drink, only a desire to pray and thank Jesus for what he was doing in his life.

Three weeks later his testimony was, that he had smoked all his life. He recalled that he was a smoker. "After these three weeks of being in the Spirit, I forgot about what I used to be like," he smiled. "I reached in my pocket for a cigarette. Not finding any and having no desire to smoke, I gave up smoking."

He told us it was the same with alcohol. "It's a foreign substance with no appeal for me anymore."

He kept hearing the announcement that we had a Bible College in affiliation with the Mission.

He knew a few First Nations men who had joined the Bible College.

He told Matthew, "I don't think it can do any harm." Matthew agreed. He came and enrolled in the College the next day.

People who had heard his testimony welcomed him.

It became evident that he couldn't write complete sentences. His writing was in large often illegible letters, but he tried.

He admitted that he hadn't read a book in thirty years. "I look at the pictures in magazines and get the general idea."

He asked me, "Will that mean I can't read the Bible?" I told him he would read the Bible, but it might take time and lots of help learning to read again.

We teamed Alex up with one of the third year students. Alex was determined to read and to improve his writing skills.

Alex assured me that he was going to read the Bible if it took the rest of his life.

He was not a great student but he persevered.

For the first few months, Alex was totally motivated and eager to learn all that was offered. With the help of his tutor, he managed to hand in all his assignment

I had Alex come into the office and we had a long talk. I told him he should give his testimony to the class. He was reluctant at first, but he agreed and gave his testimony.

He told us that he was raised in a big family on a reserve over the mountains in a small settlement ten miles from the nearest town.

"There was a power station there and a few worked for the power company. My dad couldn't hold down a job as he was an alcoholic like me.

I should say an alcoholic like I used to be," he laughed.

"I was a real ringer, but I'm changed. No more in condemnation, thanks to my precious Jesus."

He went on with his testimony. "There were no jobs where I lived and no jobs for me in the town over the mountain. I went to a small city and looked for a job. With my drinking and laziness, I wasn't worth hiring. I depended on the government for many years to support me and supply my needs," he thought about those years.

"One day the circus came to that small city. I happened to be almost sober as I had run out of money. Somehow, I was always strong in the back. I heard they were hiring people to do circus jobs. I stood in line and was hired.

They didn't ask questions, no resume or nothing like that. Only one question. "Are you in trouble with the law?" I told them I was arrested for being drunk and disorderly, but the charges were dropped. I got hired," he smiled.

"I stayed on that job as a carney for twelve years. I made enough money to keep drunk for a few years. That's what I did. A bunch of us all got paid on the same day and we all go drunk on the same night," he laughed.

"I'd have been with them still, except I got into a bit of trouble over some gambling debts. I was threatened with a knife to my throat.

I told the boss to give my pay to charity. I hit the road looking for another job.

My references were not that great as being a carney doesn't equip a person for many jobs out there.

I got terribly discouraged. I felt I wasn't worth anything. A piece of junk ready for the scrap heap. It drove me to drink even more.

That's when this Mission straightened me out and put me on the road to recovery. I'm forever grateful for what they have done in my life. I was a hopeless alcoholic and, they disciplined me. I needed that. They told me not to come back drunk. I was kicked out because of my bad behaviour and my addiction. They did it out of love for my soul. I had lost my soul, but the Holy Spirit reached down and put the love of Jesus into my heart. I regained my soul and I'm spiritually alive. Praise the Lord!"

He went on to say, "You can't buy that love for the Lord. It's worth a million, but it's free for those who ask and are willing to change and turn to Jesus."

Everyone encouraged Alex and they were moved by his testimony.

It is necessary that students attend classes regularly and complete assignments on time. Alex did neither. At times he would be absent for weeks on end. Now that he was sober and a Christian, he was courting a lady in a different city.

I asked him if he would like to have a leave of absence. Keep the credits you have earned, do your business and come back to the Bible College when you settle down.

Alex agreed and was absent from the College for six months.

I wondered if he was going to come back.

To everyone's surprise, he came back and told me he was ready to get back to work on his courses.

Alex helped in the kitchen as everyone does. He kept people laughing as he loved to tell jokes and pull tricks on others. He was so happy to be working for the Lord. Still better, he liked to be with Christians.

After a month, Alex gave another testimony to the class.

He told us, "I used to laugh at Christians. I thought they were weird the way they always smiled and were nice to each other.

I wondered why they were happy and I was miserable and could only be happy when I was drunk and drinking with my buddies. The truth is I was happy as a result of being drunk and out of my mind. But I paid for it the next day when I had a hangover and was broke."

At another meeting with Alex in my office, Alex asked me if I was ever drunk.

I told him when I was about eighteen, I was at a house party playing cards and drinking cheap wine. I had to run out of the house in the snow and heave everything I had had for supper. I assured him that I knew what it was like to be sick and hung over.

"That was a lesson I had to learn and I'm glad I learned it when I was young."

In the College, we studied the life of Jesus and what happened before He started His ministry. We were studying about John the Baptist. Suddenly Alex got up and proclaimed, "I've got to get baptized!"

The students laughed and clapped. I assured him he would be baptized.

We have baptism classes so people know what they are doing and have a realization of why we are to be baptized. Alex asked to join. I told him we usually advertise the times of the classes and enrol people. There and then he told me to enrol him.

We advertised and three people signed up for the baptism class.

We scheduled the baptism for the fourteenth of March. We hoped for a nice bright sunny day. It turned out to be a windy, blustery day. That didn't deter our four candidates for baptism.

It also did not keep many of the students away as they feel that they are witnessing a miracle when a person gets baptized. The going down of the old self and the rising up of the new man. Born as a human and now born of the Spirit.

A surprise guest was the girlfriend of Alex who came from a smaller city to witness his baptism.

After everybody was dried off and were back at the Mission for a celebration luncheon, I got to talk with Alex's girlfriend.

She told me that she was a nursing assistant. She said they let her help patients who need her help and also help the nurses lift or move patients.

"Some day I will become a nurse but for now I am an aide.

Funny thing is I do the hard work and the nurses tell me what to do. But most nurses are really nice to me."

She told me how she met Alex.

"We were in the mall of this smaller city. Alex was with his nephews and nieces. He treated them really nice. He joked with them and made them laugh. I thought I'd like a man like that. I had been married to a man who beat me and was mean. I didn't want another man who did that," she shook her head.

"He saw that I was alone. He invited me to join his family. Soon he had me laughing and having fun with the kids. I was hooked. He asked me for my phone number and asked me out. We've been dating for over a year now. He told me how he was changed by the Bible College and the Mission."

I asked if marriage was in the big picture. She told me he wanted to finish Bible College first. "I'm a Christian and I understand."

In order to receive a 'Letter of Recognition", it is imperative that a person attend classes and do the assignments for at least five months which is half a year. To graduate after one year a person must hand in the essays and written sermons and attend class a minimum number of days. The person will then be commissioned and receive their certificate.

I went over this with Alex. At first he was aiming at six months.

He missed a few days but he did the very minimum in order to get his Letter of Recognition.

There was a big celebration at the Mission. Alex was allowed to preach a sermon he had practised at the college.

He brought two litre bottles of pop and everyone toasted his achievement.

I thought that would be the end of his studies.

That was not to be. He settled down and came to class for the rest of the term and graduated.

His graduation was a time of jubilation and a time of decision.

He came to my office and told me that two more years was a long time to wait to get married.

I didn't know what to recommend. I asked him what were the alternatives? He told me he didn't have any.

I told him we would pray about it.

We prayed and he went back to his village on summer break and courted his wife to be.

When College resumed, Alex was not present.

He phoned me a week later and told me he was getting married in her city. "You're invited along with the students from the College. We put off the date so you can bring an outreach up to our wedding."

I made the announcement to the class and everybody wanted to make our first outreach to the city of Alex's new wife.

At the counsel meeting it was agreed that the outreach would coincide with the planned wedding.

The wedding was a happy affair as Alex was now filled with the Spirit.

His wife beamed. The relatives of Alex were all present and making this a joyous celebration with their joking and laughing.

The relatives of his wife were more sedate. They enjoyed watching the antics of Alex and his extended family.

The outreach was a great success as it was in the same city where we met Ben. There was a Mission that we always visit. Not only do we visit their Mission but they come for a visit to our Mission and Bible College once a year.

The day after the wedding of Alex we went to their Mission.

The second and third year students knew the Pastors and they knew some of the regulars. For them it was a reunion.

Our worship team joined theirs and there was powerful singing and playing great music to the Lord.

We told Alex that the day after his wedding we were going to the Mission to join them in worship.

To our surprise, Alex and his wife took time from their honeymoon to come to the Mission and have a session with the whole gang

We prefer that our students complete three years of schooling and training in order to prepare them to do ministry.

With Alex being a mature student in his early fifties, the denomination made an exception. It is their policy that a person can plant a church as a missionary church. When the church reaches a more mature level it becomes a beacon church.

At the point were the church is solid and on its own it becomes a full fledged church.

As well, there are courses and training every year for new Pastors who plant a church.

Alex decided he would plant a church in his home town. With this request came the possibility of being ordained.

I helped Alex with his application for ordination. I signed it as the sponsoring Pastor.

One of the Mission Pastors worked out the logistics with him. The church became a reality and it grew.

Not only did the church become a reality, but Alex was ordained

His ordination party was a big day at the Mission. He brought his wife and many relatives and friends. They joined in with the people from the street and made his ordination a joyous occasion.

As well as his church in the village, Alex started home churches in the surrounding native reserves. He was welcomed as their pastor and his ministry bore fruit.

His wife was accepted as a nurses aide in the town's hospital where Alex ministers.

God worked out all the logistics in answer to our prayers.

Alex phoned and asked us to have an outreach to his home town at his new church.

We spent many fun filled days in his town, meeting his people and ministering to individuals we met on the street and inviting them to our church services.

Alex was a great influence on the students and gave them an idea of what it was like to plant a church and effectively minister to different cultures.

Alex, to this day, has remained loyal to the Lord. He did not graduate fully from the College but he took the plunge and made a go of his ministry.

We gave him books to read in order to learn the basics necessary in order to do ministry. He has attended the denomination sponsored workshops. They explain the principles of effective ministry.

Alex occasionally returns to the Mission and drops in on the Bible College. He signs up to be a guest speaker at the Mission and draws a crowd.

Alex is happy and his followers are happy in the Church they call their own. He also has house churches in outlying areas, which depend on his coming to share the gospel.

Quite a difference from the smelly man, who came drunk and disrupted our worship and ministry.

He is now a man making a difference in the lives of others who need to clean up their lives and find the Lord as he did.

He teaches them how to invite the Holy Spirit to come into their lives with power and bearing spiritual gifts.

Alex was radically changed by the power of God Almighty who sent the Holy Spirit to dwell within and lead him on the path of righteousness.

The great thing is, this demonstrates how God can use the most undesirable as well as the most worthy of persons to do ministry after being trained and filled with the love of God and His Son Jesus the Christ.

CHAPTER NINETEEN

MEDINA
Moslem

Proverbs 7:1, My daughter, keep my words and store up my commandments within you. Keep my commandments and you will live; guard my teachings as the apple of your eye. Bind them on your fingers; write them on the tablets of your heart."

Medina came to the Bible College with her husband. It was a mixed marriage as the husband is Caucasian and his wife is Oriental.

The husband spoke for the wife, "My wife wishes to enrol in your Bible College," he told the student at the door.

He was told to stand in the lineup for new students.

It was the end of August and two, third year students were doing the enrolling.

Becky was enrolling all of the first year students. She completed filling out the form of the student in front of the married couple.

The husband stepped forward with his wife behind him. It was all very strange to his wife.

I watch the new students in order to get some idea as to how they will function in the College. I could see that this lady relied a great deal on her husband. Her confidence level seemed very low. She appeared quite timid.

Becky asked the husband, "Who is enrolling? Are you both coming to the College?"

The husband told her that his wife was enrolling.

Becky asked if she could speak to his wife. The husband stepped aside and motioned for his wife to come and answer the questions. She looked to her husband. He motioned for her to speak up.

Becky started the process of enrollment. She asked the name, address, phone number and age. All the routine questions. The husband answered half of them.

I learned that her name was Medina. Her husband offered the fact that people call her Dina for short. He told Becky that their last name was Hughes. He spelled it for her.

Dina gave their address. The husband looked pleased that she got it correct. Dina also gave the correct phone number. When asked how old she was, Dina looked to her husband and asked if she should give such private information. The husband nodded his approval.

I was wondering if she would need his approval before answering questions in class.

When it came to spouse, the husband was proud to tell that he was the spouse and his name is Norman "But you can call me Norm for short. We shorten everything," he joked."

Becky had Dina sign the application. Norman wanted to sign also. Becky complied although it was not necessary.

Becky got through making the application and asked if there were any questions. Norm said, "No, not really." Dina put up her hand indicating that she did have a question or two.

In her broken English she asked about bus service. "My husband is at work. I must ride the bus as there are broken hours."

Becky looked at her address and gave her two options. One involved the underground and the other was an express bus. She thanked Becky.

Norman had his own method of coming to the College, which involved two transfers.

Becky told Dina to phone bus information, "They know the best connections."

Becky asked if there was anything else.

Dina put up one finger. Becky nodded.

"Outside, I saw many not too nice men. Will they hurt me?"

Becky told her, "I feel safe but I usually walk with a friend."

Dina asked, "Who will be my friend?"

Becky answered, "I'll be your friend. Phone me and tell me the time your bus arrives as Hornel and McDaniels. Becky gave Dina her cell number. Dina thanked Becky.

Norman looked at the line-up they had created and told Dina, "We were lucky to get here when we did, look at that lineup."

The couple walked out hand in hand. I wondered why he was making her come to Bible College, or was she the one who wants to come. I realized the answers would be forthcoming through a testimony or through my interview.

I knew the Bible College would work things out, but I wondered how she would manage at the Mission where these, 'not so nice men' hang out.

When I thought about it, this was the first time we have had two oriental ladies enrolled. We have had oriental men but not ladies.

The next Monday, classes started for another year. The enrollment was up over last year. I had to teach another two sessions each week in order to accommodate the the overflow.

I watch as people come into the classroom the first day. Where they sit and who they come with gives me some idea of how they will fit in.

Dina came a bit early. She noticed Anna, the other oriental girl, sitting in the front row. She went and asked politely if she could sit beside her. Anna was all smiles. She moved the chair back in order for Dina to sit down.

I could see a friendship forming. I was pleased that Dina went to Anna as I needed someone to help Dina get settled in and someone to show her around.

I looked over again and they were engaged in conversation. Dina was no longer shy and introverted. She was doing her share of the talking and smiling.

Anna told Dina that she had come for two months the previous year. She explained that she had credits but did not graduate.

During the break, I heard Anna telling Dina what she could expect and what was expected of her.

Dina was older than Anna but that didn't dampen their enthusiasm.

Not only was Dina older she was also taller. She carried herself in a refined and dignified manner. She is tall and slender. Her dresses I would say were petite.

By the end of the week, I noticed that Dina, guided by Anna, had made only one quick tour of the Mission. Normally, the students like to hang out at the Mission during the noon hour.

They play the instruments and talk to everyone they know from the street.

Dina went to the Mission at noon hour when the noon meal was being served.

The meal is served after the morning service which starts at eleven. There is an altar call when the students and staff pray for those in need of prayer for healing of the body, mind and soul.

Some students bring a plate of food from the Mission and eat at the College.

Dina brings a light lunch from home and eats it in the company of Anna who also brings fruit and some fresh vegetables. The two offer each other special morsels. They often include me in their offerings; sharing their oriental goodies.

Two days after her trip to the Mission, Dina asked if she could speak to me. I wondered what was on her mind. After class, I welcomed her and asked her how things were going.

Dina told me she was not good at understanding, "English is not my first language. The Christian is not my religion."

I told her we take that into account. "You are bright. You will understand as you study more. "

Dina told me she speaks and writes in five different dialects in her country, but English is number seven. "I took English in school. I know much, but not what is taught in the Bible College. There are many big words." I agreed.

I asked if there was anything else.

"Something very important, I think," she replied.

I waited for her to collect her thoughts.

"My husband does not like me to go to the Mission at night. It is not safe for a lady standing on the street with all the men who are not so nice."

I knew I had a problem on my hands as the Mission is the training ground. It is where we live out the scriptures and fulfill the great commission of Jesus the Christ.

I took the Service Manual from the bookshelf and pointed out all the commitments a student makes upon enrolling in the College.

Dina told me that Anna had told her about all of them. "It is my husband, he will not allow me."

I arranged to meet with her and her husband. In the meantime I told Dina to come to the College and we would see what could be arranged.

I ran off a copy of the most important obligations and gave it to Dina to show to her husband.

She looked at the list and smiled. "He will blow his stack," she said.

I wondered where she got that saying. From what I saw of him at enrollment, I figured he has blown his stack more than once.

I welcomed them into my office. I was surprised to see how mannerly and cordial he was.

Dina was not the wallflower she appeared to be at enrollment.

The first thing Norman told me was that Dina really liked coming to class.

"She tells me so much about Anna. She also tells me the teachers are very good and understanding."

I thanked him and got down to the business of the Mission. I told him we cannot make any exceptions because it would open a floodgate of excuses and reasons why students could not comply with training at the Mission.

Norman understood. He asked me what I recommended.

I told him, "It might be best if you brought her that one evening a week which is compulsory, and take her home safely."

He shook his head. "I don't feel that safe myself. I don't even drive this main road going by the Mission if I can avoid it."

I told him I felt the same way myself when I first came down here. Now it doesn't bother me. I know enough good guys who come for the action on the street, and are willing to protect me.

He asked me if she could do something up front where it is safe.

I told him she could sit up front after setting up the Mission for the service and then mopping the floor after everyone has gone.

He told me that his wife doesn't know how to mop a floor. "Where she was brought up they have servants and a house boy. She didn't even know how to cook as they have a cook who does it all."

I told him we would teach her. I added that after that she would be working and serving in the kitchen.

Norman told me that was pretty tough. "I didn't think it would be so strenuous." I pulled out the manual and showed him the rules. He told me we had a deal.

Norman and Dina got up to leave. He said, "She's really getting into what you're teaching. She's preaching to me already," he smiled.

Dina had heard the testimonies of a few students. The week after the meeting with her husband, Dina offered to give her testimony to the class.

She told us that she was born and raised a Moslem. "My father took me to the mosque. Girls had to stand to one side. They could not pray. I didn't pay much attention as it was for the men to understand and pray," she explained.

"My father has much land and works very hard. He would work in the field and then go to the jungle to get meat. I would watch for him to come home because what he hunted would be our main meal. Sometimes he would come home with a dead monkey or snake around his neck. At other times it might be a wild boar.

When he couldn't go to the jungle, he would fish for eels in the river. At night he would go to the lake with dynamite. The fish would die from the blast and come to the top of the water. It was easy and fast fishing.

On his way home he would dig in a fallen coconut tree and gather the big juicy termites and we would have a feast. Sometimes he gathered honey from the trees where the bees were busy making honey.

My father had to do much hunting and fishing as he had three wives and three families to provide for. If he did not provide and was lazy, he would be in trouble with Islam law.

Not only field work, hunting and fishing, but he had to buy smuggled goods and sell merchandise in the market and door to door to make money to buy from the store, what was needed for his families.

He would buy from the pirates who held up boats and made them give what they had bought in the city when they were on their way back to their island homes. Sometimes they raided larger boats and there was a lot to sell in the market.

I am learning your ways from the Bible. I don't understand that much, but I do know they are different from the ways my father taught me. He knows the ways of Islam. He reads the Quaran. I don't read this book as it is for the men to read and practise. All I know is my father told me if someone throws a pebble at you, you throw a grenade at him. This is not what the Bible teaches, I'm sure.

He also taught me I must get even. Never let anyone get away with coming against you. The Bible teaches to forgive and love your enemy. I was taught to hate my enemy and get even. It is a much different teaching."

I later asked her which teaching she thought was better? Dina said the Bible was much easier in this country.

She said there is much more. Maybe another time.

"Now that I am in your country I must learn the ways that are best for me and my husband."

When Dina went to sit down, Anna gave her a hug. The students had a lot to think about after her testimony. They were amazed at the differences in the religions and culture.

I was glad we were studying the Gospel of John. It tells who Jesus is and how we must react to his teachings. Lessons that not only Dina has to learn, but also all of the students must learn and imitate Jesus the Christ.

Dina came with her husband to the Mission in order to carry out her commitments and gain hands on experience in operating a ministry and mission.

Norman found out that it is not as dangerous as he thought it would be.

He fitted in just fine. He sat at a table near the kitchen talking to some of the regulars from the street. He learned a lot about the streets and why people migrate to this area of the city.

After the service, I asked him how he made out. He told me he learned a lot about street life and street people, a subject he knew nothing about.

Dina thanked me for letting her mop the floor. I told her she could come back any night she wanted. She shook her head. Norman escorted her to the door.

After the next few times Dina came to the Mission, she gave another testimony.

"I wanted to be a doctor, but my father could not afford to send me to university for seven years. Instead, I went in for teaching. I didn't like teaching, so I became a midwife. In the province I delivered babies. The husband would give me two chickens or a baby goat for my services. I wanted pesos, but the people were poor and often lived in unsanitary conditions.

I went to live with my aunt in the capital city. I was hired by the most famous hospital. It is where rich men bring their wives to deliver their babies. I was happy in that maternity ward.

I showed a baby boy to his father on the other side of the glass window. When I walked out of the nursery, this well dressed man asked me to raise his new born son. He offered me twice the salary. I became his governess which meant I was in charge of all the staff. There were two cooks, six maids, two drivers and two guards.

I must make certain all ran smoothly. I had my own driver and maid. I ate the same food as the millionaire and his wife. I had many privileges in the country clubs and the five star hotels. I just had to sign for anything the boy and I desired. I travelled around the world with them and cared for their son.

I raised his son for twelve years," Dina reflected.

"My nieces were in high school and I must help send them to university. I did not want them to become maids or nannies. I must go abroad to make dollars. I was sponsored and came to this country. I worked as a nanny and trained to become a nurse. I worked in many different hospitals. That is where I met Norman after his operation. So here I am."

The men clapped and some congratulated Dina.

The first outreach had been planned the year before. It was to go to the church and the ministry of Alex. We always do two visits a year to his church in the valley by a big river many miles away from our city.

Dina handed me a note written by Norman. He explained in length why Dina could not go on outreaches. Number one she has never been away without him. Number two she doesn't know how to act on such a trip. Number three she might get hurt as she doesn't know how to protect herself. And on and on.

I had a short meeting with Dina. She told me as long as Anna was on the outreach, she was confident. "My Norman wants to protect me at all times. Sometimes he's too much for me."

I phoned Norman and told him outreaches were mandatory. He said he doesn't like that word, mandatory. He agreed she could go but he must go along on the first trip.

I told him the seats on the bus were all taken. He offered to drive her to the town. I told him she must go on the bus as that can be the best part of the trip.

He told me, "It's up to Dina, but I know she will never go without me."

The next day, Dina said she was going on the outreach. "I am very excited. I know it will be good for me."

I wanted to ask her how Norman was taking the news. I didn't ask.

As usual it was a great outreach. Anna took good care of Dina. They both mingled with the students and enjoyed every minute. Dina had her first experience at going door to door talking about Jesus and inviting people to come to our services.

The students in charge asked Dina to read the scriptures at the second service. I could see it was a big deal to her, but she carried it off.

Dina and her husband had come for several nights to the Mission. He was impressed by the testimonies. Dina signed up to give more of her testimony at the Mission.

"My father has much land. My mother and I had to go many miles to dig sweet potatoes on his farm. I didn't like digging in the hot sun. My mother would dig so as not to kill the plant. I was bad. I dug so the plant was uprooted. My mother would yell at me. I pretended I was upset. I would sit under a tree in the shade and watch my mother work.

My father had a pet monkey. I didn't like his monkey as my father showed love for the monkey, but my father showed only little love for me. I was jealous.

I would take a stick and run it across the wires of the monkey's cage. The monkey would screech and yell at me. When the monkey was on my father's shoulder, he would pull my hair. I would get even when my father was not around.

Sometimes the men in my village didn't do what it says in the Quaran. If a person was caught stealing, they would cut off a finger.

Sometimes my father would take me to the town square when a man was accused of a bad crime according to Islam law. The leader of the mosque would hear the case against the man and rule. If the verdict was guilty, the man would be blindfolded.

The executioner was a big strong man. With one swipe of the bolo knife the head would fly off and roll on the ground. Blood like a fountain would spurt up and the man would take a few steps and then stumble and fall.

This didn't bother me as much as when my father took me to the cock fights.

My father raised beautiful roosters. Brown with gorgeous coloured neck feathers. I got to love the roosters and my father would let me carry them. My father would massage their legs and we would carry them around the property and onto the road. They each had a name and a personality.

At the fights, if my roosters lost and got cut up badly, I would cry all night.

You might wonder why I came to Bible College. My husband told me I must learn the religion of this country. I told him that I had heard the Moslems call Christians infidels. For that reason alone, he was certain I should learn the religious ways of his people and compare it to the ways of my people.

I am learning and I have a feeling the ways of your people will win. I am learning about a great man Jesus and a great God. I have the feeling that as I learn more, I will be totally convinced."

At the Mission another night, I had a session with Norman. He told me that he didn't know that Dina was raised a Moslem. He went on to tell me that after they were married, she went from being totally loving and sweet to becoming the complete opposite over the slightest provocation. "One word will set her off," he explained.

He told me about one of the signs that twigged him to the fact that he had a problem on his hands. He went on to say, "It was after we were married for a short time. We had a party at our house. The guests were gone and I was helping clean up and doing dishes. I was washing dishes and Dina was drying. Playfully, I flicked a few spots of water at her. She put down the towel and ran into the bathroom. I heard water running.

I thought she was washing something. She came out with an ice cream pail half full of water.

She was coming at me. I started to run. She doused my back.

I quickly twigged onto this abnormal behaviour.

The next day, I asked why she had to get even all the time.

It was then she told me about being raised a Moslem. My dad told me, "In all circumstances you must get even, or people will think you are weak."

He went on to tell me that the first few years of marriage were rough at times and great at other times.

He explained, "There has been culture shock on her part. She doesn't have any family in this country. I am the only one who loves her. I want the best for her. I figured that if she became a Christian and lived out her faith, we would both be blessed."

I asked if there was any change? He told me she is definitely showing signs of forgiveness and not always getting even. "But every now and then she slips back into her Moslem ways. The thing is, she recognizes what she is doing and stops. Sometimes it takes a few hours alone in the bedroom to think about what she has done and what Jesus would do," he laughed.

Norman told me, "One day I was driving her to the house of a friend. A driver in the lane to the right of me swerved in front of me and into the next lane to my left. He went across that lane to make a left hand turn.

I watched in amazement as he did it without getting smashed into. I said, "You idiot, how can you be so crazy."

Dina asked me to pull over and stop. "I want to get out," she told me.

I pulled over and asked her what was the problem? She told me, "You called that man an idiot and a crazy man. You don't even know him. I will get a taxi."

"I promised I would never call anyone an idiot or crazy man again."

I asked, "What about the future. What vison do you have for yourself and Dina."

Norman thought. "I see a bright future for the two of us. I know I am much more settled in my thoughts now that she is becoming a Christian. Your College is really making a difference in her life. I love what it's doing for her and for me."

I asked, "Has it changed you at all?" He told me he has been significantly changed.

"I now have compassion for the men and women in this part of town. Before coming down here I looked down on them. I was scared of them. Now I know they can be changed and become good citizens and good Christians."

He went on to say, "I know Dina looks at people in a much different way."

Dina graduated after the first year and was commissioned.

Norman made it a great occasion and threw a big party for her at his home.

Dina was much more confident and knew she wanted to learn more. She enrolled on her own for the second year of College. She was now helping people with their studies and witnessing to her friends from her country.

Anna went through the second year with Dina. They both graduated the second year College and received their diplomas.

At her new church in the suburbs, Dina was introduced to a seven year course.

The course is given at night. This course leads to ministry and mission work in her country and other countries.

Dina told me that Norman is enrolled in the men's section of the course. "We both go together as he did not want to go alone."

Dina explained to me that Norman needs to learn more about the scriptures in order to be able for the two of them to do missionary work in her third world country.

She explained that Norman must work to support them so she must sacrifice not finishing her third year so Norman can get to know the Lord and how to do ministry.

A year later, Dina came for a visit. She told the class that they were in her country for three months. "We are now partners with a church and we have three mission projects which we support financially and in prayer."

She told us that they support children aged four and five in preparation for going into grade one at pubic schools. "Some parents cannot afford the enrollment costs, so we subsidise their tuition fees and school supplies as well as supplying food and clothing."

The other ministry is with young boys and girls who are abandoned and put onto the street by their parents to beg in order to make money to support themselves. These children are apprehended by human resources and taken to a safe house where they are cared for and get their schooling.

As Norman said, both he and Dina have been radically changed as the result of her coming to the College and his coming to the Mission with her.

Dina and Norman are now in the fourth year of the seven year course.

She explained that she will take six months of the year to go and witness and bring Moslems into the faith and a relationship with Jesus the Saviour of the world. She will also do her children's ministry in her country.

A radical change from an insecure Moslem lady, bent on getting even to a Christian who has become a forgiving lover of Jesus the Christ.

CHAPTER TWENTY

NICK

Abandoned

1 Thessalonians 5:5 "But you brothers, are not in darkness that this day should surprise you. You are all sons of the light and sons of the day. We do not belong to the night or to the darkness."

NICK was a regular at the Mission. He was on the scene before I came to the Mission. He would come early and sit at a table at the back near the kitchen. I soon realized that anyone who sat at his table would hear the word of God

Nick took on the role of street evangelist. Anyone who would listen was a target for the scriptures he had memorized and put into a presentation to be preached for the glory of God.

I sat with him and listened to his witnessing in order to know that what he was preaching was biblical and not heretical. I was impressed with his knowledge and understanding of the word of God.

I got a laugh out of some who were not ready for his stream of biblical verses and his mini sermons. They would get up and move to another table. Some would curse at him and tell him he was crazy. That didn't phase Nick. He was on a crusade and he felt in his heart that he was doing the will of God.

One day I sat with him. He comes an hour or more before the service every day. I asked him where he came from. He told me in a dumpster at the back of the Mission. I was going to tell him to get real. I looked at him and realized that this was a painful admission on his part.

He continued, "I'm a throw away baby. I learned that my mother was a prostitute who accidentally got pregnant. When I was born, she threw me in the dumpster at the back of this building. It's all in the police reports," he confided.

"A drunk heard me crying and dug in the dumpster, picked me up, wrapped me in his jacket and took me to the police station. That tells you how much I'm worth."

I told him that in the eyes of the Lord, you are worth a great deal.

His eyes watered. He found this emotionally painful. There was a pause.

"From that time on it was one foster home after another. I'm an expert on how these homes operate. But its not always the foster parents fault. I would be in a home where they really cared for me. When my Social Worker realized that we were bonding, she would take me away from them and place me in a new home. It was devastating, but I had to follow orders. At times I would run back to my previous home and ask them to hide me. They would keep me overnight and amid tears tell me they had to turn me in."

I asked if there were any really special homes?

Nick told me that there was a home where the Bible was read at every meal. He said that they prayed and studied the Bible as a family before they went to sleep.

"I really liked that family and I still visit them. They gave me my first Bible and taught me how to read it. Mr. Jacobson made out a reading list for me to follow. It was fun because for every bible verse memorized there was a star placed opposite your name on a chart next to the fridge. I was winning the month the Social Worker made me move to a new home."

"It's nice you still have people who love you," I offered.

By then there were people joining us at the table. I excused myself and told Nick we'd have to talk again some time.

He said, "I'd like that."

I encouraged Nick to come to the microphone and give a testimony.

From this testimony I realized how great was his command of the Bible.

Being new to the ministry, I had not developed the evangelical ease that Nick exhibited.

After listening to two of his testimonies, which were really mini sermons in a shotgun style, I told the Senior Pastor, "Nick should be preaching, in the Mission. He preaches much better than most of the other preachers and the students."

The senior pastor of the Mission told me, "If he gave up his drugs and cleaned up his life, I'd rent the biggest and best theatre in the city and have him preach. He'd fill the house night after night."

I didn't leave it there, I begged Nick to come to Bible College. He wasn't certain he would be welcomed. I assured him he would be more than welcome. He enrolled the next week.

He was very familiar with the Bible and he had memorized countless verses. These he used in his witnessing and in his mini sermons which he called testimonies.

We were studying the doctrines of Divine Healing and Anthropology as well as Eschatology. Nick had never studied these doctrines. He was keen to learn what they were all about.

Nick played a game by matching verses he had memorized with the doctrine being taught. When we were studying Divine Healing, he would quote the verses and stories in the Bible which applied to the healing ministry of Jesus.

He took his studies seriously. He wanted to learn everything. Not only learn but have command of the concepts.

He particularly liked it when we studied Anthropology, the study of man. It involved the study of the families in the Bible. He made a list of the families starting with Adam a Eve and their two sons Cain and Able. Noah and his three sons, Shem, Ham and Japheth. He told me he had a list of families right up to the time of Jacob and his twelve sons. "I really like Joseph. I want to be like him," he told the class.

This study fascinated him. One day when things were slow as it was early in the morning, he invited me to his table near the kitchen.

He told me his Christian family had moved to a city far away. I told him I was sorry.

He went on to explain how many families he now belongs to. It was over fifty families and counting. I didn't understand his little game.

"I am part of every family in the Bible," he smiled.

I felt sorry for him. He so desperately needed a family as he had no mother, father, sisters or brothers. No uncles or aunts, cousins or any relatives. Now he had imaginary families. Every family in the Bible has become his imaginary family.

He went on to tell me about how David and he went up the mountain with the sheep and a bear came to attack and eat one of the lambs.

"David and I looked after the sheep for his father. David is really strong. I'm not that strong. David had a long stick. A bear attacked one of the lambs. David ran toward the bear and jabbed the stick into its ribs. I stood ten feet away waving my cloak and yelling at the bear. The bear ran away as fast as it could go."

He told me about the brothers of David and how they put him down.

"I was always there to cheer him up and make him feel good. He's a great brother and I really love him."

I felt like crying. Here is a grown man in his early thirties wanting so desperately to be loved. I felt that this loneliness caused him to do drugs

At times he missed lessons and I knew drugs had got the better of him.

I took Nick for lunch at my favourite restaurant,

He told me , "I think I told you that I was a throw away baby. At times I wish they'd have let me die. I went from one foster home to another. In some they told me they loved me. At first I was thankful that they gave me a warm place to sleep and good food, but soon I learned I couldn't trust them.

The Bible has been my constant companion, my only hope. Jesus told me he would never leave me nor forsake me. I trust Him."

He went on to tell me how he started drinking alcohol when he was twelve years old, marihuana at fourteen and heroin at sixteen.

I asked him what drugs did for him. He told me they gave him hugs no mother ever gave him. It's a comfort I need, when I think of how cruel life has been.

I wanted to put my arms around him and hug him, but I didn't do so as we were in a restaurant.

Nick remained in the class for one year and graduated. I watched as he received his certificate. I expected him to be overjoyed, but he pushed it against his body, not wanting to look at it. I realized that most of the other students had family and friends to help them celebrate, but he had no one.

My wife, Kristina, knew his story and what was happening with him. She went and sat beside him and congratulated him. He looked at her and smiled. He uncovered his certificate and started telling her how he was commissioned and could now do his ministry officially.

Kristina stayed by his side. They invited me to join them for the snack and fellowship. Three students joined us and we had a great graduation.

On the way home, Kristina told me how she wanted to invite him to our house and adopt him. I told her that was a great idea, but he is too involved in the downtown eastside ministry.

I told her, "His happiness is spreading the gospel and bringing in the lost sheep as a helper of David."

She didn't understand the part about David. I explained it to her.

During the summer, Nick came to the Mission. I reminded the senior pastor that Nick was now eligible to preach as he had completed his first year's study.

I got the same story, "When he is drug free, I will rent the largest theatre..."

I didn't bring up the matter of his being commissioned again.

I encouraged Nick to give a testimony when the Spirit moved him. I knew that I was undermining the senior pastor in doing so, but we always have testimonies. So what if the Bible is preached in a mini sermon.

In the second year of studies, Nick asked a lot of questions which were answered. He was especially interested in the end time prophesies.

I gave him books to read and we had long sessions talking about the coming of Jesus for His church at the rapture.

One day Nick told me , "Rapture is my only hope. Please tell me I won't be disappointed by being left behind. I do love my Lord. I need something to hold onto."

I felt his desperation and his emotional pain. I could only point him to the scriptures telling of the prophecies describing the coming events and the promises of Christians being removed from the coming wrath, which is the Tribulation.

Nick poured over these prophecies and was gaining hope when he read that Jesus was coming for those who were eagerly awaiting His return.

Nick cornered me early in the morning and read the scriptures he had found in the Bible. He asked again what he had to do to be certain he would be taken with the Lord at the rapture.

We went over the verses and I explained them to Nick. He lit up and told me he was ready. I told him to read,

1 Thessalonians 1:10, "... and to wait for his Son from heaven, whom he has raised from the dead -Jesus, who rescues us from the coming wrath."

Nick knew what he had to do in order to be ready to meet his Lord and saviour. He looked down and nodded his head. He said , "I know, I have to clean up my life. Knowledge is not enough is it?"

I explained that everyone has something to change, something to give up and something to grab onto. Only you know what that is for yourself.

I repeated the scripture in Psalm 139:23

"Search me, O God, and know my heart; test me and know my anxious thoughts."

I told him, "I might think I know, what is necessary for your deliverance, but only you can make your life ready to go before the throne of God Almighty."

I asked Nick if he would like a booklet I had written on Eschatology and the Book of Revelation. He took the booklets and they became his constant companion. He couldn't get enough of the promises of God relating to the end times.

When the class had a break after forty minutes of lecture, I saw Nick take the booklets from his pocket and review what had been taught.

One day he pointed out what he thought was an error in my booklet. He went to a passage of scripture as his reference point. I was a little embarrassed that I had made a mistake. I read it over twice and realized that it had been based on another scripture which verified it.

Nick laughed and said, "I thought I'd got you. I still think I had a good point."

I told Nick I was really pleased with his spiritual growth. "You're becoming my star student."

I felt this interest in the end times might be the means of getting Nick off drugs and off the street. If I could only channel it in the right direction.

Kristina invited Nick for Thanksgiving dinner. He declined telling her he had people from the street who needed him at thanksgiving as they have not much to be thankful for.

"Many have lost their families. I know how that feels. I have the family of God, but they have nobody," Nick explained.

Nick started missing a day, then two days and finally he came and told me he had a new ministry and wouldn't be coming to College for awhile. He told me he had moved to a new room in a hotel which was filled with the toughest men from the street. He told me, "Some of them belong to gangs and have lots of money. They carry guns and knives. It's sort of scary."

I asked him what kind of ministry he was involved in. "Is it a street ministry or something else?"

He told me he witnesses to the residents of the hotel in which he now lives.

"We have a common room with a shared kitchen. There are chairs and a chesterfield and an easy chair. These guys sit around and talk about drug deals and what they shop lifted and how they're going to make big money. Some talk about guys they're going to get even with. I know they mean that they are going to beat someone up or even kill them.

I have to listen to all this crap while I get my breakfast and lunch ready. At first I ate in my room, but now I sit and eat while they're talking. If there's a break in the conversation, I tell them about Jesus and about the great news of the gospel. I quote Bible verses and now I tell them about the doctrines. I tell them about the end times and all I have learned at Bible College."

Nick went on to tell me, "They really need Jesus as they are corrupted in their ways and their thinking is only toward evil at all times," He paused and recalled what had happened as a result of his witnessing.

"At first they don't want to listen and they even hit me and tell me to take off. They call me a nut and a screwball. I've been threatened with a knife and had my life threatened.

When this happens I go to my room and I wait. A knock comes to my door and secretly, one, or at times two of them want to know more about Jesus. I tell them what I have learned at Bible College and I share the gospel with them."

I asked, "Isn't it dangerous?"

He shrugged. "I get hurt a bit, but Jesus died for us."

I told him he was welcome to come back to Bible College any time.

He told me,"I've got the text books and I'm studying them. If I can't understand something, I know where to get an explanation," he smiled."

He confided that he could never plant a church. He went on to say, he could never do a conventional ministry."

He smiled and said, "Then again, how many students can minister to the toughest guys in the gangs and the toughest guys on the street?"

I agreed that he had chosen the most difficult ministry in the country. I encouraged him to continue doing the ministry God is calling him to do.

Over the years, I have kept in touch. I sometimes meet Nick on the street. If he acknowledges me, we go for lunch or if he's in a hurry, we have coffee and a piece of pie.

If he ignores me when I'm on the street, I don't take offense. I know he is with someone he is ministering to and he doesn't want to ruin his chance of bringing them into the kingdom.

One day, my wife was coming from the Mission at noon. She saw Nick passing by. He stopped to greet her. She asked him why he had no shirt. He told her someone had ripped it off his back. "He didn't agree with the gospel I preached," he laughed.

My wife insisted on buying him a shirt. He said he'd take the money and spare her the trouble. My wife knew the money might go for drugs, but she had to let him know she trusted him. She knew his life story and how he trusted noone except his Lord and Saviour.

Nick walked Kristina to the bus stop. They had to go through the throng on the street. Those who were dealing drugs and others trying to sell their stolen goods. Some who were wanting to buy drugs as well as those who were trying to sell their bodies for a quick fix.

Nick waited for the bus to come in order to protect my wife.

He recognized Jesus in her and he knew she loved and cared for him. He needed a shot of love from a beautiful lady.

The bus took a while in coming.

Nick told her while they waited for the bus, that nothing can fill the hole in his soul except the love of Jesus.

Kristina prayed for him and told him we are there for him any time he needs us. She thanked him for being kind enough to walk her to the bus stop.

I often see Nick in the alley at the back of the Mission. This is where the addicts hang out. I observe him from the window. If he is relatively free from drugs, and not ministering to anyone, I invite him into the kitchen and give him a plate of food. We talk and he tells me what he is doing for the Lord.

He is always in a hurry. He doesn't stay long, but we have a bond which will never be broken.

Two of the favourite verses of Nick are:

Matthew 16:19, "I will give you the keys of the kingdom of heaven; whatever you bind on earth will be bound in heaven, and whatever you loose on earth will be loosed in heaven."

Galatians 6:7, "Do not be deceived: God cannot be mocked. A man reaps what he sows. The one who sows to please the sinful nature will reap destruction; the one who sows to please the Spirit, from the Spirit will reap eternal life."

Nick has put these verses into a powerful and touching sermon.

Nick dreams about pleasing God and inheriting eternal life. He tries so hard to do works that will be pleasing to God and to Jesus.

Often to the point of risking his life in order to save the souls of those who are lost on the street and in the hotels of the downtown east side, skid row.

A ministry which I would not dare attempt.

Six months ago, Nick told me that he had given up his drugs and he had even quit smoking.

He explained,"It happened after a service at the Mission. Some of the students prayed for me. It was as if a bolt of lightening hit me and really rocked me. I fell to the floor and saw a brilliant light. I can tell you it was really bright. It filled me with the Spirit of God.

While I was still in the presence of God, the students kept praying for deliverance. from a demon and an evil spirit. I felt something lift. It was as if I were set free."

He told me he was shocked as he didn't believe he had a demon or an evil spirit. "I know many Bible verses. I tell people about Jesus!" he exclaimed.

I told him that his experience with God and the Holy Spirit was incredible.

"You have been set free from those spirits which bound you to drugs and alcohol. God needs your temple to be free from contamination," I explained.

Nick told me that every day he tells God the Father, "I belong to Jesus. He's my brother and I long to be in union with Him."

His deliverance from spirits which bound him to substance abuse was the greatest news I had heard for a long time.

I told the senior pastor that Nick can now preach in that theatre as he is freed from his addictions, evil spirits and demons which bound him. He is now ready to serve the Lord and preach the gospel.

The senior pastor said, "We'll wait and see how he makes out over the next few months."

Every time I think about Nick, I pray that he will now live a life filled with the Holy Spirit and filled with the joy and peace from the Lord.

For some months after that, I didn't see Nick in the alley at the back of the Mission. I also didn't see him on the street

One day I ran into a friend of Nicks. He told me three or four months ago, Nick was at another mission where they let him preach. "It was really powerful preaching, I was definitely moved, by his message," the man explained..

He went on to tell me, "That night there was a travelling evangelist listening to him. The two of them talked for a long time after the service.

Nick and the evangelist got up and walked out together. He hasn't been seen on the street since that night."

I thought about it and realized that Nick is probably preaching up a storm in First Nations villages along with the travelling evangelist.

Nick told me, during one of our talks a few months ago that God had warned him to stop defiling his temple with drugs and alcohol. He said he had to clean up his life and follow the commands of Jesus in the Bible.

He told me that when he was about to shoot up in the alley, he heard a voice say to him, "Satan wants you." I rebuked Satan as that was shocking to me. I keep telling God, "Satan can't have me, I belong to Jesus the Christ."

Nick told me for years he used the excuse of being thrown in a garbage dumpster and abandoned by his mother as permission to do drugs to forget the pain.

"I guess I never fooled God. He wants my whole body mind an soul without blemish. That's what I aim to give him," he laughed.

Nick didn't fool the Senior Pastor and he didn't fool God. They knew his preaching didn't come from being filled with the Spirit. They knew there was something missing.

Prayer and receiving deliverance at the Mission, allowed God to warn Nick and put him on the road to recovery. He is now filled with the Holy Spirit and preaching in the Spirit. He has been radically changed and is changing the lives of those he is preaching to. He is fulfilling the great commission to go and preach and teach as he is now filled with the Holy Spirit.

CHAPTER TWENTY ONE

WILLIE

Chasing A Dream

John 11:25, Jesus said, "I am the resurrection and the life. He who believes in me will live, even though he dies; and whoever lives and believes in me will never die, Do you believe this?"

We had a pastor visit us from a smaller city many miles from our large city. We learned that he ran a mission which was similar to our Mission. He visited us for a week, staying in the dormitory, and visiting the Mission and the Bible College. He arrived in June, just as the Bible College was winding down. He asked if he could teach a lesson to get the feel of teaching at this level.

He was told he could teach a lesson on the 'Attributes of God'. I gave him the outline and some pointers as to how to prepare the lessons. I told him to follow the text and add from his own knowledge and experiences.

He enjoyed the company of the students and was amazed at the number of persons from the street who came twice a day to the service and stayed for the food.

He particularly liked the Bible College. He kept telling me that they need such a college in their city as it would be of great service to many native reserves in the area.

He was asked to preach once at the morning service and again at the evening service. He preached a message of love and renewal. This message has been preached a number of times but it is always fresh coming from a guest speaker.

Before his message he told how he had founded the mission in his city. He explained how it was a struggle to get it started, but now he has some assistants who are capable and they carry most of the load.

He kept telling us how badly they needed a Bible College. "You are fortunate to have good teachers and a fine program. Perhaps I will have such a program along with my mission."

In the middle of the week he was given a tour of the big city. We didn't want him to think he had seen the beauty of the city only on skid row.

He marvelled at the rapid transit and the ferry boats. He was taken to a large park which had every flower in full bloom.

"Maybe some day our city will have the beauty of your city," he commented.

He came as a visitor to our Counsel meeting. We discussed issues relating to the operation of the dormitory, the Bible College and those issues with the Mission that needed our attention.

It was a time when students made a commitment to come back for one more year.

We also talked about outreaches for September and October. Pastor Ernie, from the smaller city, suggested we visit his Mission. We told him we usually go to native reserves as we are mainly involved in the First Nations ministry.

It was suggested that we could visit Roy's reserve as it was in the vicinity. Another suggestion was that we visit Hilda's reserve which is only fifty miles from the smaller city. The counsel agreed to visit both reserves if possible.

We assured Pastor Ernie that we would visit his mission for one or two nights on our way back from the reserves.

Classes resumed in September. Most of the student from the previous year returned.

There was a time of adjustment and a time to resume friendships and get organized in the dormitories and in the Mission.

There were sermons to prepare and assignments to complete. Music to practice and runs around the sea wall. The formation of a soccer team and weight lifting in the weight room.

The outreaches to organize and a number of things to do.

The outreach to Pastor Ernie's mission and the reserve of Roy was scheduled for November the 29th. This was a longer outreach , as the travel would take four or five days. Stop overs were scheduled. Ten days were allotted for the outreach. The third year students did much of the planning.

It was decided to go to the reserve of Roy and make this our second stop over.

It was not possible to arrange a visit to Hilda's reserve at that time as there was a conference being held and many administrators were going to be absent.

The students were told to bring warm clothes and expect colder weather.

Our first stopover was in a larger city which we reached the first day.

We were warmly welcomed by the ladies group of a large downtown church. They had a great supper prepared.

We are always surprised at the warmth of the welcomes we receive at our stop overs. It's great to belong to the family of God.

Henry thanked the ladies. He told them how beautiful they are and how great the meals were. The ladies smiled and accepted the compliments.

The next day we reached Roy's reserve. Once again a welcoming committee. Roy was really happy to be among his people. They were happy to know that he had chosen the higher path and was at a Bible College in the large city.

They put us up in the old church building

I remembered when I was a boy of five or six being in a church with a pot-bellied stove in the middle of the aisle. The stove in this church brought back memories. The church is beautifully adorned with richly varnished dark woods. The organ is a pedal organ. There was also an old piano which needed tuning..

We were billeted in the adjacent church hall which only had a stove. I looked for a thermostat but there was none. We figured that if we let the heat from the stove in the church get hot enough it might help heat the hall. We all ended up sleeping in the Church as it was easier to heat.

When we unloaded the van, we felt a cold nip in the air. By the time we got ready for bed, the building had cooled considerably. One blessing was that they had dumped a load of firewood near the back door of the hall.

The guys and a couple of the girls took turns waking up and stoking the heater in the church.

The next day we went from house to house and visited the residents. We were invited to the band office meeting room for lunch, prepared by the wives of the band council. We met with the members and were asked if we had any questions. They answered a few questions from the students.

A band member then asked the students what they thought of the program at the College. The responses from the students were all positive and complimentary.

Roy spent the next night with his parents. He arranged for others to stay in houses as the old church was too hard to heat.

A wind from the north brought freezing weather. It went down to twenty below.

I went out to warm up the van ready for our trip to Ernie's mission.

The starter wouldn't crank over the engine. I didn't know what to do.

I motioned for a resident, a young man, to come over to the van.

He told me he'd get it started. I left him and went over to the band office.

I wasn't used to this extreme cold.

I watched as he lit a fire under the motor of the van. I panicked and was tempted to go and stop him. I watched. He seemed to know how big to make the fire.

An older man in the band office sensed my concern. He looked out the window. "He's doing good. You chose the best man for the job."

I was relieved.

The young man had the keys to the van. After half an hour or more, he got in the van and started it up.

We arrived at Pastor Ernie's mission at two in the afternoon. He welcomed us and introduced us to Willie.

Willie came from a reserve close to that of Roy. They knew each other from playing sports on opposing teams. Willie told us they were related. Roy asked how?. That led to a study of the genealogy of the two families.

We enjoyed the evening service. It had some similarities to our mission. The crowd was smaller but the people were similar.

Willie welcomed those who came to the mission. He knew everyone of them and served the older ones. In some ways it was more personal than our mission which is more transient and faster moving.

The next day, Willie had a long talk with the students. He wanted to know everything about the mission and the college. He seemed interested.

After lunch ,Willie cornered me and I had to answer all his questions. He wanted to know if he could stay in the dormitory. How far was the dormitory from the College and the Mission? Could he eat at the mission? How much was the tuition? A multitude of questions.

He told me he didn't graduate from high school. "I wasn't that bright. I'd rather be hunting and fishing. I couldn't keep my mind on what the teacher was saying. It bored me as I knew I'd never need all that information to live on the reserve. Now I'm in the city, I could use more of that teaching."

Pastor Ernie asked if he could send Willie to the college in the big city. I told him he would probably be a good candidate.

Three weeks after we got home, I went to the bus station to bring Willie to the College. He was pleased to live in the dorm. The mission was grateful to have him come and work in the kitchen as he had experience.

I thought he would have more understanding of the Bible and spiritual matters. I asked him how long he was at Pastor Ernie's? He told me two months.

Three weeks later he gave a testimony at the Mission.

"I still don't understand a lot that is being taught at the college. I have my own native beliefs. At the college they think I should live by their beliefs. I guess I'll have to see how it goes. I was brought up to believe in the ways of my ancestors. They are down to earth. At the college their beliefs are pointing to the sky.

When I look at my life, I realize I could have done better. I'm counting on the college to teach me how to improve my lifestyle and my life in general.

I have a wife and four kids. I haven't seen them for a couple of years. One of those years I spent in jail. I would like to see my kids, but I can't as I deserted them and their mother doesn't think I'm worth anything.

I guess this is my last chance to make something of myself. Pastor Ernie told me I could help him when I graduate. It's worth it if I get a good job in the church.

I quit drinking last month. I knew they wouldn't like it if I was a drunk I've been a drunk for twenty years, but now I quit. I still smoke as that isn't as bad. You don't do silly things after puffing," Willie laughed. "Maybe some day they'll talk me into quitting smoking. As I figure it a man must decide to make a difference in his life. I know it's up to me and I believe its for anybody who wants to be a man with dignity and integrity."

I realized at that point Willie was still on thin ice. A drunk for twenty years and only one month sober.

I told the captain of the house to watch Willie and be certain he didn't come home drunk or leave the house after curfew. I asked him to inform the guys to be watchful.

It wasn't that we wanted to kick him out of the dorm and end his education at the college. I know from past experience that if you nip such behaviour in the bud you can stop it more quickly.

Willie could read at a grade five level. For the college we demand a grade nine level at the minimum. Willie was matched with a tutor, who was a student from the third year.

It was the girl's turn to tutor as we don't push all the hard work onto the guys. I don't do the matching. It is done by a formula. In this case it was Cindy, a first nations lady, who would tutor Willie, a first nations man.

Cindy was a happy lady with a smile for everyone. She had her issues like everyone else. When she knew it was her turn to tutor, she was quite happy.

We have all the books and the level tests for reading and math. Cindy had received training and was ready to go.

Willie was happy to have a young, first nation's lady as his tutor. They got along quite well. According to Cindy, Willie wanted to talk more than to do his lessons.

I had a long talk with Willie. He wanted to do the talking, but I told him to listen. We came to an agreement. He would upgrade and stop socializing with Cindy.

"She's the teacher. You must respect her," I warned.

There were not only problems with his reading but there were problems in the dormitory. Willie had quickly formed his idea of what being a Christian should look like and act like.

Anyone who horsed around or who joked and had fun, was not a Christian, according to Willie's idea of Christian behaviour.

I seldom saw him smile as he was too busy being the policeman at the dorm. Nobody could live up to his standards.

The guys are Christians and they like to laugh and be filled with joy. They have given their life to the Lord and they live their life for Him. They also have in house jokes which make them laugh. They remember previous students and what they did. Willy was out of the loop and couldn't figure out what was so funny.

The captain of the house took him aside and told him his stay at the dormitory was being jeopardized by his criticising and being a bore.

Willie stopped his foolishness and started getting along at the dorm. and the Mission. He started to smile a bit, which appealed to more people.

Christmas was always a busy time with turkey dinners and all the trimmings. Those who didn't go home for Christmas pitched in and helped prepare and serve meals at the Mission.

Willie took it upon himself to make certain everyone was cared for. If a person from the streets looked lonely, he would go over and sit with him or her and cheer them up.

Willie never learned to play the guitar or the drums. He felt his calling was to preach the gospel and let others do the singing. I never heard him sing. I guess he didn't have a good voice.

After Christmas break, Willie put his mind to studying his lessons and getting his reading and math up to a reasonable level. He told me that during the Christmas break he really did a lot of reading. "It helps when you read the Bible," he discovered.

The next decision Willie had to make was one regarding his graduation. He was three months short of the full year as he came in December. We have a correspondence course they can take and they can get help over the summer break. It was decided that with this extra study, Willie could get his first year certificate by September or October.

Willie was given a few months to decide. He came to the office and took half an hour to tell me that he would go and help Pastor Ernie for the summer. "Get away from the skid row of the big city."

At graduation, Willie received a Letter of Recognition. He smiled but didn't display his framed letter.

The next day he took his possessions and caught a bus for the smaller city of his friend, Pastor Ernie. He phoned the Mission a few times. I took one of the calls and listened to him for half an hour telling me how wonderful things were in the smaller city

It was summer and a bit of a break for the staff

In the middle of August, Willie phoned from the bus depot. I wasn't there but another staff member picked him up.

Two days later, I went to the Mission to sign a few cheques. Willie heard that I was there. He came in and I could tell by his demeanor that all was not well.

He asked me to come over to the dorm as he had something to tell me that was not to be told in the Mission.

I agreed to meet him there in twenty minutes.

When I came in the door, Willie exclaimed, "I can't believe a Pastor could stoop so low."

I interrupted, "Whoa, settle down."

I sat down and Willie told me how his mentor, Pastor Ernie, had been making love with a young girl. "She's only sixteen, can you imagine?"

He went on to tell me how he would be at the mission and Pastor Ernie would let him hold the fort while he went and made love with this girl.

"He had to go in the afternoon while her parents were out working. Not only that but he made her pregnant. What a rat," he blurted out.

"I was home when this young girl knocked on the door.

She told Ernie's wife that her husband had made her pregnant and she needed money for an abortion.

Ernie's wife was crying and I had to console her."

Ernie came in smiling, I told him to wipe the smile off his face. He saw his wife in distress and blamed me. I told him what I thought of him. He said we had to pray about it.

"How can you face God when you've knocked up a young girl and brought shame on your wife and on your life?" Willie asked.

I had it out with him. I grabbed my stuff and came home.

Willie said, "I thought Christians..."

I put up my hand and stopped him before he got into hot water. "You can't judge all Christians by one man's bad behaviour and sinning," I said.

Willie stopped his ranting and calmed down.

"We have to pray for Pastor Ernie," I encouraged.

"I can't call him pastor. As a matter of fact I don't want to think about him." Willie stopped to ponder his situation.

"He told me I'd take over his mission some day. That was my dream."

I put my hand on Willie's shoulder. "God has something better. Wait and see."

Willie went on the first outreach of the new school year. We went back to Alex's church by the river. Alex took us over the mountain to his house church. The trip over the mountain was scary for me and I'd been there before.

Willie came from the flat prairies. He had never been over a mountain with switchbacks and steep climbs and steep droop offs. He sat by the window and looked down. He turned and grabbed John who was sitting beside him. John laughed. He told Willie to hide his head in a pillow.

Willie said, "Then I can't see when to jump."

Peter was the driver. He told Willie to chill out.

To make matters worse, Edgar told Willie, "Look down at the bottom. See that car? It went over the bank and rolled down into the ravine, five people died."

Willie knew they were trying to scare him. He quit looking out his window and watched others in the van. Nobody was upset. Stacey was doing her nails and Becky was reading her Bible.

The students enjoyed the meeting at the home of an elder in the small settlement where Alex lived and grew up. The house was filled with Alex's people ready for the service. Alex conducted the service which was quite informal.

A young man recognized me from our prison ministry and we had a long talk. He wanted to know about my wife and how Martha was doing.

The students joined in the worship in song and really rocked the house.

We got back to Alex's church at midnight. Some of the guys were hungry. A big meal was prepared. I ate my share.

My wife and I had the office as our bedroom and we turned in.

Willie graduated. He did some upgrading and received his first and second year certificate.

From then on he kept asking me about his ministry.

"You told me I would have a ministry when I graduated," Willie stated.

"I'm sorry Willie, I told you when you had your ministry, I would recommend you for ordination."

"But aren't you going to give me a ministry?" Willie asked.

"God doesn't have a list of ministries that I am to give to people."

I reminded him of Ephesians 2:10:

"For we are God's workmanship created in Christ Jesus to do good works, which God prepared in advance for us to do."

He agreed that perhaps he misunderstood. I told him that I only teach, "I don't prepare good works in advance for people to do."

After his finals and graduation, Willie was given a break. He became a pastor in training at the Mission. He told me some day he would be the Assistant Pastor.

Later, it was brought to my attention that Willie had adopted a harsh manner of preaching. His message had become one of hellfire and brimstone for not coming to the Lord.

I told him that this message is not for skid row. They have enough grief on a daily basis. We must preach hope, love, peace and joy, I informed him.

He told me that the Book of Revelation was filled with hellfire, brimstone, and burning sulphur.

"That's for the unrepentant ones who blaspheme God and are steeped in sin.

These people from the street have to be given another chance. They have to be told about a Saviour who died for them, who loves them and wants them in His kingdom with him."

This time Willie listened. I added that it was the senior pastor who wants you to change the tone of your message. That helped to seal it.

I watched as Willie carried out his duties. He grew in the faith as he prayed for healing and people were healed.

Willie went from a recovering alcoholic to a well informed spiritual pastor in training with a ministry that God has prepared in advance for him to carry out.

Willie has been radically changed in many areas of his life

CHAPTER TWENTY TWO

RANDALL

Buddhist

Isaiah 41:10 , "So do not fear for I am with you; do not be dismayed, for I am your God. I will strengthen you and help you; I will uphold you with my righteous right hand.

RANDALL came to the Mission and stood a short distance from where the service was taking place. One of the members motioned for him to sit down, but he shook his head and declined. At some point in the service, he would disappear.

For some months, I never had an opportunity to speak to him. He was always smiling and took pleasure in the music and listened to some of the Word of God, but he didn't speak to anyone.

He is of Asian descent, but I didn't know which country. Later on, I learned his parents were from China. He is always dressed neatly and is well groomed. Long hair in a pony tail which accents his oriental looks and makes him look younger than he really is.

On Saturdays, we rent the Mission for the afternoon to a group who were ministering on the street, but now desired to minister in a Mission.

I opened up for them and oversaw the service to make certain they complied with our rules and preached according to our interpretation of the doctrines and scriptures.

They were on fire for the Lord and complemented the Mission.

Randall was loosely affiliated with this group. I learned that they were Taiwanese. Randall helped set up for the service, served in the kitchen and charmed the young ladies.

It was at a Saturday service that I had the opportunity to speak to Randall. He was very polite and told me he was a new Christian.

I invited him to take part in the Bible College. He said he'd think about it.

The next Saturday, I told him we were waiting for him to show up at the College.

He smiled and gave no answer.

I had given up on his coming to the class.

A few weeks after that, he came to the Mission and smiled as he observed the service. There was the singing of gospel songs by a student. This was followed by testimonies telling what God was doing in the life of the believers. Finally the Word of God presented in a sermon and the altar call.

On a Monday morning, half way through the lesson at the Bible College, Randall came in and took a position a short distance from the class. He was leaning against a post, smiling as he listened attentively.

A student set up an extra chair and invited Randall to sit down and join the class. He declined.

Randall monitored the lesson.

I watched to see if the lesson grabbed his attention. At times he would nod his head in agreement. At another point in the lesson his eyes opened widely as something new to him was taught.

After our prayer to close the study of God's word, he disappeared.

I was thankful that he had completed monitoring half a lesson. I hoped it might spark an interest in the Bible College.

A week later, Randall came to class early. He paid his tuition and told me he felt good about coming to the College. "I feel relaxed and the people are very polite." I thanked him for his kind words and handed him the text books and the work book. He thumbed through them and made note of the pages we were studying.

I told Randall that we have tutorials, "You can go over the missed lessons and do the essays and written sermons, and work towards graduation."

He told me that he wasn't going to preach. "That's not my gift." He informed me.

I countered with, "But you do have gifts, everyone has a spiritual gift or maybe three or four."

"What are spiritual gifts?" He asked

I told him that they are gifts given to Christians who will use them to edify, the church. He didn't know what edify meant. I told him it is to build up and make more powerful, the church, the body of Christ.

I explained, "If I use my spiritual gifts and another person uses their spiritual gifts we have twice as much power and twice as many blessings from the Lord?"

Randall thought about what I had said, but he did not really understand.

I invited him to read first Corinthians 12:4 to 10 and verse 27 to 31. I also mentioned Romans 12:6 to 8

I opened my Bible to these verses and we read about some of these gifts and discussed them. I asked which of the gifts he believed he had? I also asked, "Which of the gifts would you like to have?"

He thought for a moment, "I like to encourage people to do things that are good for them."

He thought for a minute and replied, "I feel merciful towards those in addictions and those suffering pain and being in a wheelchair or whatever."

I told him the greatest thing is, if we use our gifts we will not lose our gifts.

He asked me what gifts I practice. I told him that I have the gift of teaching for one.

He smiled, "That's rather obvious."

I told him I also have the gift of knowing. I had to explain that this is from God and must be used in conjunction with Jesus the Christ and the Holy Spirit.

I went on to tell him, "I know , through the Holy Spirit's leading, what is wrong with a person physically, mentally and spiritually."

He asked me for an example.

I told him about a man who came to the mission and needed healing. He asked me to pray for him for healing. I asked, "What specifically." He said, "You pray for whatever you think is my problem." I was put on the spot. I quickly got in touch with the Holy Spirit and determined through listening to the Holy Spirit, that it was his stomach that needed healing. I prayed for relief from ulcers and any other pain in of his stomach. After praying he told me I was right. I told him it was the Holy Spirit who was right.

Randall asked if there was another example of my using Spiritual gifts.

I told him how another young man asked me to pray for a painful back caused by an accident when playing street hockey. He told me he was checked and fell on the cement curb and hurt his back. He told me it had been painful for years."

He didn't divulge the region of his back that was painful. I allowed the Holy Spirit to direct my hand. My right hand went to the lower back. I prayed and felt a vertebra pop out and a neighbouring vertebra pop in. His back was healed.

The next day he told me there was still some pain. I told him he was healed and the pain would go away. I explained to him, "Your testimony must be, 'I am healed. My back is healed."

Randall agreed that Spiritual gifts were great if used for the glory of God.

Randall stuck with his studies and turned out to be a model student. He got along with everyone. He always had a smile and a kind word to share.

He came to the Mission and loved to work in the kitchen, greeting the people who come in from the street. He displayed his love and concern by his actions.

He started a new fad. It was for people to buy a special treat to share with those people who come off the street. He gave them a sucker wrapped in a bible tract or whatever he thought might make a difference in their lives.

It was when we were studying Eschatology, the 'Study of Things to Come,' that Randall lit up. He wanted to learn more about the future. He found it fascinating. and full of mystery.

In Randall's testimony at the Mission, he explained that both his parents were Buddhists. "I was brought up in that faith. Their talk is about Nirvana and reincarnation. They taught me the Eightfold paths to Nirvana which is a release from the endless cycle of death and rebirth on the earth. I know you don't believe in this cycle of death and rebirth, which is called reincarnation. I must tell you that I still reserve the right to believe in some form of reincarnation.

Our belief is not like the Hindu religion which teaches that people will come back as cows or snakes or pigs.

Buddhists are told they will come back as humans in many situations and cultures until they reach Nirvana, the complete state of being one with the universe.

I still have a hard time not believing some of the things my parents taught me. The reason I came to Bible College is to learn the truth.

The truth is very important to me.

I have read some of your Bible, which is very interesting and enlightening. I have told you what I have learned from my parents. They will not change their beliefs.

I am now learning the differences between the two religions. In the College, I am learning more every day. I believe I will soon be able to argue the differences in my parent's religion and Christianity and come up with a clear vision of eternity.

One of the great differences is that Buddhists must work for Nirvana. The Christian believes and has faith in God's grace for salvation.

I am trying to understand fully. It is difficult because it is so easy," he laughed.

"You do not call it Nirvana, but in some sense it is. Those who believe and give their life to God's precious Son, Jesus the Christ will have eternal life in the heavenly kingdom. Buddhists will argue this is Nirvana." Randall shook his head.

Randall promised, "I will have more next time as I am filling my mind with new thoughts."

Our study of Eschatology, (Things to Come) led Randall down a new path, as there was nothing like it in the Buddhist religion.

He was totally involved in the thought that he could be taken from the earth and go before the throne of God Almighty. It was as if he was afraid he'd miss out on the coming rapture if he didn't know all the facts.

After class, he would corner me and ask questions about things which baffled him. When I showed him the scriptures which corroborated what I had taught or what was not taught as yet, he'd get excited.

He was not the first end-times student who was full of curiosity and questions.

The study is so intriguing and so well documented in the Bible.

Randall wanted to share with the class research he had done on the internet and in magazines. I had to filter that which was genuine and based on Biblical prophecy with that which was possibly from false prophets.

I spent many hours after class listening to the findings of pseudo-prophets whose prophecy did not line-up with Biblical prophecy.

At times, I was fascinated with his findings, but after prayer and some filtering, I would come to the conclusion for or against his findings. I pointed out the scripture of Jesus telling His disciples, "For false Christ's and false prophets will appear and perform great signs and miracles and deceive even the elect." Matthew Chapter 24:24.

I taught Randall to sort out that which is Bible based and that which can at times be suspect.

When we started studying the Minor and Major prophets, Randall was really interested when it came to prophecy and their predicting "Future events." And what would happen "In the Last Times." It made me smile, as I knew he was eagerly awaiting the return of Jesus the Christ to take him before the throne of God.

I pointed out to him that he would receive a crown.

2 Timothy 4:8, "Now there is in store for me the crown of righteousness, which the Lord, the righteous judge, will award me on that day and not only me, but also all who have longed for His appearing."

That made Randall's day. He read that verse over and over again and he read it aloud. His countenance lit up. and he went home happy.

After Christmas break, he gave a testimony to the class.

"As I told you before, my parents are devout Buddhists who feed their ancestors in order that they will be happy and my parents will be blessed. They have a special place in the house. It is an altar to their god, Buddha. There is always fresh fruit and incense placed there by my mother.

My sister and I are embracing Christianity. We have no special place in the house for placing a symbol of our God and His Son Jesus the Christ.

We decided this Christmas we would put up a tree and decorate it.

We went and bought a small tree and some decorations. My father was home when we brought the tree into the house. I have never seen my father go so ballistic. He demanded we take the tree from the house.

"It will bring a curse on the house. Trees are for outside. You decorate your tree out near the dog kennel," he commanded.

So much for our tree. He did allow us to put up some decorations as long as they did n't come too close to the altar to the dead.

This is just one of the many superstitions of our people. Red is for luck. I tried to tell my father that there is fate but not luck. He told me I was speaking foolishness, which in our household means, shut up," he laughed.

"When I have much more knowledge and wisdom, I will bring my mother and father into the arms of Jesus."

Randall completed his studies in the second year and graduated with honours.

Randall told me that his funds were running low and he might have to stop coming to the College if he couldn't afford the tuition. I told him to come even if he was short and unable to pay up front. "We will carry you for as long as you need assistance and have a desire to learn. We have sponsors who are committed to helping students like you," I informed him.

For some reason, he didn't want to hold down a full-time job. He did have a part-time job working at nights.

Randall told me his money was short this month. "It's usually enough but for some reason I am overspending," he explained.

During the summer there are supporters of the College who will hire students.

I told Randall about these jobs and I told him he could have first pick of the jobs that are listed. He wasn't interested in a full time five day a week job.

He told me that Jesus is coming. "I don't want to be slogging at a job I detest and miss the big event."

He went on to say that working night shift three nights a week made him available afternoons, when he attended most of his classes.

Randall went on many of the outreaches. He went to the smaller city when Alex got married. He also went to the outreach at the church Alex had planted in a smaller town near the river. He told me he really liked that size of town and that type of ministry.

"Alex gets to travel over the mountain to his house church and to all the reserves. I'd like that."

I reminded him of the time we went to the island where Wallace lives. "You told me that kind of ministry was miles above any other. You thought it would be great to have a boat and visit small inlet villages, where there was no pastor in residence." He agreed that he had a great time at the village and on the fishing boat.

Randall told me he has to get a partner to go with him when he does his ministry.

I asked him about the young ladies who were with the ministry which rented the Mission on Saturdays. He nodded and smiled. I wondered if there was any particular young lady he was looking at.

Randall completed the three year program. His marks were in the nineties which earned him a scholarship to the prestigious College. He would only need two years of study to be a graduate in their four year program. He declined.

The other thing on his plate was being ordained. He had already applied and was waiting for his interview. I was certain he would be accepted, but there can always be a hitch that I'm not aware of.

We were short a teacher in the College for the coming year.

There were a few people who applied, but they were not of the caliber we were looking for. Others wanted a big salary which we couldn't afford.

I presented my idea of having Randall team- teach in the College with myself as his partner. The staff, teachers and Pastors agreed that it would be O.K. until we found a teacher who would be a volunteer.

Our budget did not allow us to hire anyone who demanded equal pay with other colleges.

We all taught out of a love for the students and the Lord. Most of us were Volunteers receiving no salary.

I had taught for twenty-six years in the public school system and retired early as I had the means to retire.

When someone asks what salary we receive a year at the College, I tell them I don't know as my treasures are being stored in heaven where God will protect them.

Randall fitted in quite well. He taught the lessons I had prepared from the previous years. We went over the lessons and I taught him how to add his own thoughts and research on the subjects.

I learned from the students that he also had his own methods of getting closer to the Lord and the Kingdom of God.

Upon talking to the students, I found that they loved what he was teaching. I couldn't argue with people being filled with the Holy Spirit and being at one with the Lord in their thoughts and minds.

There was never one complaint, but only favourable compliments about Randall's teaching.

Randall was ordained. There was a big celebration. Randall and a few students, cooked at the Mission and made a sumptuous meal. The students pitched in and helped decorate the Mission. I met Randall's sister and some of his close friends. The Taiwanese group from the Saturday ministry were there. It was a great occasion.

Randall taught for a year and a half. They were pleasant years as we were on the same wave length and we shared what we had learned regarding the signs of the return of the Lord for His chosen ones.

He would ask me what I thought on various subjects. I'd share freely knowing that he was hanging on every word.

He met a lady who became the love of his life. She is a beautiful and a charming young oriental lady from a good family.

At first, she supported his ministry, which now included preaching, teaching and being a staff pastor.

Being in a Mission church on the Downtown eastside has its moments we'd like to forget. People swearing, fighting, being belligerent and disrupting the service.

On the whole, the regulars, who come off the street, are well behaved. It is the new ones, who have to be disciplined, who are the problem. Many do not like discipline. They rebel and become obnoxious.

His girl friend and my wife have had encounters with intoxicated and rebellious men and women, to the point of being threatened with violent acts such a being hit or pushed around. That turned them off and scared them as they were not able to defend themselves.

At one Sunday service a young man kept speaking out and being rude. My wife and I were sitting in the front row.

A student went over to talk to this young man. The offender jumped over two rows of pews, picked up a chair and hurled it high into the air. My wife ran and hid behind the pulpit.

Fortunately, the chair landed in an empty space and no one was hurt.

Randall's girl friend was upset as was my wife.

That incident, as well as many others which included swearing and men wanting to fight close to where they were sitting, was enough to turn the girlfriend of Randall against the Mission.

Because of this, Randall's lady steered him to a church in another end of town which catered to the middle class intellectuals.

He kept coming back occasionally and then stopped coming to the Mission.

I have kept in touch and he e-mails me quite often. We go out for coffee and for lunch. These meetings have become less frequent as he has a full-time job and is married.

I have fond memories of Randall and marvel at how much progress he has made in the spiritual realm. He has become very mature in the faith.

In his last e-mail he told me he and his wife are planning to start a home church. They have the backing of a large denomination. Because of his graduating from our College and his teaching experience, he is already ordained in their denomination.

Randall told me that he and his wife will also do mission trips to third world countries when their house church can be left in the care of a staff pastor.

The downtown eastside does not appeal to those who need the safety of a refined and spirit filled church. Randall could handle skid row people but his wife needed to worship in a more sedate and quiet setting.

Randall and I have a secret agreement that we will be together in heaven and learn more of the universal truths from Jesus the Christ when we are in the presence of God Almighty.

Randall has given up a religion that sees Nirvana as the potential goal with reincarnation and the eight steps to completion of the soul and the worship of Buddha.

He in now completely immersed in the Christian religion. He is looking forward to the New heaven and the New earth in the presence of God Almighty as the potential goal of his and his wife's life.

He has been radically changed.

CHAPTER TWENTY THREE

WALLACE

Seeker

Romans 12:1, "Therefore, I urge you brothers, in view of God's mercy, to offer your bodies as living sacrifices, holy and pleasing to God-this is your spiritual act of worship. Do not conform any longer to the pattern of this world."

WALLACE came to the Mission with his father. I have known his father for a number of years and it was great to be introduced to his son. I could tell that Wallace was well educated and would be a good student, if he opted to come to Bible College.

On that first visit, I sat and talked to his father and put forward the idea of Wallace coming to the College. They looked at each other and the father said they would consider the invitation.

I wondered which part of the area up north they came from. I had spoken to the father on numerous occasions but he had never mentioned a town with which I could specifically locate where they lived.

I knew that Wallace's father had been a lumberjack and a fisherman, which meant they must be near the coast or possibly near a lake in the interior. Wherever it was, Wallace was a good representative of that region.

A few days later, Wallace showed up at the Mission without his father. He asked if he could enroll in the College. I told him we would be pleased to have him.

He had a cheque made out for his tuition. When I accepted it and gave him the texts, he thought that was great.

During the service, at the Mission, he was scanning both texts and nodding his head, giving his approval.

I smiled, knowing that he would be special.

Wallace is a handsome and presentable, First Nations young man. His clothes are designer and he is always impeccably groomed.

I noticed that at the College, he made friends with the intellectual guys and girls. Curtis took notice of him and the two of them hit it off. I thought Wallace would seek out another first nations person, but he became friends with Curtis.

Peter wanted to get to know Wallace so he joined the two and they became the three who were always together.

Wallace had a smile and a word of encouragement to share with everyone. This boded well with him when he made friends with the girls. He brought a ray of sunlight into the classroom and into the Mission.

His written assignments and tests set him above the majority of the students as he is a serious student, wanting to know all the angles and gain all the information available in each subject area.

When we studied the 'Doctrine of Soteriology" (the doctrine of Salvation), Wallace knew he had to make a more lasting and deeper commitment to God and Jesus the Christ.

He explained in his testimony that he was baptised as a child.

He felt he must now be baptised as a true believer in order to have the Holy Spirit come and dwell within him and control his life.

When he approached me, I agreed to the baptism and arranged a time for him to tell the class why he wanted to be baptised and what he planned to do after baptism.

His baptism turned out to be a grand event. Wallace's father, uncles, aunts, cousins and their friends came for the celebration. We had to put out the folding chairs in the Mission and arrange more tables for the food that was to be served after the baptism. His family and friends had brought food enough to feed an army.

As usual, we went to the ocean for the baptism. The weather cooperated and we had a beautiful sunny day. It was great to see so many people in the park which borders the ocean. People walking by stopped to witness the immersion of Wallace. We celebrated the going down into the water and cleansing of the old man and the bringing up of the new spiritual creation.

After that, I had a flood of those wanting baptism. I considered it a blessing that the Holy Spirit is working so powerfully in the Downtown east side.

The next course we studied, after Wallace come to Bible College, was the 'Doctrine of Divine Healing'. It included the stories of the healings of Jesus the Christ and healing as the Will of God the Father. Methods of Divine Healing and all that is involved in the process; including the vessel and their part in the healing process

Wallace wanted to know everything about 'Divine Healing'; every facet.

I explained that Salvation can lead to healing as healing is often contingent on a person's being saved and believing that God does heal.

In our discussion, I also pointed out that there are cases where divine healing took place first and because of this healing, the person turned to Christ and was saved. That ended any controversy.

As I taught about faith and healing the question was put forward about how much faith a person must have. Wallace sited the parable in which Jesus says:

Matthew 17:20,"... if you have faith the size of a mustard seed you can say to this mountain move from here to there and it will be done.":

Curtis asked, "Why are not all people healed after prayer for healing?"

Wallace wanted to know, "What impedes the healing process?"

Becky asked, "How can we retain healing?"

I gave them a list of twenty five things that can impede healing and by which people can lose their healing. I prefaced it by telling them that there is healing power coming from God and you can be vessels of God's healing power.

I told them how God has used me as a vessel many times when someone has come to me asking for healing.

Stacey asked, "If people come for healing and you pray for them but healing doesn't happen; wouldn't that be embarrassing?"

I told her, "What if they ask for healing and you refuse to pray and you were the only one God could use as His vessel. Now that person will have to suffer pain or sickness the rest of their life, because you were afraid you might be embarrassed if healing didn't happen."

That struck a chord and the students knew they must ask for the gift of healing and use it for God's glory.

All the questions were answered during the course presentation.

I read First Corinthians 12:31, "But eagerly desire the greater gifts."

Everyone agreed that the power of divine healing was a greater gift.

I also told them they had to ask the Holy Spirit for the greater and all spiritual gifts. Why? Because the Holy Spirit lives within you and is the giver of gifts.

The Bible tells us that the Holy Spirit came down with power bearing (spiritual) gifts.

Wallace asked for and knew he had the spiritual gift of healing. He was really enthusiastic and excited. One night, he prayed for a girl who came to the Mission. She told him she had a sore back and had terrible pain when sitting and walking. A few days later, she told Wallace that her back was healed, no pain after months of suffering.

She thanked him for his healing touch. Wallace told her it was the touch of our Almighty God that healed her through the stripes of Jesus which he bore when going to the cross and while being pierced for our transgressions.

I was listening to the conversation and realized that Wallace was really growing in his knowledge and understanding of spiritual matters.

Wallace gave a testimony at the College.

"I was brought up in a Christian family. My mother is devout and she prays the rosary every day. Mine is a Christian home but my mother doesn't read the Bible. She has a Sunday Missal which she often reads. It gives her some insight but she never shares it with me.

My father likes to go to religious gatherings and feels that through osmosis he will be filled and saved. I love my father and now I will be able to teach him and hopefully he will be filled with the Holy Spirit rather than basking in the glow when at church, but not being a candidate for glory once he leaves and goes into the world.

I am learning so much at the College. In our church we don't have the Holy Spirit. We talk about Jesus but we don't walk with Him. We learn the commandments but we don't keep them. We can do much better.

People in my village need someone to tell them to read their Bibles and do what it says."

At another time he told the class how God had healed the young lady with a bad back. He told them how he , touched her back and prayed in the name of Jesus the Christ for the healing process and it happened.

"To think God used me!" he stated in surprise.

When he gave this testimony, it opened up the healing ministry again.

Wallace was told by Darryl that he could heal himself through prayer and touching the affected area. Wallace looked to me for verification. I told him that we had covered that concept, but perhaps I went over it too quickly.

When Wallace understood the implications of healing himself, it was like receiving a special gift from heaven.

At the time of the lesson, he told us he had no symptoms or pain. He related that he did get headaches periodically and now he could be set free from all his aches and pains.

I gave an example of self healing. "When I was at a hospital on a visit, I was attacked by an incurable virus. They called it a Super bug. The doctor prescribed an antibiotic which I took, but it had no effect. I could only pray, which I did.

Of all places to lodge, it attacked the inner lining of my nose.

In our medicine cabinet I found a salve which I hoped might work. It was a prescription for a rash. This salve actually took away the pain for a day or two, but it didn't heal the infection. It took two years of praying every day and night for the pain to subside. At times, I prayed continually as the pain was excruciating and constant.

God heard my prayers and healed me. I thank him daily for that healing."

The students now believe in the healing power in the Word of God, in the stripes of Jesus and the sanctifying work of the Holy Spirit.

Wallace put great effort and enthusiasm into all his studies. So many new concepts that he had never explored; were now brought to life and took on real meaning in his life.

Wallace went to the Mission nearly every night hoping someone would come forward at the altar call and ask for healing He gained the reputation of one who had the gift of healing. He was called upon many times to use that spiritual gift from God.

Wallace went on every outreach. He loved to see new places and meet people who he could talk to and witness Jesus the Christ to them.

We took an outreach to Darryl's reserve. It's on the shores of a large river which comes from the mountains. The men were fishing for salmon. Wallace had fished for salmon, but in boats. These men were using a casting rod with spinners and hooks. This reminded Wallace of the times he used the same equipment when he was younger and not ready for the hard work on the fishing boats

He talked to the men as they waited patiently for a bite and a catch.

They were his people, but not from the same nation. He shared information about his nation. They all knew one of the travelling evangelists and laughed at the times they spent listening to him preach. "Maybe some day he will come this way," the smallest man said with a sigh.

Wallace invited them to the church service that was being held that night. He informed them that it was near the sweat lodge. They all knew the church.

"I was there once," a tall man explained.

Wallace left them and said, "You come to the meeting. We came a long ways to put on a service for you and your family."

Wallace joined the other students in a door to door blitz of the small reserve. People were very nice. Many had an excuse why they couldn't come. Others promised to come. That night there were nine people who came to the service on time.

The lack of people at the service didn't dampen the enthusiasm. There were fourteen students and staff and nine more from the village They filled one quarter of the small church. The sound of worship in song to the Lord brought in a few more teens, children and some elders to join in the worship of God and His Son.

Wallace read the Bible verses and Darryl preached a sermon based on the Book of Acts of the Apostles. It was well received.

On the way back from the outreach we went to a ski resort town. It was late fall and there was snow on the mountains. We went to the top of the mountain on the chair lift and from that viewpoint marvelled at the beauty of God's creation.

Wallace graduated and was presented with a certificate commissioning him to go out and preach the gospel, teach and lay hands on the sick and they will be healed.

Wallace already fulfilled the great commission in various ways.

Many of his relatives attended the graduation ceremony. He introduced me to most of them. They were all well dressed and very presentable. They were a happy family and they held Wallace in high esteem.

For the Summer break ,Wallace went back to his home many miles from the downtown east side.

Wallace returned to Bible College refreshed and ready to learn.

A week later he came in for a chat. He told me about the greatest healing anyone could image. I love these revelations. He said he was on the plane coming from his town up North.

Wallace explained, "Everyone was seat belted and ready, when there was a commotion near the back of the plane. A distraught woman was yelling,

"He's having a heart attack! My husbands dying."

Attendants and the pilot ran to the back of the plane. The stewardess got the wife under control and they put the man on a stretcher and carried him out"

Wallace said he started to pray for healing. As the man was carried by, Wallace made it a point to reach out and touch him while praying for the healing touch of God Almighty.

He said he felt the healing energy go out and into the man.

Wallace confided that," Twenty minutes later, the man and his wife walked back into the plane. He looked a little pale but otherwise he was healthy."

Wallace said he thanked God for His healing power.

The woman kept saying, "It's a miracle. I'm so happy."

Wallace wanted to tell her that God healed him, but he was too shy.

Eight months later, Wallace told me that he had enrolled in a course at a college that would be his life's career. He went on to say that it was related to healing.

I agreed that it was important for a person his age to have a career and possibly two careers as one must earn a living.

He qualified for the second year at the Bible College.

He took the classes while waiting for his classes at the new college to begin.

He received his second year graduation certificate.

Once more his family made it a great celebration.

He thanked me for the opportunity of coming to Bible College.

"I learned so much and I still put it into practice," he told me. "I have the text books and I will study on my own. If I need help with any concept, I'll give you a call," Wallace laughed.

"Seriously, in the back of my mind, I think about having my own church, but it is not feasible at the present time," Wallace lamented.

Wallace has kept in touch and comes to the Mission mainly on weekends when he has finished his home work for the course he is taking..

I was honoured to be invited to speak to his class at the Medical College. I spoke on the topic of Divine Healing.

His profession is in the pharmaceutical field. The students in his class were enthralled with the idea that God heals without invasive surgery and medications which have side effects.

As necessary, Wallace calls me for references when he sends out his resume. After sending out his first resume, he called to inform me that he had had three offers from pharmacies and was praying about which one to accept.

His father comes to the Mission occasionally and keeps me informed as to what Wallace is doing. His concern is that Wallace has no lady friend with which to make him a grandfather.

I was surprised to see both Wallace and his father in the Mission together one Saturday night, a year later.

What was my sermon that night? If you guessed that it was a healing sermon, you're right.

Wallace came to the Bible College with some knowledge of religion and left with a greater knowledge of the Scriptures and the Doctrines and how to apply these in his everyday life.

He is now Spiritually mature for such a young man. I"m certain he is still gaining more knowledge and understanding of God's wisdom and using God's miraculous power as he reaches out to those in need.

Wallace had been to church with his mother. A church which did not teach him the meaning of the scriptures or the doctrines. These are important to our understanding of God's attributes and God's mighty power and His role in the universe.

After coming to the Mission and the Bible College he has been changed radically and given spiritual gifts to use for the edification of the body of Christ. He was also given the power and authority to reach out to others who need the Lord and need healing of the body, mind and soul.

CHAPTER TWENTY FOUR

DARRYL

Street Person

Psalm 51:11, "Do not cast me from your presence or take your Holy Spirit from me. Restore unto me the joy of your salvation and grant me a willing spirit to sustain me."

DARRYL lived on the streets of the Downtown Eastside for forty-three years. Wandering aimlessly, living a useless and meaningless life. Doing drugs and drinking alcohol to deaden the memories of better times.

Occasionally, thinking about the children he had fathered and the wife he left behind on the reserve.

Sharing needles with other addicts and getting infected with deadly infectious diseases

His life was lived with no set pattern and no goal. He had no hope of a better life. Doing what he had to do to get a fix and get through the day.

That was before he came to the Mission on that life changing night.

The Gospel Songs were sung by a group of youths and their leader gave a powerful message.

Later, in a testimony, Darryl said the message was directed at him and stuck in his mind.

He came back the next night to a different group and another powerful message .

In the summer we have young people come and do the services. These two groups were from the same church in a big city miles away in a different country. There were over thirty of these young people so they broke them into two groups. One group ministered in the Mission and the other group went onto the street to minister to those wandering aimlessly and without hope.

Darryl testified that this was the beginning of his journey off the street and into a saner, more realistic and fruitful life.

I remember the first time Darryl came to the Mission.

It was a hot summer evening in mid summer.

We were short staffed as the students had gone to the beach.

They were enjoying their summer break from class and working in the Mission.

The person who was scheduled to be the overseer, asked if I would cover for him. It was summer and the young people always have something exciting to do. I came to the Mission and was in charge.

Darryl was seated at the back of the Mission. The group we had in that night were spirit filled young Christians. They really lived their faith and they influenced the men and women from the street. They particularly influenced Darryl.

The next time he came to the mission, I noticed he sat in the middle of the Mission. No longer hiding in the back row.

I said, "Hello, nice to see you again." I greet many people in a night, but for some reason Darryl stood out.

The next night was the end of August and the disability pay cheques had come in the mail. Our attendance on those nights drops from eighty or one hundred to twenty or thirty if we're lucky. Darryl was one who didn't show up at the mission.

When he did come back there was a regular service with singing, a message a time for testimonies and an altar. call. This night, Darryl came early. It gave me a chance to talk to him.

Sometimes, I think I should talk to someone and they rebuff me and tell me to mind my own business and leave them alone. I'm aware that they are not in the mood for a friendly chat.

When I first came to skid row, I was taken back by such gruff rejection. I thought it had something to do with me.

I now smile and say hello. It's up to them if they want to go further with the conversation and the relationship.

Darryl was well mannered. He welcomed my presence and was pleased that I had taken an interest in him.

When he was able to open up in conversation, he asked how a person gets involved in the Mission. He told me he has lots of time as he doesn't have a job and is on disability pay from the government.

I took him into the kitchen and introduced him to the cook. I asked the cook if he needed any help.

The cook looked at me as if I was from outer space. He said, "Look around. How many helpers do I have?" We usually have three or four. That night he had two who were working really hard. The cook handed Daryl a knife a chop board and a bowl of onions. He gave a demonstration on how he wanted the onions cut. He watched Darryl cut the first one. The cook corrected him and went to another area to prepare a fruit salad.

I figured Darryl might last a week or two as we have a steady flow of those who are eager to work. When they are trained and useful to the operation, they often disappear.

Others come to the Mission but want to be served rather than to serve. They'd rather talk to their new found friends than cut onions or potatoes and make a fruit salad.

With Darryl, we now had another helper in the kitchen. We also had a man to go on road trips in the city, with the assistant pastor. They go daily to pick up whatever meat, vegetables, day old bread and other foods which are donated to the Mission.

Darryl was not lazy. He often did more than he was asked to do. Soon he was taking responsibility for the working of the kitchen He got along well with the cook as he was not a loud talker and someone who knew everything but never did anything right.

After working for almost a year in the kitchen and setting up in the Mission, Darryl asked if he could come to Bible College.

I had never thought of him as a student, as he was older and seemed happy to work in the Mission and not go any further.

He knew all the students as he worked with them and taught them how to operate the machines in the kitchen and taught them the proper way to cut and slice.

When he asked me if he could enrol, I was pleased to have him join in with the other students. I knew he had been on the street and I wondered at what level of education he would operate.

We soon learned that he had not read a book for thirty years.

He concluded, "That is not going to stop me, I'm going to graduate."

Darryl exhibited that resolve as he strove to do his best in the kitchen.

He carried over that same resolve in his assignments at the Bible College.

"I will need help getting my reading skills back. I haven't used math except to count my money each month," he laughed.

He went on to tell the class that he had two sons and a daughter. He told how embarrassed he was when his daughter phoned him a couple of years ago and he was plastered. "I made such a fool of myself, I can't forgive myself," he remembered.

"I haven't seen my sons for a few years. They've given up on me.

They grew up on the reserve. Their mother raised them. I couldn't make money as I couldn't hold a job. I'd get paid and have a party. Three days later I sobered up and went to work. My job wasn't there as someone more reliable had my old job. Soon nobody would hire me.

I went on the street. Sleeping under bridges or in doorways. I ate what I could get. Sometimes I dug in the dumpsters outside the restaurants. I didn't care if it was clean as long as it filled my gut. I sometimes went to other missions where they served food.

I started sharing joints with people on the street or at a bus stop. This wasn't bad as I'd get a bit of a buzz. It didn't cost me much as four or five shared a joint. I went from there to cocaine and to heroin. I became a heroin addict. That's where my troubles started for real. There's more but at a later time."

Just as he was punctual and reliable in the kitchen, he carried over those traits in the College. Always reliable and hard working.

He later told me that the reason he took so long to do the assignments is that he has to read the directions ten or twenty times in order to understand what had to be done. He also had to do his assignments with limited knowledge and understanding of the scriptures. "I've never read the Bible in my life," he told the class.

We encouraged him every step of the way.

Not only did he come to the Bible College but he also worked in the Mission becoming the cook's helper for a year.

Because he lived close to the Mission in the Downtown eastside, he was asked to do extra duties which saved the staff time and effort. He just had to walk a block to the Mission and College, whereas the staff had to ride a bus for an hour or drive twenty minutes or more, in rush hour traffic.

Darryl never complained. He was happy to be a member of the team operating as a volunteer and a student.

Darryl gave a testimony which made us sit up and take notice. He told how he had been suffering from HIV and Aids as well a Hepatitis C, for a number of years.

"If I didn't have a needle to give myself a fix, I'd watch someone shooting up and borrow their needle. I didn't care as I figured I'd be better off dead than alive, which I now know is stupid."

He said he was on medication. He told us, "Someday I'll be cured. I keep praying for healing and I know God heals those who have faith."

This made the staff wonder about the safety of our students, and other volunteers. Also the safety of those who come into the Mission.

We had a medical expert on these three sicknesses come and teach the staff about precautions they could take. The nurse practitioner assured us that we were not at risk as long as no blood was spilled and no co-mingling took place. No open wounds and if no sexual union happened.

It eased our minds to some degree. Still there was great concern.

"What about an accident on field trips?"the bus driver asked.

"What if he cuts himself while working in the kitchen and accidentally his spilled blood gets into an open wound of another person in the kitchen or even in the Mission?" the cook asked.

"What if he gets into a scuffle, which happens when dealing with drunks and people on drugs, or people with mental problems who are off their medication and blood is spilled, what then?" the Assistant pastor asked.

There are still some underlying concerns among the staff and the volunteers.

Because Darryl was not concerned, it sort of calmed the nerves of those he works with. He admitted that he had to be careful.

After eight months of worship services and Bible College, Darryl was able to read much better and his writing became more legible. He bought a computer in order to fulfill the requirements regarding essays and term papers.

Every lesson was new to him. He had no knowledge of the Bible or the doctrines. It was fun to watch him be amazed at what he read and heard taught at the College. It opened up new horizons and new and wonderful promises of God that he could expect to receive now and inherit later on.

In my chat with him in my office, he told me that he was sorry he wasted so many years living like an animal. Having no direction, wandering aimlessly the streets of the downtown eastside. "I was a pathetic mess of a man. My children didn't want to look at me let alone visit that old drunk," he informed.

"My wife tried to talk me into coming home, but I couldn't pull myself away from skid row and the drugs. I had to have that next fix."

He looked at me and smiled, "But now I'm a new creation. I contacted one of my sons. He wants to come and visit me."

Darryl learned about the gift of Divine Healing.

He not only learned these lessons, but he practised what he was taught in the lessons on healing yourself through prayer and petition.

He began trusting in the Holy Spirit to deliver healing. Believing the Word of God for healing and thanking Jesus for what He did on the cross. "For by His wounds we are healed." 1 Peter 2:24.

He tells everyone who asks for healing, "By the stripes, the wounds of Jesus our Lord, you are healed."

Darryl told me that daily he spoke healing for his body through, "My Spiritual Medicine."

This is a healing process I have compiled. Read daily, it does bring healing to those who believe and trust in God for their healing.

This is a one page prayer and petition I have written as preventive medicine and healing medicine without side effects. (Insert #1) At the end of this story.

Darryl told me he reads this healing medicine every day and it works.

When he came to the Mission and the College, he was bent over and could not straighten up. He told me his muscles were atrophied and his immune system was compromised. Aids and Hiv along with Hepatitis C wracked his body with pain.

He explained that he took all these ailments to the Lord and asked for healing. He told me privately, while both of us were in the kitchen, that one by one his ailments were losing their power and Jesus was triumphing.

I told him that was great.

A month later, Darryl came back from the doctor's office with good news. He explained that his HIV and hepatitis C counts were so low they hardly registered. He said he was cured by God and the working of the Holy Spirit, who answered his prayers. Not only cured of HIV and Hepatitis C but also Aids. We were amazed at the power of God to heal so much so quickly.

Now, he keeps telling me he might be late for class as he is going to the doctor. I never ask why he is going to the doctor, but I have a good idea. He must keep track of any recurrence of these diseases.

After two years, he had finished the first years course. When he received his Commissioning Certificate, he was very proud. Everybody clapped and showed how much they cared for this man who was a real street person, but now is a Christian and is going to Bible College in order to prepare to do a ministry.

At the Mission, he meets many street people he knows and ran with on the street. Many are still stuck in their addictions and destructive habits and ways.

They notice such a change in Darryl, recognizing him as a man of God. They know that he is with the Mission and he is now in charge of services.

The street people respect him and honour him.

He told the class, that as he walks the streets of the Downtown Eastside, people who have been to the Mission come and ask for prayer. He went on to tell us that as he walks home or to the market, he is often stopped and ends up praying for those who tell him their troubles.

It is evident he is in the Spirit and is walking with Jesus toward the Kingdom of God.

Darryl has now completed the second year of Bible College and is in the final year. He will probably graduate by the time you read this account of his life.

He has also brought his family together. A son he hardly knew is now his best friend. I was talking to his son and he told me he wants to become a nurse and then go to Bible College and become a Pastor.

I asked him, "Then what?" He told me he wants to have a mission in a third world country. In the Mission he would have a church and a medical facility.

What a surprise! I knew his son when he was on the streets, doing much the same as his father. Now he is healthy and clean of all diseases, is married and has a child.

The three sisters of Darryl are all married and have children. He ministers to them and they have come to the Mission for the Sunday service. All three sisters have given their life to the Lord since Darryl started ministering to them and their families.

Darryl shakes his head as he tells me his son and his sisters sometimes slip back to their old ways and he has to pray them back into the presence of the Lord.

Darryl feels he is prepared to plant a church and minister to his First Nations people. He is laying the foundation for his ministry, by going to the reserve and cleaning up around his mother's house; planting a garden, trees and flowers. He says it is his way of letting those on the reserve know that he is now one of them. No longer an addict and drunk on the streets of the big city.

On an outreach to a town in the interior, Darryl led a group of young people in reaching out to a community. This group of fourteen, on fire young Christians, were invited to come to the community and make a difference.

This town has twelve churches, all of which are not moving ahead. They are functioning in opposition to each other. There is no common thread holding them together. People were not coming to church. Those who do attend the churches are going home spiritually dry.

One church had good music and built their reputation on the ability to do worship in song. Their problem was the word of God was not powerful and uplifting. Members often left the church after the music stopped.

In another church the pastor ran a taxi business. In the middle of the service he was dispatching taxis by phone. His congregation dwindled as they felt this was not appropriate behaviour for the pastor of a church..

Another church was taken over by a local businessman who set himself up as a pastor without any training. He was from an Asian country and had problems with his English. Half the time people couldn't understand his sermons or his counselling.

Darryl was sent with his team to bring these churches together.

The one common thread was that they didn't have a functioning Sunday School. Darryl had two young members of his team teach people from the community how to operate a Sunday School and become teachers and leaders.

His team showed them how to do crafts and make the lessons interesting and get some excitement into their lessons.

He also got the church leaders together and held three seminars aimed at finding common ground and building the spiritual community rather than being splinter groups in opposition to each other. They were given a book which explained how to do effective ministry.

This group of dedicated Christians from the Bible College, made three twelve hour trips to this community .The reports from the leaders of the churches involved indicates that there was significant improvement.

Darryl set up a time each month when these church leaders would meet.

They were to discuss what more they can do to improve relationships in the spiritual community in order to attract more followers.

Darryl has changed in so many ways it's incredible. He is filled with the Holy Spirit and not only talks the talk but walks the walk of faith.

He inspires all who know him as he is a prayer warrior. He brings people into the kingdom of God as he lives a life filled with the Spirit and an abundant love for Jesus the Christ.

Darryl has been changed in many different ways.

Changed from being a street person who was on drugs and disease ridden and bent over in pain, to a man of God, walking upright and filled with the Holy Spirit.

He now walks tall as a prayer warrior on the streets of skid row. He has been radically changed after coming to the Lord and obeying the commands of God and Jesus the Christ

INSERT #1

MY SPIRITUAL MEDICINE

READ three times a day until healing takes place.
Read once a day as preventative medicine.

I pray that every organ in my body operates normally. Every gland secretion happens according to God's plan. Every heart beat in perfect rhythm.

The life of God flows within me bringing healing to my whole body.

The life force of the Son of God rushing into my body to destroy the works of Satan.

I am free from unforgiveness and I forgive others. The love of God is in my heart.

Jesus bore the curse for me, therefore I forbid growths and tumours to inhabit my body. My strength and health is restored daily. I forbid any malfunction in my body.

Christ's life energizing every cell of my body. I am dead to sin and alive in Christ.

Thank you Father for my strong heart. My heart pumps blood to every cell in my body and cleanses my arteries of all matter that does not pertain to life.

I command my blood cells to destroy every disease, germ and virus that tries to inhabit my body. I command every cell of my body to be normal. I ask this in the name of Jesus Christ. I deny the right of sickness to exist in my body, because I have been redeemed by Jesus and delivered from the authority of darkness.

My immune system grows stronger every day. I speak life to my immune system.

Father God, I make a demand on my bones to produce life giving marrow which will produce perfect blood that will ward off sickness and disease.

Body, I speak the word of faith to you giving my body healing power to cure:

(Name your affliction) Such as Asthma, Arthritis, Diabetes, Cancer or any other condition in the name and by the blood of Jesus the Christ. By His stripes (wounds) we are healed.

I make a demand on my mind to think clearly at all times. No distortion allowed.

The same Spirit that raised Christ Jesus from death lives in me and quickens my five senses. It restores my sight and hearing by the life and wisdom of God Almighty.

The life giving power and complete health of my body is assured by the Word of God. I speak the words of healing to God Almighty and Jesus the Christ, knowing that your word will not return void.

Thank you for my healing. The words I speak aloud for healing are your words from the Holy Bible.

Psalm 107:20, "He sent forth His word and healed me."

Matthew 9:22, Jesus said, "Your faith has healed you."

Luke 6:19, "Those troubled by evil spirits were cured,... Power was coming from Jesus and healing them all." (I claim this power today)

Acts 3:6, Peter said to the cripple, "... In the name of Jesus Christ of Nazareth. Walk. He jumped to his feet and began to dance."

Psalm 103:3, "Who forgives all your sins and heals all your diseases.

James 5:15, "The prayer offered in faith will make the sick person well."

Acts 10:38, "Jesus went around healing all that were under the power of the devil, because God was with him."

Luke 5:18, "And some men came carrying a paralytic, and Jesus healed him."

Mark 6:13, "They drove out many demons and anointed the sick with oil.

1Peter 2:24, "...by His wounds we are healed."

It is best to memorize Bible verses for healing and send them up in prayer every day.

Spiritual Medicine has no harmful side effects. For faster healing double the dosage.

God bless you.

CHAPTER TWENTY FIVE

MARIA

Battered and Abused

Ephesians 2:8, "For it is by grace you have been saved, through faith -and this is not from yourselves, it is the gift of God."

Many people come into the Mission. Some come once or twice others become regulars and come for years. I take note of some, as they stand out and are intriguing. One of those who intrigued me was Maria.

She came with another lady who had been to the Mission a few times. I knew Flora quite well as she was the one who made arrangements for a memorial service for her brother who had passed away at an early age from a drug overdose.

I knew her brother well, as he would come to the mission under the influence of alcohol and cause problems by speaking out during the service and yelling at the staff when corrected.

I wondered what the connection was between Flora and Maria.

Maria is a middle aged lady. Slight of build but strong looking. She was not that well dressed and her hair was long and stringy. She looked as if she had come through a tough time. She never smiled and was intent on telling Flora all her problems.

I thought, "We don't need more problems. We've got enough of our own."

To my surprise, Maria came back to the Mission on a regular basis. Sometimes with Flora and sometimes alone.

Cindy and Stacey started talking to her. They told me later that this lady needed help. Stacey informed me, "Maria has been through some rough times. I feel for her. She needs our caring and our love."

I told Stacey to let her work in the kitchen or do something to take her mind off her problems. She followed my advice and started to care for Maria making her welcome and being her buddy.

Maria let Stacy know that she wasn't ready to work in the kitchen.

She was particularly interested in the music. She clapped her hands and at times got up and did a little dance when the beat was strong. She would stay and listen to the testimonies, preaching and the word of God.

Stacey asked her if she had a Bible. She told Stacey that she had never owned a Bible. Stacey went to the store room and brought a New Testament for Maria to read and call her own. Stacey went through the Bible and pointed out the gospels and the letters and epistles.

I watched and thought perhaps she might come to the College.

After a month or more, Maria gave a testimony at the mission.

Maria told us that she came from a reserve which was on a large island, "The reserve takes up the whole island. There is a road that goes from one end of the island to the other." She went on to say, "There is the large settlement near the eastern part of the island. It is here where the band office, the auditorium and the school is located. There are also a few stores. The main pier is there and that's where large boats are docked.

My mother and father and most of my relatives live in a cove which is on the south side of the island. It is a short drive to the store and the facilities at the bay.

One of my brothers is on the band council. He moved from our cove to be closer to the action.

I married a fisherman who has a big fishing boat. His family and ours are related but not closely related. An uncle of mine married one of his aunts.

Our life was good. My husband worked hard during fishing season and then hired on as a lumberjack on the mainland. He came home every night and every morning he took our boat to the mainland where he works.

One night he didn't come home. I was worried. There were no high waves but there was always the danger of a dead head, a half submerged log, which could damage a boat or turn it over.

The next day I got the news that my husband was in the hospital. I had my dad take me in his boat to the mainland. At the hospital, they told me he was transferred by helicopter to the big city hospital. I asked what was wrong.

I had to talk to my doctor. He had bad news

My husband was paralysed from the waist down. My doctor told me,"He is strong and the paralysis can be reversed through therapy." He went on to tell me that there was no guarantee.

From there it all became a blur. We have two girls that had to be cared for. I made two trips to this big city and stayed for weeks. His condition did not get better. He wanted to come home. He went to rehabilitation for four months.

Before he came home, our house had to be made wheelchair accessible. His brothers and my brothers worked hard with an architect to make our house ready for my husband.

For a short time, he was happy to be home. Then depression set in.

I had a hard time dressing him and moving him into the van and driving him around. He'd get angry with me for the least little mistake. He'd also get angry for no reason at all.

He had a stick and he'd hit the girls if they didn't behave or if they breathed too loud or if they were too happy. Any reason. He also started hitting me with his stick. I grabbed the stick and threatened to hit him. This made him really angry Our relationship went downhill from there. I couldn't stand the sight of him as he was a completely different person from the man I married.

I knew it was difficult to be useless from the waist down. Especially for such an active and strong person. I hung in and tried to make him happy. I'd have the girls give him little crafts they had made. They would spend hours gluing, painting and colouring in order to make their father happy.

At first he went along with it and praised the girls and told them their offerings were beautiful. As his depression got deeper, he would not even acknowledge these gifts or their trying to show love.

I had a nervous breakdown. The pressure became too much. There was no love. The only love I received was from reading romance novels. I relied on the love expressed in these novels to fill the gap left by my husband's cruel remarks and his hitting me for no reason.

I went to live with my mother and father. The girls, now in their early teens, went to live with my sister.

I had a meeting with members of the band council and they gave me enough money to come to the mainland for a rest. A time to get my life together.

I have known Flora from the times we went to school on the island. She brought me to the Mission. I can now smile as I have a support group and the promise of greater things to come. I have a great deal to resolve," she explained.

"By the way, I have stopped reading romance novels. I will rely on this Bible for my love and my peace of mind."

People were impressed with her testimony. Some of the students hugged her and told her she would overcome with the help of the Lord.

After that, Maria started serving in the kitchen. She had refused to do anything up to this point, but now that she opened up, I felt she had started the healing process.

I watched her work in the kitchen. She no longer had that haggard look. She started smiling at the people she served. This smile was also for those she now greeted as friends.

It took another two weeks before she decided to come to Bible College.

By now she knew all of the students and she was warmly greeted. She looked around to see where she could sit. Stacey made room for he and told her that would be her place.

Stacey sat her beside Becky another first nations lady.

Maria soon got involved in the process of learning.

In a short testimony to the class she told how she had never read the Bible. Jokingly, she told the students that she could teach them all about romance novels, but she didn't have a clue about what is in the Bible.

"You'll have to excuse my ignorance on these spiritual matters, but I am here to learn. I'm now registered with my band as a student. They support me and they want results. PLEASE help me and don't laugh at me. I'm going to master this religious stuff if it kills me."

The students applauded.

I had a chat with Maria and encouraged her. I told her, " I'll appoint a tutor who will answer all your questions and give you understanding of what is being taught."

She thanked me. "This means so much to me. I had no hope . I was drowning in self pity and in my problems. I read where Jesus says cast all your burdens on him and he will give you rest.

I feel that peace when I'm with the students and when I can reach out to others as I serve them. They're worse off than I am. I pitied myself, now I have compassion for others who come to the Mission."

I told her, "Keep busy with things that matter to you. God will work out those matters over which you have no control."

She looked at me and smiled. "How come you people have the right answer to all my problems?" she asked with a smile.

I assured her it comes from a relationship with Jesus Christ and His Father.

She told me that some day she's going to have that relationship.

In class, she sat beside Becky on one side and Peter on the other side.

He takes lots of notes as he too has much to learn.

Maria has started to take notes. She checks with Peter and at times copies from his notes. I noticed that they were getting along really well

We were just beginning the study of the doctrine of Anthropology. When Maria reviewed the text she shook her head in disbelief. I heard her say to Peter, "I will never be able to learn this." Peter assured her that it would be explained and you will know all about anthropology in the spiritual sense.

The first study was the nature of man with his environment and the nature of man in relationship to God and to a person's soul.

Maria's favourite saying was, "That's great."

The first scripture tied it together.

Genesis 2:7,"And the Lord God formed man of the dust of the ground and breathed into his nostrils the breath of life, and man became a living being."

I liked to tell the class that when they were born that God breathed life into them and gave them a purpose and a reason to live. When you were born, God and the angels celebrated as they had been waiting for you to come to the earth and make a difference for the kingdom of God.

They then learned about the soul and the spirit. Paul, the Apostle of Jesus, tells us that if our earthly tent, which is our body, is destroyed, we who believe and trust in God will have a house in heaven not built by human hands.

This was all new and fascinating to Maria. When the verse from first Thessalonians 5:21was read, she had problems understanding it. Peter told her he would explain it to her.

1 Thessalonians 5:21, "May your whole spirit, soul and body be kept blameless at the coming of the Lord Jesus."

Not only did Maria and Peter work together in the kitchen, but because they both had a valid driver's license they were given the keys to the van. They did the pickups and the deliveries of vegetables, meat, bread and all that was donated to the Mission. They also moved people from one apartment to another, and they picked people up and drove them to the bus depot and the airport.

Maria liked to drive, but Peter thought it was more appropriate for the man to drive. I laughed when Maria would demand the keys. Peter would tease her but would give in and let her drive.

Maria lived in the co-ed dorm in the women's quarters. Her room looked out on the back alley. She didn't think to draw the blinds when she was getting ready for bed. Where she came from on the island there were not that many people. She was shocked to realize a man was in the back yard and was watching her strip off. She was horrified. She quickly pulled the curtain, then closed the window.

The next day she told Peter and some of the girls. They told her to cover her window and it would be alright. Peter told her he would catch the pervert.

The trap was set. The peeping tom saw Peter and took off. That ended it.

Peter played his hand drum in his room. Maria knew that this was his way of praying. He sang in his native language which was not understood by any except Roy.

Maria wanted to learn to play the hand held drum but Peter told her it was only for men. She asked if he could teach her to dance a ladies dance. Peter taught her the bird dance.

At the College, the students planned a talent show night to be presented at the Mission on Saturday night of the next week.

Some of the girls sang and some danced. Others played the piano or the guitar and sang. Dan made music with his trumpet which he played down at the beach. Roy and Peter formed a team and played their drums and danced. Jack teamed up with Curtis and they did a vaudeville act with jokes and singing. Maria wanted to form a duet with Peter but he told her he had promised Roy he would be his partner. She opted instead to sing and dance with Stacey.

It was great and the people who came to the Mission that night really enjoyed the annual talent show.

Maria was really pleased to be presented with a native cloak with the insignia of a killer whale. It was heavy black felt with red trimmings and a red killer whale. It had white buttons around the border.

She showed it to Peter and he had her put it on. "Now you can do your dance in style," he laughed.

He played the drum and Maria danced. She swooped from one side to the other as a bird flying in the breeze.

Maria was no longer the sad, shaken and depressed person who came into the mission with her friend. She was loosening up and showing the brighter side of her personality.

She graduated after the first year and was very pleased with her commissioning.

In her talk to those present at the graduation ceremony she thanked everyone for making this the best year of her life.

During summer break, Maria went to her home on the island to visit her parents and her children. She stayed the full two months of summer break on her island.

Three days before Bible College resumed, she appeared at the Mission. Not only did she appear but she came with her two teen aged daughters. They were new to the large city and intrigued with skid row.

They were both very beautiful and slim. They were dressed in designer clothes with new Nike runners.

I was happy that she was with her family. We helped her find a place she could afford in native housing.

My one big concern was her bringing these two beautiful girls to the streets of the Downtown east side. I watched when they came to the Mission. The oldest girl, a sixteen year old young lady was not shy and she talked to everyone. It shocked me when she went outside with a young man I did not approve of.

I mentioned it to Maria. She told me her girls knew how to handle themselves. I took this to mean, 'mind your own business.'

From then on I tried not to think of the bad things that happen to girls on the skid row of the large city.

It was no surprise to me when Maria came to the class one Friday morning, freaked out. She told us how she trusted her daughters. "I told her never to smoke, never let a man take advantage of you. Don't take a drink. I took her around and showed her the young prostitutes and told her they were now slaves to sin because of drug dependency."

Maria went on to say, "It came so close. I had this feeling I should check on Sherrie last night. I opened her bedroom door and she was gone. She'd crawled through the window. I started running along the street. I saw her getting into the car of that rat, Domingo. I ran in front of the car before it was started. He threatened to run over me. I banged on the hood. He had Sherrie get out of the car.

Sherrie started to cry. I asked her if anything had happened. She sobbed, "He touched me. I told him no and he laughed."

Maria continued, "Sherry told me that she had promised to meet him and it was her fault."

"First thing this morning I shipped them both off to the island to let my sister look after them. I will get them back when I graduate and go home to do my ministry."

Maria continued her studies. She told the class that she was going to plant a church after she graduated.

"On my reserve they don't know Jesus. A priest comes once a month and tells them they are forgiven. Be good and that's all. They desperately need the word of God for salvation. They need redemption and reconciliation with God and Jesus.

My family all needs to come to Christ and make him Lord of their lives.

I believe I am the one to bring that message to them so they can be saved by my precious Jesus who shed His blood for the forgiveness of our sins and for our salvation."

Not only did Maria graduate after three years, but she was also ordained. Both were great times in her life. She celebrated with her friends and some members of her family who came from the Island to share in the great occasions.

Maria persevered and did go to her island to minister to her people. At first it was great. Her ministry was producing fruit.

Two years later she came to the Mission and invited us to her new ministry in a smaller city.

She gave a testimony in the Mission. She told how her people on the island, had rejected her. They told her the priest was their hope. She was forced to leave.

"It was not only that, but my husband and his family caused problems for me. They disrupted my services and turned people against me. My ministry fell apart."

She went on to tell how she has now teamed up with another graduate from our college who graduated two years before her.

They have a unique ministry in this smaller city. A restaurant owner allows them to bring people in and minister to them in the back booth. They take people from the street and witness to them. They buy their meals at a discount rate as the owner claims this to be his ministry. "Sometimes we can't pay. He puts it on our tab or writes it off," Maria laughed.

They also rent a large house in a run down part of town. They provide shelter for the homeless and the disadvantaged. She told us that they have a service each night. "We provide food, when we can afford it and when it is brought to the house as a donation."

Maria explained that she plays her guitar and sings at the services.

"Sometimes I play my hand held drum and sing prayers to the Lord."

Her partner preaches and counsels those in need. They both lead in prayer and have nights of prayer and praising God Almighty and His Son Jesus the Christ..

Maria told me that her daughters come to visit her quite often. The oldest girl, Sherrie, is in university taking nurses training and her youngest daughter is completing grade twelve. She wants to become a lawyer as she is very much interested in helping her native people.

I have been invited to visit them and observe their ministry in action. I hope to take the next outreach to this ministry by the waterfront.

Maria came to the Mission loaded with grief and anxiety. She left the mission with new hope and a plan to serve God the rest of her life.

She has been radically changed. Now a servant of God and a friend of Jesus filled with the Holy Spirit. Reaching out to others who need the healing touch of a loving Saviour.

CHAPTER TWENTY SIX

PETER

Worships Creation

1 Peter 2:9, "But you are a chosen people, a royal priesthood, a holy nation, a people belonging to God."

PETER came to the Mission on a Friday night. It was a good night as a couple did the worship. She played the guitar and sang gospel songs and her husband played the drums. Our resident pianist joined in and the place rocked.

I kept looking at Peter to observe his reaction to the service. The speaker that night was an evangelist from over on the Island. He had everyone saying 'Amen' in agreement to his preaching and clapping as they got carried away in the Spirit.

After the service and the fellowshipping was completed, people started drifting away.

I began piling chairs making the Mission ready for the sweeping and mopping of the floor. Peter came over and told me he'd take care of the chairs. I thanked him and backed off.

I went to the front and prepared my sermon for the morning service and my lesson for the Bible College. I looked up now and then to see how Peter and two others were managing. Peter was stacking two chairs to the other volunteer's one. I thought, "He'll make a good employee in some company if he works that hard."

When they were finished sweeping and mopping, I thanked them and told Peter he could come back any time and help. He nodded but said nothing.

Peter is a tall, slim, handsome young man with sharp features. I wondered which First Nation tribe he belonged to. I figured it would be Cree if he was from the prairies.

Peter came back again to the Mission and I greeted him. He kept looking at the kitchen as if he would like to help. I had one of the students go and talk to him. I selected Roy as I figured they might have something in common. They talked until the music started.

After the service, Roy told me that they belonged to the same nation but to different reserves. They lived more than a hundred miles from each other. Roy also told me that Peter would like to work in the kitchen or wherever he can be useful.

I knew he was a good worker as he had stacked chairs and mopped the floor the first time he was at the Mission.

I informed the staff of the Mission that we have a good worker who wants to get involved.

Peter was not into drugs, alcohol or any substance. He didn't smoke and kept to himself. He was a loner. However, if anyone engaged him in conversation he could talk on any subject. I determined that he had a fairly good education and was a prime candidate for the Bible College.

I didn't want to rush him into coming to class. I wanted him to make the decision himself. We always advertise the Bible College during the announcements at the Mission. We tell them that anyone can enrol if they want to better themselves and get information about spiritual matters.

Upon watching Peter over two months, I determined that he probably had a form of worship, but I wasn't certain what form it took. He was self assured and set apart from others.

It was September and classes were resuming. Students were coming to the Mission to greet each other. Matthew had returned early. He introduced Peter to his classmates. Peter became interested in knowing what the College was all about.

He had long discussions with various students, male and female. They all urged him to come to the Bible College.

Two days before classes began, Peter enrolled. I was there when he signed up and paid his tuition. I told him how glad we were that he would be coming to the College. He nodded and smiled.

I found out later that he had moved into the co-ed dormitory. I wondered why the co-ed instead of the men's dorm. I didn't ask why.

Peter fitted in quite well. He chose to sit beside one of the ladies from the dormitory. Usually the guys sit on one side and the girls on the other unless there is an attraction to one of the opposite sex. In Peter's case, I thought perhaps he liked to sit in that part of the room.

Peter gave his testimony to the class. It was necessary that they give a testimony within two months after entry into the Bible College.

Peter told the class that his father was an elder and was on the band council. "He wants me to go to university, but I am not ready. I must prepare myself mentally in order to excel in an institute of higher learning. My father sent me to this big city as I was brought up on a reserve and had no idea what it would be like to live in a big city. I am here to observe how people think and how they live in a congested area.

At home, I mount my horse and take off across the prairies. I love to feel the wind in my face and have a strong horse under me. Here I breathe polluted air and have to walk on pavement. I prefer my home and my way of life.

Perhaps I will stay for a while in your city. I believe the great spirit sent me here to this Mission and this College. It will give me a taste of city life. So far I am not too impressed. I would like you all to come to my reserve. It is one of the most progressive reserves in the area. We have a large band office, a huge recreational centre and many amenities. Our band will build a Casino in order to give us a higher standard of living for our people.

How long I stay depends on when I hear a voice telling me to move on."

His testimony gave me much more insight into who Peter was and how he operated. His believing in the great spirit made me wonder how he would react to our God Almighty and our Lord and Saviour Jesus the Christ.

I asked Peter how come he came to our city and to our Mission. He told me that a travelling evangelist came to their town. His mother and father went to listen to this preacher man.

Peter explained, "This evangelist told my father about your Mission and your Bible College. He told my father he had preached in your Mission. He explained how he was impressed with the students and the First Nations men who were completely changed by your teaching and fellowship and are now doing a ministry. My father sent me here to learn about the one his ancestors talked about."

I have known this travelling evangelist and have heard him speak at the Mission many times when he comes to the city. He is a man of God who does the will of God among his people. Bringing many to the Lord and some to the Bible College to learn the ways of God Almighty and his Son Jesus the Christ.

During the lessons, Peter takes copious notes. I figured he was honing his study skills for when he went to university. I knew we would probably have him with us for only a short time, but in that time he would learn a great deal.

Peter came to the first counsel meeting of the year. He sat back with the first year students. They didn't have a voice but they could have third year students put forward their proposals. There were a few changes but nothing of great importance. They had already decided on our first outreach. It was to the mission in the city where Alex had met his wife.

They had visited us many times and this was our annual visit to their mission. When we arrived at their mission, we were greeted by the staff and a few of the regulars we had met last year.

Peter wasn't sure what would take place on our outreaches. He helped carry the sound equipment and supplies we had brought with us into the mission.

That night, he was surprised to see someone from his village at the mission. They had a long talk, sharing their experiences since they left the wide open spaces and came into the cities.

I was talking to the founder of the mission. We shared notes on who was doing what at our Mission and the College. He asked about people he had met. I told him all I knew. He told me how his mission had changed. "So many transients. They're here one day and gone the next. I train them as staff and then I lose them."

I told him that was the same at our mission. The only good thing is that we have students who must serve as part of their education. He asked how difficult it was to operate a Bible School. I gave him some pointers as I was in on the beginning of the Bible College.

Peter listened to our conversation. I could tell he wanted to tell me something of importance. When I concluded my conversation, I turned and asked what he wanted.

He told me that his friend from the prairies desired to know if he could come with us to the Mission and Bible College.

I told Peter, "As much as I would like to have your friend come in our van it's impossible. We have only fourteen seat belts and we have fourteen people on this trip.

I went over to where his friend was sitting and introduced myself. Peter was at my side. I told the young man that if he could make it to the big city, I would be glad to pick him up at the bus depot and take him to the dormitory.

Peter reminded me that both dorms were filled to capacity. I told him we'd find room for him. Peter smiled and sat down beside his friend.

That night, our music and the word of God, was played to a full house. The people from the street were responsive to the students worship in song and the word that was preached. One of the new students gave a testimony. There was an altar call and six men came forward for prayer.

After the service and the place was cleaned and ready for the next day's service, I noticed that Peter sat at the drums and beat out a native drum beat. Some of the first nations girls started to dance to the beat of the drum. They were joined by others who thought this was great.

I was happy to know that we had a native drummer in our midst.

When we got back to our own Mission and back to studies, I had Peter in my office for the traditional chat.

I let him tell me about his family. He was the oldest boy and as such he must set an example for the younger boys and girls. "I must do nothing to dishonour my family and bring disgrace to my ancestors. I know the customs of my people and I am obliged to live according to these customs.

The only custom I am allowed to change is the one my forefathers learned from the missionaries.

I honour the creator as he brings us rain when the earth is parched and he gives us sunshine to ripen our crops and he brings fish into our nets.

I was told by my father that I must know about this other God.

This one who the white man prays to, as this God is the one our ancestors accepted when the missionaries came," he explained.

"But look at what the white man has done to my family and to my country. They now own most of the land. We have very little," he stopped to think.

"I do not go to the church when the priest comes for a service. I take my mother as she likes the service. I sit in the back of the church wondering what he is talking about. In the end he gives each person a hard white sliver of bread and people are satisfied. Then they all drink out of a large shiny container It is all very strange to me.

Now that I am in Bible College, I know more about God and how powerful he is. I know about his Son, Jesus and what he did for me. I am beginning to see what my mother sees in the church. She has a very simple faith, but it is strong. I need that same faith."

Peter told me he would stay for graduation.

It was only the middle of October. I was pleased that he was going to be with us for at least eight more months.

The end of November brought a cold snap. An early snow covered the ground, I was slipping and sliding on my way to the College. After class we had our monthly counsel meeting. The third year students made up the itinerary. I went over it and agreed with all that was proposed

Plans for Christmas and plans for a possible outreach. The outreach to a reserve on the island. We had been invited to help them establish some sort of ministry. They indicated that people are resorting to their old ways and many have no joy and show no love for each other.

We were aware that was happening. The last time we had a mission trip to that reserve, only a handful of people came to the services.

Peter was eager to go. He signed up on the spot.

Being a first year student, Peter could not speak unless spoken to at counsel meetings. He could not present a motion.

I knew he was appalled at the plight of the homeless and those who slept on the street or under the bridges. He approached a few third year students with the idea of making the mission into a shelter every night. They all said, "No way." He then asked a couple of second year students to present the motion. He found an ally in Darryl

At the meeting, Darryl presented the motion for a vote.

I was strictly against such a proposal. We had tried it two years in a row and both times it was a disaster.

One of the third year students got wind of the fact that this motion might be presented. He brought the log books which were kept for every night the mission became a shelter. He picked out a few of the entries.

November 28th, Four men were playing cards using condoms and unused injection needles as chips.

December 2nd, A beautiful young street girl, a runaway, slept soundly. On a chair along the wall a young man looked down at her and masturbated shooting on the floor. The volunteers had to clean up the mess.

December 15th, Someone was shooting up drugs in the bathroom. A man who was waiting to go couldn't wait any longer and he peed in the garbage can.

December 19th, A drunk peed his pants and it ran along the floor to two other men who got wet. They cursed and swore, threatening to beat him up. Two volunteers intervened and were wetted and had to go home and change.

January 4th, Seven injection needles were swept up off the floor.

January 20th, A stash of drugs was found hidden on top of the ceiling tiles in the bathroom. The drugs were taken to the police station.

February 21s,t Three men came late and demanded that Ryan serve them coffee and food. Ryan told them it was too late. One man argued then punched Ryan in the chest. Another man threatened him with a baseball bat. When he tried to phone the police a man tore out the telephone wires.

Matthew asked if we needed any more ammunition to defeat the motion.

Dan had been to properly run shelters before coming to our dormitory. He informed us about shelters. How they needed to have plastic covered mats for the men to lay on. Clean blankets and pillows had to be provided. There had to be more than one bathroom. People must be paid to operate the shelter.

The motion was defeated. That was the end of that issue.

Christmas plans were adopted. The next outreach was planned and a toboggan party was happening after the Sunday Mission service, if there was enough snow.

Christmas happened with lots of good cheer and a lot of preparation. There was a ten day break from class. Peter decided to take this time to visit a sister who did not live on the reserve and moved with her husband and family to a small town only a hundred miles from the big city.

I had been assured by Peter that he was going to graduate, so I knew he would be back after the holidays.

I wanted to take him up on his promise to teach the students some of his native dances. I remembered the time he beat the drum at the small city mission and the girls danced. There was also the time he and Roy danced at the talent night.

The reason I wanted the dancing to continue and expand is that in February there would be the annual native pow wow in one of the large halls in a better area of the city

Each year our College students are invited. We attended but we didn't have much to offer. This year, I thought Peter might teach the students his prairie dances and perhaps he could dress in his regalia and show the people some fancy dancing.

Before he went to his sisters for Christmas, I asked him if he could bring some regalia back with him from his sister's house.

I was pleased after the Christmas break, when I picked up three students at the bus depot.

Peter had remembered to bring regalia. He had a bag full of feathers and beaded buckskin.

After class, near the first of January, Peter took the hand drum he had borrowed from his brother in law and started the beat. He handed it to Roy who was a member of his nation. Roy knew the beat and Peter danced. Roy got in the mood and started to "high ya ya" and chant to the music.

I was pleased. Peter flew and circled when he danced and I knew he would be a hit at the pow wow.

To my surprise, Peter started another beat and Roy did his fancy dancing. It was every bit as good as Peter's dancing They were both great dancers.

They ended by having everyone do a friendship dance.

The next day, the First Nation's girls asked if they could learn some dances. I told them I'd try to find a woman who could teach them.

February came quickly as did every month. The Pow wow happened. There was great excitement and loads of fun as Roy and Peter danced and stole the show. The girls did a bird dance and a sun dance. They had others in the audience join in a friendship dance.

At our February counsel meeting it was decided that we incorporate native dancing in our services at the Mission in order to have natives and all people be part of the worship service.

An announcement was made at the Mission that we needed hand drums.

Added to that was an announcement that we needed native regalia.

The response was great.

We had enough regalia to clothe five women and three men.

As well, a few first nations women offered to make regalia as worn by their nation and give it to the girl students.

April came and it was time for Peter's first sermon at the Mission. He had practised preaching before the class, but now he had to choose a sermon and present it before the congregation. I was there to evaluate the sermon in order to give pointers on how to improve the sermon, if necessary.

Peter was very confident and poised. Many students have butterflies and are really nervous. Peter was composed and self assured.

I was sitting in the second row with clipboard and pen ready.

The worship team was choosing their music and warming up.

I heard an argument happening at a table near the kitchen. It was not a good sign when two men stand up. It usually means a scuffle will happen or fists will start flying. Three students ran back and pulled the men apart.

I thought how sad to have something like that happen just before Peter was going to preach. But that is the chance you take on skid row.

Peter gave a sermon on Psalm 31:24, "Be of good courage , and He shall strengthen your heart, it is for all you who hope in the Lord."

Peter told how young warriors in his nation were taught to be courageous and trust in the creator for victory .He used this verse to tell how God gave strength to men in the Old Testament. He then told about the great sacrifice of Jesus the Christ. How he had the courage to take a beating and be nailed to a cross and die a most painful and humiliating death.

Peter then explained how his forefathers were rewarded for their courage.

He told everyone present that they too must reward Jesus by sacrificing their body mind and soul to him. This is pleasing to God, this is your spiritual act of worship.

I really liked the way he gave examples from his culture and equated them with the life of Christ and what pleases God Almighty

Peter completed his first year. His sister and her husband came to his graduation. After he received his diploma he picked up his drum and announced that he would sing a prayer to God Almighty and His Son Jesus the Christ.

I felt he was in the Spirit of God as he sang so beautifully, with deep feeling and conviction.

Peter did not return to the College. The last night at the Mission he gave a short testimony telling everyone how much this year had meant to him. How he had given his life to Christ and would treasure the Lord in his heart for eternity.

"I came with no knowledge of a Saviour and Messiah. I came only to fulfill the wishes of my father that I learn of the one the missionaries taught about many years ago.

I am leaving with the filling of the Holy Spirit and the promise that I will be with the Lord forever and forever in the Kingdom of God.

I will now tell my people of this great Lord and Saviour. I will start with my family and go wherever God will send me. I will go to the far corners of the earth if that is the will of Jesus my Christ and God Almighty as I am led by the Holy Spirit." Peter came as a believer in the customs of his people and left as a converted follower of Christ Jesus. He has been radically changed for eternity.

CHAPTER TWENTY SEVEN

ROGER AND JAMES

Shame to Glory

Psalm 43:3, Send forth your light and your truth, let them guide me; let them bring me to the holy mountain, to the place where you dwell."

ROGER and JAMES came to the Mission on and off for three years.

I learned the history of both men as my wife knew the wife of James. She also knew his sister, who was very concerned for her brother. Other sources of information came from the volunteers who spoke to the two men. Also from the students who talked to them and listened to their stories over three years. Another source were the regulars from the street who were with them during their days of drugging and hustling. The two men were well known in the Mission and on the streets of the Downtown eastside.

Roger was living on the street doing drugs and getting into trouble. Wandering around filling in time chasing women and associating with others who were aimlessly wasting their time and their talents.

Roger dropped out of school after grade eleven. He had been a star athlete, playing hockey and soccer on high profile teams. He attended too many celebration parties after victories on the field and on the ice. He drank too many bottles of beer, whiskey and vodka.

After others had gone on with their lives, Roger secretly had parties alone or with others who liked their drinks. He ended up on the street smoking marijuana and trying out cocaine and heroin. He was still doing his drugs when he came to the Mission. For over two years he didn't listen to the words of the gospel songs or the word of God preached from the pulpit. He had other things on his mind.

Roger had a brother who came down to the eastside and kept in touch with him. He drove a club cab, four wheel drive Ram charger.

In the late afternoon, after work, he would park in the places Roger frequented and wait for his brother to find him.

Roger's brother couldn't understand why anyone would waste their life chasing after drugs. Worse than that he was ruining the lives of those who loved him.

Roger's brother was five years younger than him. He had idolized Roger.

He had gone to all his home games and cheered him on. He saw him win victory after victory. Roger was on the best teams and he had a lot to do with their winning trophies and tournaments.

Now, according to his brother, he's on the losing team.

Roger would find his brother and climb into the passenger seat of the truck. They would hug briefly. The brother would ask Roger if he was alright. Roger would tell him everything was great. The brother knew that was a lie, but he'd say, "Glad to hear that bro."

He'd tell Roger how much his mother misses him. "She wants you to come home for Thanksgiving. The whole family will be there."

Roger asked what date it fell on this year. His brother told him.

"Sis is worried about you. She told me she loses sleep wondering where you are and how you will manage in this cold weather. She bought a heavy winter jacket for you." His brother gave Roger a new down filled jacket.

After all this guilt was laid on him, Roger would tell his brother he was in a hurry. Before he left he would ask his brother if he could spare a twenty.

The brother would hand him a twenty and sometimes a fifty and tell him, "It's for food."

Roger would guarantee that's what he would do with the money.

With his brother out of sight, he'd motion for James to come out of the shadows. The two of them would be off and get high.

Roger told James, "I don't mind when my brother comes down to check on me. The only thing that bothers me is, he tells me about everyone who is concerned for me and lays a guilt trip on me. He then gives me twenty and leaves.

The one I get choked up over is my sister. She cries and begs me to give up my drugs and come home," Roger shook his head, "That heavy crying affects me so much I have to get really high to forget all the crap they lay on me."

James laughed and the two of them walked to where their dealer hangs out.

Before doing drugs, JAMES was a real estate agent. Successful in marketing, he built a bank account, bought a house in a shady deal, got married and had a son. He lived in suburbia fulfilling the dream of most married men who have families.

The problem was, he had no vision of the future. It had all been too easy. He relied on his personality and his sales pitch, which he had mastered. His bank account and investments grew and multiplied.

His friends were other real estate agents and investors. It was life in the fast lane. Parties every week end and some during the week. He had a list of potential customers and kept in touch with them hoping for another sale.

It was at a party that he started his downhill slide. A group of men who met secretly and did drugs, roped him in.

At first, James was horrified and shied away. He sat and watched as the men took turns smoking crack cocaine. He observed their behaviour when high and wondered if it was really that great. He opened another bottle of beer.

Many times he attended, then he went home shaking his head. "Never, it's not for me." But he rationalized that maybe once wouldn't matter.

The next time they met, James had a few shots of whiskey and asked what he should expect if he did the drug. One man told him it was sort of comforting, like a big hug. That appealed to James. His first try was free, but from there on in it got expensive.

Two hundred a day escalated into six hundred a day.

He lost his job, he lost his house, but his wife stood by him. He ended up on the street during the day, but at night he had a place to go. Not to a house in the suburbs as he had sold that for drug money. It was now to a rented apartment.

His wife worked hard and started her own business. She gave James an allowance. She had a business bank account which he couldn't touch.

James got in trouble with the law and spent time in jail.

James told two of the students. "Roger had a break and enter lined up with Hank who would steal a car and drive to an affluent part of the city. He had a house staked out. Both the husband and wife worked to pay the bills and there were no children.

I was supposed to meet them at eight o'clock, that morning, but I slept in. I have these terrible dreams which wake me up in a sweat," he paused to remember.

"I was on the street waiting for Roger to return with the loot. A young prostitute approached me. She offered me a favour if I would be with her when she did her fix. She told me she was afraid to shoot heroin alone. I had time to waste so I went with her to her room. She had enough for the both of us. She had fixed a heavy dose. I watched her do her bending and twisting while under the influence.

I was supposed to wait for her to come down , but I shot up. When I came down, I saw she wasn't moving. I grabbed her and shook her. There was no response. I knew she had overdosed. She needed an antidote badly. I picked her up in my arms and ran to the police station half a block away from her hotel room. I kept telling myself out loud that it was my fault. I kept telling myself it was my fault when I entered the police station. They took her and tried to revive her. I stood by horrified. An officer hand cuffed me and led me to a cell. I kept telling them I was innocent that it was an accident. That she injected herself. They ignored me. I was charged with manslaughter," James shook his head.

"My wife was heart broken. She told me she would fight the charge.

I spent six months in jail as my wife fought for a reprieve. It was a long six months in solitary confinement and then in general population.

While I was in jail, my wife had her Pastor come and talk to me. He arranged to have the Prison Chaplain come regularly and do a Bible study with me," he smiled.

"I faced the court. The Prison Chaplain gave a good report. The judge agreed to house arrest for five years.

It was conditional on my having a curfew every night at seven o'clock. Also I must stay away from drugs and alcohol. If I break any of these conditions, I will be arrested and serve the full five years. I hated jail and will never do drugs again."

James came to the Mission and in discussion with the Assistant Pastor told him that upon his release, he tried to get back into real estate. He was required to write a test and go before a board of review. He passed the test but failed the review. He was told his criminal record is what caused him to fail.

The next year James worked for his wife in her business which was office and residential cleaning. He kept away from drugs and alcohol and obeyed his court order.

"I now go with my wife to her church on Sundays and I participate in the service. The Prison Chaplain laid it all out and I have given my life to Christ. I still have some reservations as it has not sunk in to the point where I feel saved."

On his days off, James would meet Roger on the streets of skid row.

Roger and James hooked up and became a team. If anyone came against one or the other, they had to fight both of them. It was a safe and sure arrangement.

Roger wanted to share his drugs with James, but James knew that if he had even one fix or one reefer of marihuana he would serve five years in jail.

James tried to get Roger off the street and back to a normal existence.

He told a group of people at the Mission, "Many times Roger and I will be walking together in this area and a patrol car will pull up. I will be cuffed and searched. When I'm clean they will take me in for a drug test to see if there is any drug residue in my blood."

James shared his story with two students. "The only thing Roger and I don't share is a warm bed to go home to at night. I invited Roger to come home with me and sleep in the living room. He knew that this was not a good idea. If he was drunk or on drugs it could end our relationship. Roger knows my wife hates the idea of my being on the street."

When it came to food there were many places where Roger could go for a coffee and muffin in the morning to get him going and then to lunch at a mission. There are many missions. Roger knew all the food places. He would tell James where they were dining out for free on any given day.

Roger received assistance from the government which meant he had three days of spending big time and twenty seven or more days of finding places to get food and a place to sleep.

Roger knew where the best places were to get warm clothing in the winter and light clothes in the summer.

James told a couple of students, "I followed along with Roger. The only thing is I have to be home by seven as I have a curfew and my wife has threatened to leave me if I offend once more."

Now that James began to change and was no longer into drugs, he gave another testimony at the Mission.. He explained that he was married to a woman from an Asian country. They had met at a party. James proposed to her and they were married. She was happy in suburbia in a new house and a big car. All the appliances and furniture were top of the line.

When I lost everything I had worked so hard for, she felt sorry for me and vowed she would never leave me. She took over responsibility for the housing and all financial responsibilities. When I went to jail she down sized her apartment and worked hard to make ends meet. The lawyer fees were exorbitant.

Now that I am released and on house arrest, she has stipulations and one is that I must work for her in the cleaning business and the other stipulation is I must be home by seven o'clock or she will lock me out of the apartment and out of her life."

James revealed to others that his relatives and friends and her relatives had given up on him, but his wife stuck with him through thick and thin. "Her relatives told her to dump me and get on with her life, but she loves me and cares for me."

James shook his head, "I often wonder why she is still so loving and I am so terribly out of control at times. Since my arrest things have changed and there is still more to change."

He went on, "Now on the one day a week I get off work ,Roger and I can come for the morning service as I have to be home before seven."

Near the end of his third year on the street with Roger, James became disillusioned. He wondered what he was doing on the street trying to get Roger to get off of drugs and get him to do something with his life.

One morning at the Mission, James said he listened to the gospel songs and took notice of the words that were preached. He looked at the Christians who were full of love and caring for each other.

He decided at that moment, he wanted what they had. He paid attention to the preaching. The message was inspiring and left people with the question, "Are you doing God's will for you at this time? Is God's purpose for your life being fulfilled?" James knew the message was for him as it was the same message the Prison Chaplain gave when he was in solitary confinement.

The preacher told them, "God is stretching out his right hand of righteousness. Are you going to take his hand and let Him lead you on the path that leads to the kingdom for eternity? Or are you sliding down a slippery slope?"

James answered the altar call and received prayer.

Roger couldn't believe his friend would be taken in by a sermon which he didn't even understand.

After praying for the plate of food that was served to everyone, the Pastor thanked God for his provision,

James felt for the first time that he was thanking God for what he was about to receive. The pastor then asked for a blessing on those who prepared the food and those who were about to receive it.

James felt he'd like to belong to a God who has been so kind to him.

He remembered what the pastor said as he prayed for him at the altar. He was glad he could understand the word of God and feel the spirit of God moving in his heart.

Roger was not in that space yet. James started explaining to him that he had to change.

I heard them arguing as they left the Mission. James was trying to convince Roger that his life was a mess.

James admitted, "My life was a disaster. I've been the biggest fool on planet earth. But I'm going to put my hand into the righteous right hand of God and let him lead me out of this hell hole."

Roger looked at him as if he was deranged. He thought about it and asked James. "Are you going to desert me. Leave me here alone?"

James told him they could make the move together.

Every morning and night the Bible College was advertised and people were encouraged to come and learn more about God, Jesus, salvation and restoration.

James asked Roger."Did you hear them talking about a Bible College. I remember they said it was open to anyone who wanted to learn more about God and his Son Jesus the Christ. I think that's what we need."

Roger told him to count him out. "I didn't even graduate from high school. I can't go to any College. They'd think I was a moron from the top of the mountain."

James told him they could try it out and see what it was all about.

James and Roger came to the College two days later. I noticed them, as they were regulars on the street and at the Mission. They were well known on the street.

In the past three years many Christians had talked to them and witnessed to them. The students knew them by name and had heard their life's story. Now that they had responded to the invitation, to come to Bible College, they were warmly welcomed.

It took a week or two for them to fit in and feel comfortable.

It was a cold December day and Roger asked to live in the dormitory.

With living in the dorm came the obligation to work in the Mission. After stacking chairs, and mopping floors, Roger started working in the kitchen. He cleaned up his life. There could be no drugs or alcohol while at the Bible College and while working in the Mission.

James still worked for his wife part time. He had his wife's permission to go to Bible College. He went home each night before seven o'clock. He was no longer a regular on the street. He only came to the Mission when he was signed up for duty for the morning service.

He never did bring his wife to the Mission.

Roger and James kept up their relationship when they were at the Bible College and while working at the Mission.

For the first time in years, Roger stayed clean. He knew James was serious about the Bible College and he didn't want to lose his best friend. He also found being with the young Christians was better than being on the street. He started pumping weights and running on the sea wall.

He was given a tutor who helped him with his essays and assignments.

I was happy, because at times I wondered if they would make it for the required five months. It took them seven months to qualify for a Letter of Recognition as James had to work for his wife and missed quite a few classes. His wife tried to arrange his hours so that he could attend his classes and not conflict with his hours of work.

At the graduation ceremony the wife and son of James came to the Mission. I could tell they felt out of place. Some of the girls talked to her and told her how blessed they were to have James in the College. She looked puzzled as she thought the College was a university type operation. The girls told her the College was separate from the Mission. "You are in the Mission where we learn to do ministry."

Roger had his brother, mother and his sister come to the ceremony. They had spent some time on skid row hunting for their brother. They were still not certain that he had made such a great change in his lifestyle. They didn't expect such a difference in their older brother.

As the ceremony progressed, the wife and son of James and the sister, mother and brother of Roger, saw the caliber of the students who were graduating. They realized it was all real and was a blessing for both men and all the students.

Before James and Roger left for the summer, they assured me that they would be back and graduate.

Summer holidays came and Roger gave up staying at the dormitory.

Roger and James both appeared for service at the Mission occasionally. Then they stopped coming to the Mission altogether.

They didn't enrol in the next year's program. I phoned to find out what they intended to do. The mother of James told me he was busy with his church. I wasn't informed what church.

A year later, one of the teachers and Pastors from the College, on a bright Sunday afternoon, was walking in a park, which had a little lake.

He noticed a baptism taking place.

Intrigued, he went and joined the group of supporters and watched as the third person was being baptised.

After the ceremony, the Pastor talked to the two men who were performing the baptisms. One of them asked, "Aren't you one of the teachers at the Bible College downtown?"

The teacher looked more carefully. "James? and you're Roger."

James and Roger told how they wanted to return to College, but that summer they started their own church and it is growing. "We'd heard enough sermons to get by," James stated. They laughed.

"We figured how many gospel songs we heard at the various missions and how many sermons we heard. If you figure out that we were at a Mission most morning for three years, that's around nine hundred sermons!

And add to that there were say six gospel song a serviced and that's over five thousand gospel songs we heard."

"Then you two finally responded to the gospel songs and the message?" The teacher nodded, wondering why it took so many sermons and gospel songs to convert two men.

"We still have the text books which are full of sermon outlines. The other thing is we've got a great worship leader. People are blessed by his singing and playing," Roger told the pastor.

God has ways of bringing lost souls into the kingdom. He used Roger and James in a big way. They started their Church in a seedy part of town, where prostitutes ply their trade and where drugs are readily available.

Exactly where James and Roger were needed with their testimony and their knowledge of street life and its perils.

James and Roger came back to our Mission for a visit. We were all invited to come to their Church on a Sunday morning. I was asked to preach. The service was informal. We took twelve people and were warmly welcomed.

A few people recognized some of us from the Mission and the College. It was a reunion of sorts.

It reminded me of how our Mission got started.

Roger asked me about Bible School. How to get one started and what curriculum to use.

We have had two meetings since then.

I was offered a job teaching. I signed up for one course.

Two of the most unlikely men to plant a church, men from the depths of hell.

Men who are now on their way to heaven with the shepherd's crown awaiting them.

And also the crown for perseverance under trial for those who love the Lord, is theirs for sure.

Roger and James, from two different backgrounds placed together on the skid row of the downtown east side. Radically changed by placing their hands into the Righteous Right hand of God Almighty. Radically changed to do a ministry they were called to do for the Lord.

CHAPTER TWENTY EIGHT

KEVIN

Richly Rewarded

John 14:6, "I am the way the truth and the life. No one comes to the Father except through me. If you really knew me , you would know my Father as well."

Ted comes to the Mission regularly. It is his source of connection to reality and to a hope of redemption and reconciliation with God Almighty. He carries his Bible and reads it but he does not respond to what he reads and does not do what it commands.

Ted is a handsome well built six foot one young man, in his late twenties. He is the result of a mixed marriage.

His father, a Caucasian, is not in the picture.

His mother is Asian and very well educated. She travels a great deal.

This leaves Ted without anyone to guide him and keep him on a straight path.

When his mother is in the city, Ted is seldom at the Mission.

When she is travelling, Ted's hygiene can suffer and his moods can change without provocation.

Ted has been coming to Bible College for a number of years, off and on. He is welcomed in the class. He knows the scriptures and has memorized many verses. Ted has learned and understands many of the Bible stories and parables in the New Testament. The doctrines are new to him. He is interested in learning and understanding all the facts related to the doctrines as presented in the Bible.

One of the other teachers in the Bible College is a first nations lady. She has a master's degree in Divinity, but no teacher training. She has her own method of teaching and making people learn. Her method irritates Ted. She reads and does all the talking. She then stops and quizzes the students. If they don't have the answers to her questions, she gets upset with the students.

Ted knows the answers to the questions, but he won't answer. He told me, "I don't want to be under the supervision and authority of a woman teacher."

I have talked to him about this behaviour but he ignores discipline.

During the break, Ted doesn't mingle with the other students. He sits quietly and reads his Bible or reads his notes. He goes to the kitchen area and gets a cup of coffee and a donut or whatever is offered and comes back to his desk.

Some of the students try to engage him in conversation. It depends on his mood as to whether he will respond or not. I've noticed that when he does get involved, he responds with joking or teasing the girls. He sometimes goes too far into sexually explicit areas which are not appropriate in the College.

In the Mission kitchen, there are often four or five beautiful young ladies preparing the noon and evening meal. I received complaints that Ted stares at their busts and it bothers them. He has even gone so far as to touch their hands and other parts of their body.

I brought this to the attention of the Senior Pastor of the Mission. He asked me to ban Ted from the kitchen. We had a short discussion as to who should do the banning. I told him it was a Mission problem and as his teacher it would affect my relationship with Ted. I won and the Pastor did the banning from the kitchen.

I heard about the fiasco which happened when Ted was banned from the kitchen at the Mission. It turned out that he was not only banned from the kitchen but he was banned from the Mission for a week because of his foul language and belligerent attitude.

This was not the first time he had been banned because of his lack of control when being disciplined for his irrational and sometimes outlandish behaviour.

At one point in the past, he got into trouble because of his harassing the servers in the Mission at a noon hour meal. In order for the servers to do their serving, two plates at a time to over one hundred men and women, everyone being served must remain seated.

Ted decided to break that rule by standing at the serving table, which meant that the servers had to walk around him. He was asked by the cook to move out of the way. The servers also asked him to go sit down. The doorman got involved and demanded he sit down. All the time Ted kept eating his meal, ignoring the pleas for him to get out of the way. He stood staring up at the ceiling, knowing he was irritating everyone involved.

I was in the office and went into the kitchen. The doorman told me to do something about that Ted. He said, "I'd like to take a strip off of him."

I went and looked. As soon as he saw me, he took a chair and pulled it up near the table. They had been telling him to sit down. He figured he'd sit down but he was still hampering the servers. I could have disciplined him, but the serving was nearly completed. I didn't want to be the recipient of his foul language in the presence of the people from the street.

I brought up his strange behaviour at a staff meeting and it was decided to ban him for another week. That decision was conveyed to him by the lady teacher. He called her a witch and other choice names including a lover of the devil. This cost him another two weeks of being banned from the Mission.

During those weeks of his being banned, things ran more smoothly at the Mission. I missed him coming to Bible College as he challenged the students to be alert and become more familiar with the scriptures and contents of their Bibles.

While Ted was banned, a new student enrolled in the class. I met him at the Mission and asked if he would like to come to Bible College. He told me he had the qualifications and credentials to enter a College.

The first day he was in the class, the girls took notice of him as he was well dressed in designer clothes. He was clean shaven and his hair was combed nicely. I noticed that he was wearing shiny brown loafers with a designer emblem.

He had a twenty-four carat gold necklace and a diamond ring.

I thought to myself, "He is really a class act."

Kevin was very polite. He was attentive during to the lectures. When I asked questions, he responded but made his own assumptions. I never say, "that's not right." I went to another student who gave the correct answer.

Kevin was a little taken back and said, "That's what I was trying to say, but I put it in a different way."

The next week, Kevin gave his testimony.

"I don't live on the street or in the downtown eastside. Our house is in the Highland area. My father died in an accident. Killed by a drunk driver. It still bothers me to think about such a senseless act with such a devastating result. I was traumatized to learn of his demise. He was the best father in the world.

I have two sisters. They live in their own world into which I am not invited except on special occasions. That is how they are dealing with my father's death.

I care for my mother who has cancer. I hate to watch her suffer. I need a sedative to let me sleep as I have so much on my mind. My family causes me a great deal of stress.

Coming to Bible College is like a breath of fresh air. Everyone is so pleasant and so supportive. I really love all of you.

At school, I had a hard time as I was not an athlete. I hung with those who were different because of their being ignored by the jocks and the brains. I was an average student getting B's and C's. I always passed each grade but it took a lot of work on my part.

We have a cabin on Lake Gravely. My father loved to fish and swim in the lake. We have a canoe at the lake and a cabin cruiser docked at the marina.

Some day I'd like to take the class to the cabin for a weekend," he stopped to think.

"My life has not been exciting. As a matter of fact it is boring at times. I have some friends from school who call now and then and we go to night clubs. Maybe I shouldn't bring that into my testimony, but it's the truth.

I have to admit one thing. My mother never sent me to Sunday School and I never go to church. She told me we are doing quite well and we don't need church in our life. This is my first time studying or even reading a Bible. I hope you can cut me a little slack until I understand what this is all about. So far I've learned things I've never heard about before. I have to learn the pattern into which they fit.

I look forward to each lesson as they are really interesting."

I arranged a tutor for Kevin. I told him if he had any questions, he could ask his tutor. "He will help you with your assignments," I explained.

I was on my way home one day after class and watched Kevin get into a sporty Lexus coupe convertible. It verified that there was wealth in his family.

Kevin liked to help in the Mission. He especially liked to serve the meals. Twice a week we served a hot meal. Every other day and night we served a line-up.

At a Counsel meeting, Kevin, through a third year student, suggested we serve a hot meals more often. It was debated and the suggestion was overturned.

As a first year student, Kevin was required to make motions through a third year student who could filter the suggestions and bring forward only those ideas that were pertinent and had some substance.

Kevin put up his hand to make a motion. He was told by the chairman that he should read the manual of procedures.

After the meeting, I heard him tell another first year student that he was going to offer his cabin on the lake as a get away for the students.

Don told him that we go on outreaches into communities where we minister. I don't think they will consider a get away.

That week, Ted came back to the Mission and to the class. Kevin was totally impressed with the knowledge of the Bible that Ted exhibited. After class, he talked to Ted and told him he was really bright. Ted smiled and went his way.

At a staff meeting, Ted's mannerisms and his ways of responding to people at the Mission was discussed. It revolved around an outburst against a man who wanted to get his attention and tapped him on the shoulder. Ted turned around and told the man, "Don't you ever touch me again. Keep your hands to yourself. Who do you think you are? I hate people like you."

I was not in the Mission when this outburst took place. I remembered a time before when he made a similar ruckus over someone pointing to his shoe where the lace was untied.

Another point of concern was that after the service, Ted was playing around with the instruments, when the worship leaders were mingling and talking to the people from the street. He was told to leave the electric guitar alone as he wasn't on the worship team and didn't know how to play an instrument. He dropped the guitar onto the floor and went away angry.

It put added pressure on those in charge as there were these added restrictions put on Ted which had to be enforced.

Rumours in a place like the Mission often get started. We have to check them out and make certain they are verified. If they are gossip, we put an end to it in the Mission and the Bible College.

The question as to why he can't stand anyone touching him has still not been answered but there were rumours.

I had a similar response from a prostitute. She came to the Bible College in order to change her life and get herself off the street. I treated her with respect and made certain that no one made her uncomfortable.

After six months of College and working in the Mission, she asked me to pray for the healing of her sore shoulder.

My usual thing is to put my hand on the person's shoulder and let the Holy Spirit guide my hand to wherever the healing is required. I started to pray and instinctively put my hand on her shoulder. She startled me when she quickly moved away and told me in a loud and harsh voice, "Don't you ever touch me again. Why did you do that to me?" She ranted on calling me a pervert as she was irate.

My action was innocent, but she thought I was seeking sexual favours. I apologized and told he I was sorry.

After that, our relationship was never the same. I was afraid of her and she didn't trust me.

A few months later, she disappeared. She became one of the sex trade workers to vanish from the street without a trace.

I prayed that she went home to her parents or to a friends or a relative.

If, in fact, she had disappeared in the manner others were reported to have disappeared, we prayed that she would be with the Lord, the one she learned about and worshipped during her eight months at Bible College. She often proclaimed that Jesus was Lord of her life.

Another twist at the Bible College.

Kevin admired the ability of Ted to spout Bible verses and to answer questions on most related topics.

I noticed that the two were hanging around together. I was happy that Ted had a friend. In the three years I knew him he had never had a friend. He was a loner.

I also noticed that Kevin did not drive the Lexus to the downtown eastside. After class he would tell me he had to hurry and catch the three forty bus.

I wondered why he took three bus rides to get to his home when he could drive it in half an hour. Someone told me it involved the use of drugs.

In class, Kevin and Ted were now sitting beside each other. Ted was helping Kevin understand the concepts being taught. They were smiling and happy to be together

Ted was now dressing in designer clothes and was keeping up his appearance. He was well groomed and had a stylish haircut.

I thought perhaps his mother was in town and taking care of her son. I mentioned this to a volunteer who knew the mother. She also knew Ted and his life style.

She told me he has a friend with money to burn. "He's buying Ted clothes and taking him to fancy restaurants. I think Ted is living in the mansion of his friend."

I didn't hear it from any other source, so I dismissed it as a possibility.

Kevin kept up his studies and the two of them never missed a class.

Three weeks later, I was upset when Kevin came into the Mission alone one night and asked one of the volunteers for a Bible. He was given an old white Bible that had been around for a while. When the music was playing at the evening service, Kevin started reading the Bible out loud. I realized that he was either drunk or on drugs.

One of the students asked him to stop disturbing the service. He became cantankerous and told Matthew to leave him alone. He kept up his reading aloud.

Finally, I asked him to come into the office for a chat. He refused at first and kept on reading aloud. I sat beside him and requested he stop reading and come with me. He then complied.

I asked him about his coming to the Mission on drugs. He told me he was stressed out. "I'm not an addict. I do drugs to settle myself down. This is my way of dealing with anxiety."

I told him that Jesus does a much better job of dealing with anxiety when you pray to Him. Kevin nodded and told me he understood. He was still lucid.

He voluntarily told me that Ted had been living with him for a month or more.

"It was nice because we really like each other and get along," he smiled..

"My mother told me Ted made her nervous. She didn't want him around. She told me to get rid of him.

When I told Ted he had to leave, he got angry at me. I don't understand him. He was so nice and now he hates me."

He put his head into his hands. "The stress of having Ted in the house, put my mother into the palliative care unit of the hospital. It's my fault," he lamented.

I told him, "She has a sickness the doctors can't seem to cure. It's best she gets hospital care."

He looked up and asked emphatically, "Do you know what palliative care means?"

I told him I knew and I was sorry.

Kevin asked me if I would go to the hospital and pray that she gets better. I agreed and told him, I'd bring my wife along. He smiled.

Kevin came back to the College and became more settled.

Ted wouldn't talk to him and he stopped coming to the College.

I started teaching the Gospel of Mark.

Kevin loved the teachings. He particularly liked the healing ministry of Jesus the Christ. He made the observation that Jesus healed one after another. "It's amazing, all that were sick or infirm, Jesus healed them on the spot. Imagine a man with a shrivelled hand, that's thalidomide isn't it?" I agreed it could be.

Kevin put his hand near his shoulder and stretched it out. "That's amazing."

He thought about it and asked, "If Jesus can do restorative healing, do you think he can restore my mother back to good health?"

I brought his attention to where it says Jesus prayed and they were all healed.

The class prayed for the healing touch of Jesus to heal the mother of Kevin.

Many times at the Mission, Kevin asked everyone to pray for his mother's recovery.

As I had promised, my wife and I met Kevin in the palliative care unit of the hospital. It was the first time I had seen his mother. You could tell that she was from high society by the way she talked and acted.

She took a liking to Kristina, my wife. They talked until Kevin's mother became tired. We anointed her with oil and prayed for her healing and also for peace of mind and a relationship with Jesus our Lord.

Kevin had left the room when we were talking. He came back and told us he had three more patients who asked for a healing touch We did the rounds and prayed for those who were close to leaving the earth. We didn't just pray for healing, we also asked if they knew the Lord and had a relationship with Jesus the Christ. Two said they did but the third one told me she wasn't sure. We brought the message of the gospel to her and she accepted Jesus as her Lord and Saviour .

I told Kevin to make certain they all had a Bible to read. "You can help them understand the healing ministry and salvation as we have studied everything you need to know in order to bring them into a relationship with Jesus our Lord."

Kevin quit coming to the Mission and College for a short period. He spent his time with his mother.

When she passed away, he came back to the College.

We were not invited to her funeral. It was for invited guests only. Kevin explained that his sisters took over the planning of the funeral service.

After graduating and being commissioned, Kevin arranged a party for all the students. He took them to a restaurant with a buffet. It was in a much better part of town and was really enjoyed by all. There was lots of talking and laughing. He told everyone he looked forward to coming back for his second year.

After that he disappeared without telling anyone where he was going.

Four years later, he came back to the Mission.

I greeted him and told him how happy I was to see him.

He told me he had met a lovely lady who is his soul mate. "I now live in Romania on a farm which her father owns. We have a three year old daughter."

I asked if he was coming back here to live. He told me he was only in the city to get his papers signed in order that he can become a Romanian citizen.

He gave a testimony to the class on his visit to the College.

He told how much his time at the College meant to him. "My mother came to the Lord after much prayer. Imagine, I taught her, I became her teacher.

It got to the point where she looked forward to learning more about Jesus and God Almighty. After the Pastor and his wife prayed for her, she thought she was healed. She wanted to go home. The doctor agreed and she came home for a short time.

But God wanted her in His kingdom, now that she has given her life to Christ and is a new creation."

He finished his testimony by telling the class that he also brought his wife to the Lord.

He laughed and told us his wife now reads her Bible and shares with him what she has just learned.

Kevin came to the College with no understanding of spiritual principles. He was doing whatever felt good sexually, as well as abusing drugs and alcohol.

When he learned the truths of the Bible and started putting them into practise, his life changed. Not only his life but the life of his mother was transformed and she is now with Jesus in paradise.

Kevin has been radically changed by his relationship with Jesus the Christ and by reading the word of God and practising what he reads.

CHAPTER TWENTY NINE

MIKE

Traumatized

Matthew 10:40, Jesus said, "He who receives you receives me, and he who receives me receives the one who sent me. And he who receives a righteous man will receive a righteous man's reward."

MIKE is a tall, well built, handsome young First Nations man. He could be mistaken for a lumberjack or a fisherman. He wore his black hair long and it hung over his shoulders.

When I first saw him at the Mission, I decided not to get in his way.

For a few years he was a regular at the Mission. At times he got a bit rowdy and had to be removed. It was caused by his love of liquor.

When the music had a beat, he'd dance around and swing his hair from one side to the other. He had a happy-go-lucky attitude when things were going right. He also had a sense of humour.

One night, I was leaving the Mission around eleven-thirty. The music was still playing and people were socializing. On my way out into the darkness, I was surprised and shocked to see this big man with black hair covering his face.

He spoke in a deep and threatening voice, "Where do you think you're going?"

In my distressed voice, I replied meekly, "I'm going home."

"No you're not," he countered.

I think he could sense my shaking and my anxiety at being confronted by this big man. He shook his hair back and I recognized Mike. He laughed and it quieted my beating heart.

"Don't you do that again. You scared me to death."

He laughed all the harder.

Over the years, I grew fond of Mike. He would stay after the service and help clean up. Sweeping and mopping the floor. Washing and stacking the chairs.

If we were short handed in the kitchen, he would offer to do the heavy lifting. Carrying in supplies or anything that needed his muscle power.

There were times I asked him to be the bouncer. We needed someone with muscle to control those people who have no respect for the house of the Lord.

One night, when he was on duty, a young lady, who had been on the street, came for coffee and something to eat.

The rule is that everyone starts at the end of the line and works their way to the kitchen. She came in and surveyed the lineup. She saw someone she could use to move ahead of into the lineup.

Mike was watching her manoeuver her way to the front of the line. He went over and told her she must start at the end of the line, not jump in ahead of those who were waiting.

She used abusive language and wouldn't get out of the lineup and comply with the rules.

Mike told the kitchen help not to serve her.

When she reached the kitchen they told her she couldn't be served. She started spouting off using foul language. She knocked the water jug over getting the kitchen staff wet.

Mike intervened and had her move away from the kitchen.

She then started knocking chairs over and went into a rant and rage.

A regular at the Mission phoned the police. A foot patrol happened to be nearby. Two lady police officers, on patrol, came into the Mission. They motioned for the young lady to come with them.

The young lady from the street picked up the squeeze mustard bottle from the kitchen counter and positioned herself against the far wall from the police officers.

The gospel songs were still being played to try to soothe the situation. The officers asked them to stop the music.

In order to let people know she had a weapon, she squeezed the mustard container and mustard sprayed on some of the people in the congregation. One man got some in his hair, another had some on his shoulder and one man had it on his shoe.

The officers kept telling the lady with the mustard container to put it down. One officer told her they would not hurt her. They just wanted to talk to her. The other officer said they would take her home.

Finally, after five tense minutes, she gave the mustard container to a man beside her. She went quietly with the policewomen, much to the relief of everyone.

Afterwards, Mike told me he had dashed into the bathroom when he saw her pick up the mustard bottle.

"I knew I was her prime target as she was angry when I had the kitchen help refuse to serve her. Man, was that ever close," he laughed.

When we went on an outreach we were often short staffed at the Mission. The leader of the Mission would ask Mike if he would be in charge of the kitchen and appoint people for clean-up duties.

Mike wouldn't promise, as he knew that if a friend needed a drinking buddy he would be tempted. He'd tell the leader he'd try.

If it happened that he was available, he would come early and appoint people to tasks that needed to carried out. When Mike asked people to help, they never argued. He wouldn't bully them but he would tell them,"You're in charge of … ."

I was more diplomatic than Mike. I would ask someone if they thought they could carry out a task. If they said no, I would go on to the next person.

Over the years a number of women came onto Mike. They liked his disposition and his laughter. I would see him with a woman, but it never became serious.

Big as he was, he had an even bigger heart.

If someone needed a hand moving or carrying something up some stairs into their apartment, or any other task, they felt free to ask Mike for a hand.

The Mission had a van and a driver but they needed a helper to load and unload. If Mike was in sight they counted on him to use his muscles. He told me that's how he gets his workout. I would struggle carrying one box into the Mission and he would carry three.

Everyone had a warm spot in their heart for Mike. When he came into the Mission, people felt the warmth of his presence.

One day he came into the office. I was doing some preparation for the class I was teaching. I stopped and gave him my attention. He told me his story:

"You know me as a sometimes drunk and a sometimes happy go lucky guy.

You don't know me deep down inside. I cry a lot when I'm alone." He stopped to wipe away a tear.

"I was with my brother. We were the best of friends. We were swimming down at the river. The river was running fast as it was late spring. My brother was a faster runner and a better soccer player than me. He was a better swimmer. I was average but he was above average.

We would dive in and let the current carry us downstream and dump us off on an island in the middle of the river. We'd done it lots of times. It was a real rush.

Getting back to our village, there was a foot bridge.

Stupidly, we made it more exciting by seeing how close to the end of the island we could beach ourselves." Mike stopped to remember. He wiped his tears.

"I watched Charlie as he swept along the island. I yelled at him to beach himself. He waved and tried to get to shore. It was too late He was pushed into swifter waters. There were rocks near the falls. If you hit your head on a rock you were knocked out and you would drown," he sobbed.

I kept running as fast as I could down the river bank, yelling at Charlie to get out of the water. I was exhausted and filled with grief. I sat on the bank crying my eyes out. I still cry when I think of Charlie. He was the best brother anyone could ever have."

I went over and put my hand on the shoulder of Mike. There were no words to take away the pain. He told me it was his fault because he knew the danger but went along with the deadly game.

I told him, "There's not any fault. It was a tragic accident."

Mike countered, "I'm the older brother. It was up to me to say no. I have to live with that guilt," Mike shook his head.

I told him I would pray for him. I knew he would go out and wash away his guilt and shame with bottles of rice wine or beer.

As he left I said, "We'll see you at the Mission tonight."

"I'll try."

I knew that most of the men on skid row have a terrible story which has brought trauma into their lives. I have heard their testimonies and their tales of grief. Heartbreaking events which they can't forget.

I tell them, "Jesus is the only way you can overcome that trauma."

I have them pray to the Holy Spirit and let Jesus forgive their sins and bring them into a relationship with Jesus and his Father. If they agree, they start on the journey to recovery.

Now that I knew about Mike's traumatic life story, I can use inner healing to bring him closer to the Lord.

I talked to Mike about Bible College. I told him he would find a friend who would be closer than anyone else had ever been.

Mike said, "I know, you're talking about Jesus." Mike closed his eyes, remembering his brother.

Mike asked me. "Do you think my brother Charlie got to be saved by Jesus?"

I told Mike that God has special consideration for those who are innocent.

"My brother was innocent, He never smoked or drank. He hardly ever swore."

I told Mike that Charlie had a really good chance of making it into heaven with Jesus and God Almighty.

That lifted a load off Mike's shoulders. Yet there were still the memories.

A week later, Mike showed up at Bible College. He was cleanly shaven and his hair was pulled back in a pony tail. I didn't realized that he was so handsome.

I wondered how he would make out in his studies.

He surprised me in that he did his assignments and was a pleasure to have in the class.

He lived in a nearby hotel, which meant he could come easily to the Mission. Everyone in the Bible College is required to perform a ministry.

Mike opted to do his ministry as the janitor of the Mission and the College. He was given keys so that he could do the cleaning whenever it was convenient.

It was at a meeting of the Board, where it was decided who had keys to the Mission and the Bible College. Who should have keys was discussed. When it came to Mike, there was a division of opinion.

Some agreed that it would be a good idea as he could open up and close the Mission. He could also do the cleaning when it was convenient for him.

Others put forward the argument that he might get drunk and lose the keys. That would make the Mission vulnerable to loss of equipment and vandalism.

With a split vote of four for his having some keys and three against, the motion was passed.

The amendment was that they would give him a trial period with only one door key to each building. That would protect the cupboards and freezers. It also passed.

The Mission and College were never cleaner. He would invite some of his First Nations friends to come and help keep the buildings in good shape.

No one said 'No' to Mike. If he asked you to help, you helped.

There were times, when he would miss coming to the Mission at night. We knew his love for liquor had gotten the better of him. I learned that it was not only liquor but also drugs.

I presented Mike with the possibility of three or four sessions of 'inner healing'. I explained to him that he needed to have Jesus come and personally work at bringing closure to events in his life, which were causing so much pain and anxiety.

He didn't understand what I was talking about. I didn't bring up the trauma of watching his brother drown. I felt there might be more that needed the healing touch of our Lord and Saviour.

He told me he was busy for the rest of the month and asked if we could put it off for a month. I agreed and wrote a date and time on my calendar.

I wrote it out for him and he put the paper into his pocket. I wondered how many months he would be too busy.

At one point, after Mike had disappeared for three days, I was in the back yard of the dormitory. I noticed someone in the alley. Looking more carefully, I recognized that it was Mike.

I didn't want to intimidate him so I looked the other way. I did sneak a peek now and then to see if he would come to the gate.

When he saw me he stopped dead in his tracks, turned around and took a few steps in the other direction. He then came to the gate.

I welcomed him and he came into the yard

"I'm sorry", he said, remorsefully,"I just need a woman now and then."

Being married I knew what he meant. I told him I understood. He put me in a bear hug and tears ran down onto my shoulder.

"We do miss you and we worry about you," I told him. "Not only that but the Mission is getting a bit messy."

He let go of me and said, "Funny thing, I was just on my way to do some cleaning and tidying up."

I walked with him over to the Mission. He told me he loves the Lord and needs His love. I told him we all need the love of the Lord in our lives.

He told me, "Being with Jesus is really great isn't it?" I agreed.

For the next few weeks, he didn't miss one class and he kept the Mission clean every day.

In the Bible College we were studying the Doctrine of Salvation. It was all new to many of the students but it was particularly new to Mike.

This doctrine first of all deals with the death and resurrection of Jesus the Christ. It also deals with redemption and reconciliation.

Mike wanted to be certain that he was redeemed. I left that up to the third year students to answer. They explained it as well as I could. Mike was so happy to know that he was chosen to be a child of God because of what Jesus did for him personally. He was told he was redeemed from sin by the power of Jesus shed blood. It was all so new and exciting to the class and to Mike in particular.

When he was told that it was by the power of the trinity, God's power combined with the power of the shed blood of Jesus and the sanctifying work of the Holy Spirit, all working for his salvation, it blew his mind.

I heard him tell a group of students not to take this lightly. "We're blessed by all those great people in heaven. Now we must be a blessing to others who don't know all this stuff."

Mike seldom missed a lesson or an assignment. He was a different person when in the presence of God Almighty and when the Holy Spirit was working in his life.

I had high hopes that Mike would use his leadership skills to teach and preach the gospel and make a difference in people's lives.

He had charisma, which used in the right way, would be great for the ministry of Jesus the Christ.

He came on two outreaches and I watched as he ministered to others. Before the week-end was over, he had a following of young people and kids. There was joking and laughing. Young kids tugging at his legs for attention. Kids quoting Bible verses Mike had taught them.

Mike let them know that there was always a candy for a Bible verse memorized.

The time of the month, which I dread, is when the welfare cheques come.

Persons on skid row who have not received money for a month are suddenly rich, in their own eyes. They are now able to afford steak and lobster dinners, and the best of everything for one or two days until their money runs out.

My biggest concern is that they could now afford the best bottle of liquor and as many drugs as they desired.

It's after this time of affluence that reports of catastrophes and calamities make the rounds.

Families who are affected by a death from drugs, alcohol or a beating, come to the Mission grieving their loss. "He was such a good boy, or good girl. What went wrong?" Memorial services are then arranged.

One day, just after the cheques came, I arrived at the Bible College early as I had some copies to run off.

A friend of Mike's, who helped him clean the Mission, came into the College and handed me a set of two keys.

"Why?" I asked, in dismay.

"He overdosed and didn't come out of it," his friend replied.

I sat down and shed a few tears. I prayed that Mike would be with God and Jesus. I told God, how he had changed and how he loved to be in His presence.

I didn't feel like teaching, only praying for the soul of Mike, a child of God and a lover of Jesus the Christ.

That day we all prayed and asked God to accept our brother Mike's soul and spirit into the Kingdom.

Mike first came to the Mission with a heavy load of trauma. He was a changed man when he was at the Mission and in the presence of Jesus and God Almighty, being led by the Holy Spirit.

We don't know why he was taken so early in life just when he showed so much potential, but God knows.

Mike was radically changed. After he met Jesus and gave his life and soul to Him. He was taken by the angels to heaven to be with Charlie. He will always be remembered by those who love him.

CHAPTER THIRTY

RAV

A Gypsy

Matthew 25:16, "When the Son of Man comes in His glory, and all the angels with him, he will sit on His throne in heavenly glory. He will separate the people one from another... ."

RAV needed a place to live. Many people on skid row find it difficult to find a permanent place that suits them. There is always something they don't like. Sometimes it's too noisy. For others there is a lack of privacy. One man told me people came knocking at his door bumming cigarettes or needing a light. Some come asking what he was drinking or eating. It got on his nerves and he moved.

When I saw Rav talking to the guys at the dormitory, I thought I knew what he wanted. He is from the downtown eastside and known by many of the residents of the area. When he saw me looking at him, he came over and explained why he was talking to the students at the dormitory.

He told me he'd been observing the members of the Mission and the College and decided the dormitory is where he wants to live.

Rav was in his mid fifties and has been around for many years. I knew him and I knew about him, but I had never been formally introduced.

We walked back to where the students were and he confided to us that there were good reasons why he was moving.

The first reason was that where he was living they had cockroaches and bedbugs. I shook my head and said, "No, no! We don't need those bugs in our dormitory."

He shot back saying that he's taking everything to the laundry and he's throwing away anything that might harbor the little critters.

I asked the guys what they thought. All the time Rav is begging them to make the decision to let him come and live in the dorm.

They asked Rav if he had enough money to put his clothes and everything that might hide a bug either in the washer and dryer on high temperature or throw it away.

Rav was smiling now and he agreed to anything that would allow him to stay in the dormitory.

He also told the students that the place where he lived was noisy and there were addicts and hoodlums who thought it was funny to push him around and try to get him upset.

I had two of the students volunteer to do a complete check of everything Rav wanted to bring into the house. If it didn't pass the test, throw it away. I knew that bedbugs can hide in a tiny crack. I explained it to the boys as they had never seen a bedbug.

Rav was not that much help in moving into the dormitory as he was not that mobile. He had difficulty walking up stairs.

He had very few possessions and what he had would be considered junk.

He couldn't walk more than two blocks without sitting down. He'd been in a car accident and his knees were damaged and he had a bad hip. He rode on a red electric scooter, on which he had become quite proficient.

I had seen him ride through a crowd.

He was quite adept at manoeuvring his machine among the people on the street.

Many of these people were either loitering, buying drugs or selling stolen property.

My next contact with Rav was at the Mission. He was introduced to the other students as a resident of the student dorm.

When Rav saw me, he motored over and told me, "I'm a gypsy."

I had an experience with gypsies when I was five years old. We lived in a small village on the prairies, as my father was a grain buyer. Every year or two the gypsy caravan, covered wagons pulled by horses, came into town and parked on the outdoor skating rink area.

That Spring morning, my father took me to the Blacksmith shop where a few of the local men were gathered. They were talking rather than working as it was a government holiday.

I was five years old at the time.

Jake, the leader of the gypsies, was a tall heavy set man. There were other younger men that I knew were gypsies by their dress and by their mannerisms.

When they came into a town they would display, for sale, all the horses, cows, pigs or whatever they had picked up or had traded along their journey. They sold whatever would bring a decent price. There was a price for everything they owned. Often a price not many could afford in the tough times.

They loved to bargain. Their prices started so high no one would consider paying such a price. As they brought the price down, people were tempted by the bargains they offered.

My dad told my mother not to be taken in by their sales talk. He also told her to put everything in the house or in the garage and lock up everything including the chickens and the geese, "Don't leave anything laying around or it will disappear."

Jake kept looking at me and asked my father, "How much for that son of yours? I can use him." Hearing this I grabbed the pant leg of my father and hung on tight. My father laughed and told him I was not for sale. Later, Jake extended his hand to me. I clung even tighter to my father. Jake laughed and laughed.

After all these years I was now in the presence of a real gypsy. The funny thing is, Rav fulfilled my concept of a gypsy. He had olive skin and wore three gold necklaces, and a ring on each finger. Even his bright clothes were distinctive.

I asked Rav when he would be enrolling in the Bible College. We had a long discussion on the pros and cons of his enrolling. He told me gypsies don't like to be tied down to a contract. "We love our freedom," he explained.

I told him that only in Jesus can we be set free and you will be free indeed. He didn't understand. He just shook his head.

"I don't understand your freedom," he confided.

We made a deal. He would audit the courses and come as often as he could. He'd pay the tuition, when he could afford to. But, he wouldn't write all the essays only those that appealed to him. He would write the tests, but we couldn't fail him. I asked him if he wanted to graduate or just waste his time and our time.

He thought about it and told me he had to graduate. I told him that if he wanted to graduate he had to do the assignments.

He pointed out to me that everything can't be written in stone. I agreed and told him we'd make some exceptions, but he'd have to attend class and do the major assignments. He agreed.

Gypsies like to bargain and I think he got the better of that deal.

Later, I wondered what we had really agreed to.

I could tell from the first course of studies that Rav had very limited knowledge of the Bible and anything spiritual. He told me he had heard about God, but didn't know much about Him rather than he would help him if he fell over a cliff.

He later told me he'd never heard the name Jesus except in swearing.

The Holy Spirit was unknown to him.

I wondered how long he would come to the College and to what extent he would be involved. To my surprise, he became a regular. He marvelled at the concepts being taught. I'd watch him during class and I could see the wheels turning in his head.

His favourite expression is, "That's fantastic!"

A couple of times he'd ask, "Is that really true? Did Jesus really heal that paralytic? Even today they can't heal the spinal cord injured, they're still in wheelchairs, like me. Fantastic!"

Three months into Rav's study, we taught about what Jesus did for us on the cross. At that point, Rav gave his life to Christ. "If Jesus would do that for me, the least I can do is give my life to Him and to God."

This opened the way for a discussion on baptism.

We have a course explaining baptism and being born again in the Spirit. It is separate from our courses at the College. It is given in the evening. Rav agreed to do the study and we arranged a time for the baptism ceremony.

That opened another chapter in Rav's life. He was determined to be a missionary on the streets of skid row. He started wearing crosses on his gold necklaces and painted a cross on his scooter, with a big wooden cross on the handle bars.

One day he told me, "I've got a gift for your wife." I waited as he looked for it in his jewellery box. He handed me a beautiful silver cross with green gems embedded.

I asked, "Are you sure? It's beautiful," I exclaimed. Rave smiled.

That was the first of many gifts he gave to my wife.

Rav told me he was ready for baptism. He told me he'd read the booklet and attended the classes and he had prayed about it. "I'm ready!" he exclaimed.

The baptism took place down at the beach. He rode his scooter as far as he could and then a couple of students helped him get off his scooter and down to the water.

He had told everyone he knew that he was being baptized. Many of them came to watch him go under as the old man and come up as a new man in Christ. I was one of two who took part in the ceremony.

He was heavy, as his knees gave out and we had to support him. When we dipped him, I almost went under as he was dead weight. I strived and we brought him back up. Two younger and stronger guys helped him back to the beach. Half way up the beach another big student came and gave a hand.

Not long after that Rav completed his first year of studies. He didn't write every essay and he missed a couple of tests. He did however get high marks for participation and oral assignments. He had good marks on the tests he did write. He completed enough of the assignments and tests to give him the bare minimum credits for a pass.

Rav didn't know he had passed. He came to the Mission with a long face looking sad. I played along and told him I'd be sad too. He looked dejected and told me he'd done his best. I let him stew for five minutes. He was totally defeated.

I told him, "You passed! You graduated first year."

He was really happy. The first thing he did was give thanks in prayer. He thanked, God Almighty and Jesus his Lord and Saviour, and the Holy Spirit.

At graduation, he was really pumped up. He asked to sit in the front row.

He wanted to walk up and receive his certificate. Because he was a first year student, he was one of the first to come to the front and receive his commissioning. When his name was called, Roy and Stacy helped him stand up. Everyone clapped in appreciation.

The students knew how hard he had worked and the obstacles he had overcome to get this far.

His invited guests cheered the loudest and called out congratulations to him.

After graduation and the handshakes, his gypsy friends and a couple of young prostitutes he was ministering to, gave him gifts and took him to dinner at a restaurant. I was invited but I had other commitments.

A few days later, Rav cornered me and insisted that we go to the restaurant to talk. His choice of restaurants was unique. We were the only patrons as it was before lunch.

Rav wanted me to explain what it meant by commissioning, as first year students were, 'commissioned'.

I explained the 'Great Commission' where Jesus told his disciples:

Matthew 28:18, "All authority in heaven and on earth has been given to me. Therefore go and make disciples of all nations, baptizing them in the name of the Father and the Son and the Holy Spirit, and teaching them to obey everything I have commanded you. And surely I am with you to the very end of the age."

Rav nodded and responded, "Now that I am officially commissioned, I can go out and do my ministry?" he asked.

I told him that technically he could, but perhaps a little more knowledge and understanding would be a better plan. He asked if he could do both.

I told him that if it was God's will for him, "Yes you can."

He smiled. I knew he had a plan but he wasn't going to divulge it at this time.

Rav took my advice and continued with his studies.

He marvelled at every promise of God, every miracle of Jesus the Christ and every doctrine and concept. Every spiritual gift that we studied, was exactly the gift that he needed in order to do his ministry.

He learned to ask for the greater gifts and was certain he had received those particular giftings.

I took a great deal of pleasure in seeing his joy and his delight in his learning the word of God.

Four months into the third year of studies, Rav told me he had great news that he wanted to share with the class and with everyone on earth. I told him to go ahead.

The next time he came to class, He gave his testimony:

"I've become a pastor to the gypsies," he proclaimed. "I'm an ordained pastor," he beamed.

The students looked at each other wondering how this could be. Ordination came after three years of study.

As well, it was at the discretion of the board of governors of the denomination. Not all applicants for ordination are accepted.

One student asked me, "How did Rav qualify?"

I also wondered how he qualified. I knew he was dying to tell me.

Two days later, I met with Rav in the office. I asked him, "How did you get ordained without our knowing?"

He joyfully replied, "The Lord Jesus himself poured out His Spirit on me and ordained me, pastor of the gypsies."

I was speechless and asked the Holy Spirit for direction in this matter.

Who was I to pour condemnation on this man ordained by Jesus the Christ.

I congratulated him and wished him all the best. I did caution him to be careful about telling everyone that he was ordained. They will ask what denomination. What will you tell them?

He agreed and told me he'd be careful and give them an honest answer. "The truth is the Lord can ordain anyone who is commissioned," he explained.

I knew that he had brought many gypsies to the Lord. I also knew that he ministered to people on the street and had converted many to Christianity.

As well, he had brought male and female prostitutes to the Lord and they changed their lives.

I realized he was doing a ministry even though it was a bit different. than most ministries.

I figured that if this is the ministry Rav is called to by God, I will support it and pray for success in reaching those lost souls.

One thing I learned on Skid row is that I cannot minister to everyone in every circumstance. It takes people like Rav to minister to the gypsies, the prostitutes, the homeless and the hurting.

Rav completed his third year's study. There was much celebrating. His gypsy friends came from other areas and congratulated Rav on his being presented with a diploma from the Bible College.

Rav applied for official ordination with the denomination. I helped him make out his request and signed it as his sponsoring pastor. He filed the application.

After a few months, Rav moved out of the area. I asked him why he was moving? He told me gypsies don't live on skid row, they are a proud people.

"They are living in another municipality. I must be with them in order to minister to them," he confided.

He gave me his phone number. I asked where he was living. He told me he didn't have a permanent address, "I am staying with a gypsy friend."

He invited me to his Sunday Service, when it became operational, and told me to bring the whole class and all of his friends from skid row.

He didn't phone and after two months I phoned the number he gave me, in order to get the address and time of his Sunday service.

I also wanted to tell him that he had been given a date to meet with the representative of the ordination committee.

The person who answered the phone told me that he had moved to another municipality and had given no forwarding address or phone number.

The number he gave me may not be any longer in service, but I know that Rav is still in service to his gypsies, to the prostitutes and anyone in need of a friend.

I know that he is still serving people and bringing them into a relationship with his beloved Jesus and God Almighty. I also know that he is being led by the Holy Spirit who is guiding him, teaching him and controlling him.

The gypsies in the caravan that visited our home town were always on the move. Rav is a real gypsy who is always on the move.

He'll show up some day, as he always does, and we'll get to go to his Sunday service and meet his gypsy converts and those whom he has brought to the Lord.

Rav was radically changed from a gypsy with no knowledge of the Bible or spiritual matters to a self ordained minister who really matters in his community.

CHAPTER THIRTY ONE

MARTHA

From the Mountain

Psalm 48:1,2 "Great is the Lord, and most worthy to be praised, in the city of our God in the mountains of His holiness. It is beautiful in It's loftiness, the joy of the whole world."

MARTHA came to the Mission with a friend. She had just arrived in the big city from a small community in the mountains to the north. She was very shy and stayed close to her friend. I was not introduced to her that night, but I did take notice of her.

Martha gravitated to the older women as she was in her late forties.

The older women were known affectionately as our, 'Beautiful Christian Ladies.'

Four of these beautiful ladies had a special place along the railing. They were always smiling and lit up the room. They were First Nations patriarchs. We loved to have them join us many nights a week, as they were an example to the younger ladies. They were also honoured by the men who came to the Mission.

One of the lovely lady's son was the bouncer. She was proud to have one of her sons in the church and serving God.

Martha fitted into this group, although she didn't sit with the matrons, she sat close by and was accepted as a good person. She didn't drink, smoke, or do drugs. She didn't prostitute herself or flirt with men.

She held her head high, and humbled herself.

My wife and I did a prison ministry along with Jack and a few others.

Martha asked if she could join us and be part of the ministry. We agreed and she continued in that ministry for two years.

At the prison there was a time of greeting inmates before the service. At seven o'clock the service started. It consisted of singing gospel songs accompanied by the piano or by guitar. We let the men choose most of the gospel songs.

They had favourites like, 'I'll Fly Away' and 'Amazing Grace'.

We then had a pastor or lay person give the message, which was a word of hope in Jesus the Christ and a word of encouragement for the men.

Martha became special as she asked for, and was given the privilege of doing a solo each visit. She sang:

Psalm 48, "Great is the Lord, and worthy of our praise, in the city of our God, in the mountain of His Holiness ..."

The Psalm was sung in a quiet and heartfelt manner, which appealed to those present.

The men loved to hear her sing and always requested her solo.

Because of her quiet demeanor and her kind ways, she attracted many young men to her. They felt her love for them and they became her friends.

This happened to all of us in one way or another. My wife had many young men seek her out and want to talk. These were mainly men who had no visitors and needed to know that they were still loved.

Before the service, men would come early and talk to us. Sharing what had happened to them in the last week or month.

It caused mixed feelings when they asked us to pray for them as they were going to apply for parole. We prayed and asked God for their release. The next week many times they were already gone; or they announced the date of their departure.

We shared the joy in their being released, but also we knew we might never see them again. It affected me somewhat, but it had a greater effect on the women.

Tears were shed. Tears of happiness in knowing these men were set free, also tears knowing that they had lost a friend.

We always prayed on the way home on the bus, asking God's protection and guidance for the ones set free from prison and for those still incarcerated.

Martha came to Bible College. I knew her by now and for some reason, I expected great things from her. She was a bit reticent at first as she wasn't certain that what we were teaching fitted her previous worship beliefs.

She asked to meet with me. She came with her friend. They told me how they came from a religion which was much more formal and structured. They spoke about their rituals and their worship of Jesus but also belief in many saints.

I had had this type of meeting before as many First Nations persons had only one church on their reserve and services were conducted in this manner. I asked the two of them to give us a chance to put forward our beliefs and doctrines which were backed by scripture.

I also told them that our teaching required them to participate in a relationship they would gain by getting to know Jesus the Christ personally and be filled with the Holy Spirit.

They both agreed to come to class with an open mind and let the Spirit of God lead them in whatever direction was His will for their life.

Martha's friend asked if she could still pray the rosary and light candles. I told her what she did in prayer was her choice.

"Just be careful not to burn down the hotel in which you live," I joked.

The joke was not well received.

Martha's friend came to Bible College for a short time but did not continue.

Martha hung in and completed her first years study. She gave up her old ways and was happy to have a relationship with Jesus and with God Almighty. She confided in me that we are right in having this love affair with our precious Jesus.

She told me, "Before my studies, Jesus was only an icon, now He's for real."

At the graduation ceremony, Martha sang the song she sings at the prison. She received a round of applause.

When she went up to receive her certificate of commissioning, she radiated the glory of the Lord.

After the awards ceremony, two young men who were released from prison and came to our city, brought her gifts. They talked for a long time telling her about their new life, which included their Saviour, Jesus the Christ.

That summer she went back to the mountains and reconnected with her family and friends.

When she returned for the second year of studies she gave a testimony.

"I went home. In talking to my family and friends I knew I had changed but they were still stuck in their old ways of thinking. I tried to get them to give up their pagan ways and have a relationship with the Lord. I told them to get rid of all that was holding them back from becoming born again and filled with the Spirit of God.

I think I reached a few, but most were too stubborn. I heard they were talking behind my back saying I was the crazy one," she laughed.

"I ran out of time, but I didn't run out of words," she stated.

This caused those at the Mission to applaud her.

Martha and another friend from the eastside started a ministry on the streets at night.

They took hot chocolate and cookies they had baked at the Mission, to the street workers, the young and some older prostitutes.

She told how these young girls were so cold, standing there with so few clothes on." I feel sorry for them," Martha stated.

Two week later, I talked to her about her venture.

I warned her that there was a risk element in being out on the streets so late at night.

She told me they always prayed for an hour or more before going out on the street. I agreed that was good protection.

At a meeting, she told me that they had talked two young girls into quitting the street and going back to their parents. "We made the call and the parents were so grateful. I have their phone number and I'll keep in touch," Martha informed me.

Martha's friend and co-worker on the street, told me at another meeting, that the pimps were upset with them as their girls had missed prospects when we were talking to them. They warned Martha and her friend not to talk or come near their girls. She asked me for advice.

I advised them to either quit or to take their chocolate and cookies to a safer street. Her friend asked, "Are we really in danger?"

I told her of women I knew who were missing from the street and some were murdered. "You could be the next," I warned.

She told me that so many girls wanted to get away from that life, but they were hooked on drugs and needed money for a their habit.

Martha graduated after her second year. She went back to her mountain home and continued her ministry with people in her community.

Upon returning for her final year of College, she reported that her time at home had made her more aware of her spirituality and how it had changed her life.

She explained that she now has a better idea of her call to ministry.

During the final year at the College, she spent a great deal of time in prayer and meditation. She put more effort into her studies and made each assignment a challenge and a way of preparation for her ministry.

Before graduation, she applied for ordination.

The final decision on ordination was in her favour. There was a big celebration. By now she had many friends and admirers. They let her know how special she was to them and to the Lord.

Soon after that came graduation. Another celebration.

Martha had to make a decision as to where she would do her ministry. She told me she had ruled out ministering on the streets of the downtown eastside. She concluded it was not safe for a lady to do a street ministry in this area.

In her talk at the graduation ceremony, Martha informed us:

"I see young men and young women from my village and all villages in the country come to the big city. They drift onto skid row. I prayed to Jesus and to our Father in heaven and asked what I could do to stop this migration of our young people into life on the streets which is a hellish existence for many.

Our church back home is dilapidated and not functional. I will go home and have the men build me a church and I will tell everybody about the real Jesus. I'll tell them the truth. Every chance I get I'll tell the parents to keep their young men and young women at home on the reserve," she looked around.

"We'll create jobs for them and make them proud of their heritage," she said proudly. People applauded and gave their approval.

I have a friend who I felt could help Martha in her venture. He is a travelling evangelist who I know preaches in her area. I arranged a meeting with Martha and my friend.

They knew each other, but had lost touch. I put Martha into his care and had her tell him of her vision.

We said our goodbyes as she boarded a bus back to her village in the mountains.

She came back to visit once and told us how her ministry was growing.

"Now young men are staying away from the big city and having careers in the region where they live," she told us proudly.

I often think about Martha. I know she's safe in her home town among the people she knows and loves.

My friend, the travelling evangelist, told me that Martha doesn't have her church building as yet, but she uses the Band hall for her services.

"She has some pretty good worship leaders," He confided. " They pack the hall on special occasions. Martha has a place of honour. She speaks really good and people listen."

He told me how Martha visits many reserves with him and explains the folly of letting their young people go to the city, even for a visit.

He laughed and told me that Martha preaches the gospel better than he does. "She has a great heart for Jesus and for God and she is filled with the Holy Spirit."

A lovely, humble lady who got to know Jesus personally, is now causing many communities to grow spiritually and protect their children and young men and women.

There are many people from all walks of life who were and are associated with the College. Some for a few days others for the full three years or more. They all studied the Word of God and have a relationship with God's beloved Son, Jesus of Nazareth.

Most were filled with the Holy Spirit and had their lives transformed.

People are still enrolling in the Bible College and preparing for ministry.

Each year I get charged up as new students enrol and start their journey to be with Jesus in the Kingdom of God.

A month or so ago, a middle aged man, who heard Martha preach in her native village, and tell the young men and women to stay away from skid row, enrolled in the Bible College.

Martha had prayed for him and she was given a revelation from God that this man has been chosen by God to do a mighty ministry among his people. She encouraged him to come to our College and be prepared for ministry.

She sent a letter of introduction and recommendation.

WE were pleased to welcome him.

In six months of studying God's word and God's ways, he has made it known that the Holy Spirit is moving powerfully in him. He told us he is ready to preach or do whatever he can for the glory of God.

It's our policy to have the students wait for a year before peaching publicly. Elmer practised his preaching in the College. It is so spirit filled and inspiring that he was booked to preach in the Mission.

After the message he told the young men and women to go home to their reserves. The same message that Martha preaches in whatever setting God provides.

Elmer is still in the College and is an inspiration to the younger men and women.

God will move powerfully in those who study the Word of God and make themselves available to do His calling. Those who pray and praise the Lord from their heart, will be changed and become new creations, spiritual beings ready to fulfill God's purpose and plan for their lives.

Martha was a shy and introverted lady from the mountains. Her study, coupled with a desire to do God's will, has allowed the Lord to use her in a mighty way.

She has been radically changed into a true servant of God Almighty.

CHAPTER THIRTY TWO

PIERRE

Drug Dealer

Luke 6:46, "Why do you call me, 'Lord, Lord' And not do what I say? I will show you what he is like who comes to me and hears my words and puts them into practice."

I heard loud talking near the back of the Mission. Loud talking in a French accent. I knew it must be Pierre. He has been asked many times to keep his voice down, but when he gets excited his voice becomes louder and louder.

Sometimes people tease him and get him stirred up. We have to intercede and get both parties to keep quiet after the service starts.

Most people who come into the Mission respect what we are doing and they know they must not disturb the service. Pierre is slowly learning that talking while the word of God goes out in music and preaching, will not be tolerated.

A few days later, it was not only loud talking but an argument that broke out at the back of the Mission. The argument became more and more heated. The next thing I knew, chairs were scraping across the floor and two men were yelling at each other and threatening violence.

Pierre and another man I had not seen before were engaged in this battle of words which led to fists starting to fly. Brian, the bouncer, and two students separated the two and sent the assailant out the door.

Pierre took some time to cool off and collect himself. One of the students stayed with him and talked him down.

As I walked from the back of the Mission up to the podium, one of the street wise regulars said, "Dealer." I nodded that I had heard him and realized we had a problem on our hands.

If Pierre was a dealer, I felt I should intervene and talk to him. The problem was how should I approach this delicate subject. Is he the dealer or is the guy who challenged him the dealer?

After the service was over, I asked Pierre if he would like to come to the office for a chat. He shook his head, refusing to come. I went on to tell him that we can't tolerate the behaviour we had witnessed this evening.

He started to explain in his broken English. His voice was getting louder and louder. People were listening and shaking their heads. I extended the invitation to come to the office once more and Pierre complied.

I asked him point blank if he was a dealer of drugs on the street. He nodded and told me that he was dealing drugs, "Good money, easy stuff. I'm not doing drugs."

"Easy money but dangerous," I replied.

I then asked him about the fight. He said it was a misunderstanding.

"He gave me a ten, I put it in my pocket. He lied to me saying he gave me a twenty. I told him, get lost. Now he wants to fight me. I'm not afraid of that punk."

I asked, "Was that your first fight?" "Not my first," he shook his head.

"Do you think it will be your last fight?"

He replied, "Who knows."

"What if someone comes after you with a knife or a gun?"

"I have to take that chance," he said nonchalantly

I saw a worried look come over him. He started to squirm.

"You know we have a Bible College and a men's dorm and a co-ed dorm. You are more than welcome to come and join us. You can get funding if you qualify."

Pierre thought about it, cocked his head to one side and said, "I'll think about it." He got up and left the office.

Sometimes I get a good feeling when I ask people to enrol in Bible College and change their life. With Pierre, I figured the chances of his coming to the College was one in ten.

Two weeks later, Pierre sat talking to two students. One guy and one girl. These two were our best ambassadors. If someone wants to know about the College, we have them talk to Becky and Jack. I hadn't built up much hope of Pierre's coming to the College.

The next night Pierre asked to speak to me. I went down to his table and waited to hear what he had to say.

"I can't make promises. Maybe yes, maybe not long. But I will try."

I shook his hand and welcomed him. He told me not to build up my hopes.

"Maybe I come Tuesday, OK." I asked if he had considered living in the dorm. Once again it was, "Maybe, we'll see."

I asked what had made him change his mind and give up making easy money. He told me the police warned him. "I had just sold my last rock of cocaine. I was on my way to get more. I didn't know I was under surveillance. They put me in handcuffs and searched me. They found nothing. I didn't confess," he shook his head. "I was that close to going to jail and having a criminal record. They warned me and told me I was being watched. They roughed me up a little and went away."

I told him he was lucky. "They've got your number. You're a marked man."

Pierre told me he didn't want to go to jail. "I'm not a bad man."

Pierre came to Bible College and gave his testimony. He testified that he was an illegitimate baby. "My father, he has a wife and a mistress. This young mistress, she gets pregnant. I come out. My father does not want my mother to know. He makes her send me to an orphanage. This orphanage is run by nuns who are very strict.

As a baby, I don't know nothing. When I was two or three, I started to learn. People come for babies and young children to adopt. I wanted a mother and a father to love me. When big people come, I do my best to get them to adopt me. I push my way to the front. Nuns pull me back and get upset. They tell me, "No, You must wait for people to see that you are a good boy."

"I kept wondering why others got to leave and make these people smile, but they didn't choose me. I was very sad.

As I got older, the nuns made me do the hard work. I gave up hope of ever being adopted. I was now twelve years old. I was strong from the hard work in the orphanage.

One day a big man and a big lady came to choose a baby or a cute girl or a curly haired little boy. I was not going to leave my room, but a nun made me go downstairs. She combed my hair and gave me a used, but nice suit to wear. I was made to shine my shoes and told to smile.

To my surprise and amazement, the big man pointed to me and said, "We'll take that one." I looked behind me, maybe another boy or girl was hiding. The big lady said, "He'll do just fine."

"I went down to their truck. I was squeezed in between the two big people. I was elated. I couldn't wait for them to hug me and tell me I was a good boy and that they loved me.

I didn't know we were going to a farm. We drove and drove. Finally, we turned into a driveway. I thought I was in heaven. A big house, barns, animals, machinery open spaces, pastures, big trees. It was the answer to my prayers," Pierre stopped to think.

"To my dismay, I soon realized that I was their unpaid hired man. There were no hugs and kisses. I sat at the table but was not allowed to talk. The food was good, but the people were cold and distant. They talked about the prices of cattle and grain. I didn't understand. After supper I was told to go to my room. "Get some rest, it's a busy day tomorrow," the big man always told me.

"I was better off in the orphanage. At least I had kids to talk to and to take care of. There was a lot of laughing and joking. Some of the nuns liked to laugh and play tricks. Now I was alone and very lonely.

During the first year, the truant officer came to the farm and told the big man and woman they must send me to school. This upset them, but they had to comply. Before I went to school, I had to get up at five o'clock to do the chores and do whatever work was necessary. I caught the school bus every day.

I liked the school. It was my escape from the drudgery at the farm. When I got home I worked some more.

The big man kept telling me, "You're a useless young man." Or he'd say, "Don't you have a brain in your head?" or "You'll never amount to anything."

At school, they realized I was so far behind the class and that I might never catch up. I took that to mean I was dumb.

I stayed on the farm until I was sixteen. My counsellor at the school heard my story and told me he would help me. I ran away from the farm and those wicked people.

My counsellor at the school intervened. He set me up at a house where the people were nice and caring. It was such a relief. I was in a small city and was able to do as I pleased. I made friends and we were happy to play baseball and soccer.

After graduating on a conditional pass, I had a hard time getting a good job as I only had grade eleven and I probably failed that grade."

Pierre laughed and said proudly, "Now I am in College." Everybody laughed with him.

Pierre took his studies at Bible College seriously. He was a good worker and never shied away from helping and doing his share. He told me we should get a janitor as the place needed a major overhaul. I looked around and agreed that some paint would brighten up the place.

At the next counsel meeting, I brought forward Pierre's suggestion All agreed that a work party should be formed to make the Mission and the College more presentable. Pierre volunteered to head the work party. A budget was set and the work went ahead.

Pierre was in his element. He had a perpetual smile on his face throughout the renovations. No more loud talking and arguing. He was beginning to fit in and be a student.

At my monthly sessions, I ask what is the goal of each student. Some want to have house ministries, others want to plant churches, others want to counsel.

Pierre told us he wanted to start a Mission just like ours in a big french speaking city where he lived in the orphanage. He smiled at the thought.

"But I will need help to start and run my mission." A few people said they would help. Pierre countered, "You must speak french, it is a french city."

Things were going smoothly for Pierre. We were studying the Doctrine of Divine Healing. When we came to the study of 'Inner Healing" Pierre asked for counselling. I did the counselling.

I had told the class that they could do anything according to the purpose and will of God for their lives. I used the scripture:

Ephesians 2:10, "For we are God's workmanship, created in Christ Jesus to do good works, which God has prepared in advance for us to do."

At the beginning of the counselling sessions on Inner Healing, Pierre told me he needed that healing. "I have a tape in my head that keeps playing over and over. It's the big farmers voice which keeps telling me, "You're useless. You're so dumb. You're good for nothing. Don't you have brain in your head? You'll never amount to anything."

I told Pierre that we will erase that tape and replace it with the words of Jesus in the Bible. He agreed and we had many sessions where we went over Bible verses and planted them in his mind. Verses like:

Philippians 4:13, "I can do everything through Him who gives me strength.

Romans 8:28, "And we know that in all things God works for the good of those who love him, who have been called according to His purpose."

Revelation 21:7, "He who overcomes will inherit all this, and I will be his God and he will be my son."

These are but a few of the Bible passages that we planted in the mind of Pierre in place of the toxic messages put there when he was on the farm and some from other sources.

In further counselling, there were others in his life who had had an adverse effect on his self image. With the help of Jesus the Christ and the Holy Spirit, we confronted the issues and resolved them one by one.

It warms my heart when I see people change so radically. His self image improved to the point where he wanted to face a challenge in his life. He came and showed me the brochure from a Computer College which promised great things for those who completed the course. It was a two year course at a College not far from the Bible College.

I asked him if he could handle both courses. He said he'd try.

He had graduated with the one year diploma and was commissioned. He had also completed his second year with good marks. His third year was more than half completed when he enrolled in the Computer College.

It was impossible for him to take both courses. He chose to complete the computer course first and then come back and finish Bible College.

Pierre would come to the Mission once in a while and keep in touch. We enjoyed his stories and the students shared the news of what was happening at the Bible College. He gave his testimony at the Mission.

He challenged all who came off the street to get their life together and make something of their life. He told them how he is going to computer college and will have his own company some day.

He went on to tell them about the toxic tape in his head which caused him to have low self esteem. He told everyone that they need to know Jesus and God. He ended by telling them that the College will teach them all they have to know about the Bible and the commandments of God.

He finished by saying, "If you have a problem in your life, let the Pastor fix it up like he fixed up my life real good."

I was prepared for a flood of those wanting Inner Healing, but it didn't happen I did help two others and then the requests stopped coming.

I was invited to the graduation of Pierre at the Computer College. It was a friendly affair. Only six people were graduating. Pierre was the centre of attention as he had passed with honours.

I suppose others thought their sons or daughters were the centre of attention.

That summer, Pierre returned to the big french speaking city near where he was born. Before he left he told us he would be back in September to complete his final year at Bible College.

A postcard saying he was doing well was our last communication.

Pierre went from being a drug dealer with a grade eleven education to a Bible College second year graduate and a degree from a Computer College.

He has been radically changed in many ways. He now has a good self image and a career. He also has a walk with the Lord and is commissioned to do ministry.

Before he left for his French city, he told us he would make big money at his computer business and he would open a Mission and Bible College just like ours. Our prayers for this venture are with Pierre.

CHAPTER THIRTY THREE

DON

Ex Convict Addict

Psalm 62:8,11 "Trust in God at all times, O people; pour out your hearts to him, for God is our refuge. One thing God has spoken, two things have I heard: that you, O God are strong, and that you, O Lord, are loving.

I can usually tell when a person comes to the Mission after being released.

They come from prison looking healthy and refreshed. filled with joy at being free at last. Many want to take part in the Mission and some of them come to Bible College. We share their exhilarating feeling of freedom and welcome them with open arms.

The problem for many is that they get back onto the street and take what it has to offer. What it has to offer is destructive to the body, mind and soul. I watch them go down hill and eventually either move on or get buried.

We do memorial services upon request and grieve with the mourners.

For the fortunate ones who go home or move away from the street, we often get a phone call thanking us for giving the message that life on the street is not God's plan for them. The message goes out from the pulpit that God does not want people to waste their time, resources and their life living on skid row, being a slave to their addictions, lusts and desires.

When DON came to the Mission, I was pretty sure that he had been in jail and was recently released. He had that fresh, macho look.

I didn't speak to him right away. I nodded, in order to acknowledge his presence. I don't push myself onto people. I wait for them to come back to the Mission a few times. When the right time comes, I will welcome them and talk to them about coming to Bible College.

My introduction to him was when the Captain of the dormitory came with Don and introduced him. The Captain told me that Don had no money, but he needed a place to stay. Don interrupted and told me he would pay in full when his money came through.

"I've got a wife," he said, "she's sending me some money from our account."

The captain told me he was taking Don to Human Resources and he would receive money from the government's emergency fund. Don told me that Darryl will be with him when he gets the money from the government.

"I'll give him money for the rent," Don confided.

I gave the O.K. We gained a renter and a Bible College student.

Don seemed alright. I was waiting for his testimony, which was usually given at the Mission and again in front of the class. He is tall and well built with broad shoulders; good looking and well groomed. He has a perpetual smile which brightens up the room.

At the Mission, after the gospel music was finished, it was testimony time.

Don was nervous and I felt he might be holding back a bit of information.

In his testimony, he told how he was brought up on a farm, but he wanted to explore and see what city life was like. He went to the city when he was twenty and got a job in a car wash. This city is hundreds of miles from our city. Don went on to tell how he got into trouble and was charged with some minor offenses. For these he received a fine and some community hours.

"I tried to clean up my act, but I kept hanging with the wrong crowd. I got myself in more trouble and this time I got a short jail sentence.

When I got out I swore I would clean up my act. I went home and helped my dad on the farm. On Saturday nights I'd get hooked up with other farm hands and we'd get plastered.

After a few weeks of that, I was introduced to weed. It gave me a buzz, which I thought was great. I only used on week-ends. I was happy enough to have a toke once a week.

One of my school buddies, a farm hand on his father's farm, introduced me to cocaine. That led to crystal meth.

My father is a great guy and a hard core Christian. He got wind of what I was doing on weekends. The truth is, I had a stash in the hay loft. I think my dad smelled the weed burning. However it happened, he asked me to get help. As a matter of fact he insisted I get help to take away my drug habit.

I was ashamed more than anything, so I moved to the city again. I should have taken my dad's advice, but I was young and naive. I thought I could kick my habit on my own and in my own way.

The need for drugs did me in. I ran out of money and I needed a fix. The guy I was running with talked me into a break and enter job. He told me he had a place staked out. He explained where it was and I knew it was in a classy part of town. We got caught and I did more jail time.

There was another serious offense, but I dodged it.

When I got out I met a lady. She helped me get a place to stay and get back on my feet. I told her I'd pay her back when the money started coming in. She helped me get a job which paid big bucks.

We got to the point where we planned to get married. I was on cloud nine.

The bubble burst when I was pulled over for speeding. They did a computer check and found that I had an outstanding warrant for my arrest dating back three years.

I had pushed it out of my mind and hoped they would forget about it. Assault and battery with the intent to maim. I was drunk and can't remember exactly what happened.

I was devastated and my lady was so shook up she asked for time to think about it. That's the last I saw or heard from her.

Any excuse I made would not have made a difference. I did my two years and now I'm clean. I've got a wife who will join me when she gets things together.

I'm going to Bible College and I'm turning my life around. I want to make my dad proud of me. He'll love the idea of my becoming a preacher."

People clapped and a few came up after the service and shook his hand.

Don was smiling and felt so much better at having it all out in the open. For him it was a new life with a beautiful wife.

Don came to class regularly. It was evident that he came from a Christian home as he had a good understanding of the basic principles of Christianity. He liked to pray and sing gospel songs. During class he had answers to most of the questions. If he answered wrongly, he'd say, "I remember now."

It got to be a bit of a joke as others would say, "I remember now, how could I forget?" Don took the ribbings with a smile.

Two months passed quickly but there was no wife. Don would take long walks by himself. He got the reputation of being a loner.

Then came a startling discovery. The guys in the dorm told me he was displaying signs of drug dependance and he was on the verge of drug abuse. They knew the early signs.

I had him come to the office for a visit. We talked about his long walks and I asked him what thoughts he entertained. He was shocked and asked me, "What are you thinking?" I told him, "I've been informed that perhaps you're flirting with the idea of having a hit or a toke." He buried his head in his arms and sobbed. "It's the pain." he sobbed, "My muscles ache." I asked him if he was ready for a session at a rehabilitation centre.

He shook his head and exclaimed, "I can't do that."

I asked him, "So what will you do?"

"I'll fight it. I'll pray and let Jesus take away the urge."

I agreed and told him we would pray and ask for release from his addiction.

I offered another recommendation, "Every time you leave the house or the Mission, I want you to be with a buddy, understand." He nodded his approval.

I asked for volunteers and three of the students agreed to help him.

After that everything ran smoothly for Don. He was no longer distant and hiding his secret desires. It was all out in the open. I heard some students pray with him and our prayers were answered. The pain and the desire for drugs lessened and then went away.

I was at lunch with the students and sat at a table with Don and four others. Two guys and two girls were talking and joking. Don was day dreaming. One of the girls said, "A penny for your thoughts." Don came back to reality and told them he was thinking about the farm and his brothers family "You really love the farm don't you?" Cindy asked.

Don nodded, "It's my real home."

Darryl asked, "Will you and your wife end up on the farm?"

Don shook his head in the negative.

He told all at the table, "My wife and I were travelling from one city to another. I took a short detour and went to the farm. My brother's wife answered the door and was in shock when she saw me. She invited us in and called to my brother in a disturbed voice. He came out of the den where he had been doing the books. He told his wife to get the kids upstairs. I felt like a pariah, something unclean. I asked where my father was. He told me he was in town at a church meeting. I told him we were just passing through and wanted to see the farm.

My brother told me, "That's a good idea." He headed for the door and put on his coat. He invited us outside and we walked around the buildings. He showed us the improvements and told about his plans for the future. They didn't include us. He all but ignored my wife, which really hurt me as she's an angel." Don looked out the window and shook his head. "I felt his disdain and his contempt. To him I was something foul as I was a drug addict and an ex convict. There was no invitation to come back or wait to visit my father. Only a curt goodbye.

We got in the car and I was shaking. I had to pull over and let my wife drive into town. That's probably the last time I'll see the farm."

There was no more joking or laughing that day. His story affected us all.

The good news, a few days later, was that his wife, Lorna was on her way. I really wanted to meet this angel, who was his wife.

The next day, we were in the Mission. Don walked in. I looked and thought, "I didn't know he had a daughter."

Don was introducing his daughter to everyone. She was no older than sixteen or perhaps seventeen. He brought her over to were I was and introduced her as his wife. I looked in disbelief. Don saw my reaction. He smiled proudly.

Don was forty or more and this was his wife? It was incredible. I forced a smile and welcomed her into the Mission family. I had two of the lady students come and attend to her needs.

Don and Lorna were given the largest bedroom in the co-ed dorm. It had a view of the alley where addicts did their thing. I prayed that she wouldn't get hooked.

At Bible College, she had a hard time fitting in as she had very little knowledge of the Bible. I heard Don tell her not to answer any questions unless she knew for certain the answer was correct.

Don adored his wife and catered to all her needs. They always walked hand in hand. Don had stars in his eyes. We stopped the buddy system and relied upon Lorna to keep her husband clean and free from drugs.

I had my usual little chat with Lorna in my office. Don waited outside. She told me that her parents were not happy with their marriage. They thought she was too young to be married and that she should marry a much younger man. She confided that she was very happy and needed Don as much as he needed her. She was quite mature for her age.

She told me, "His family treats him like an outcast, but really he is so kind and gentle." She told about their visit to the farm. "Don was really hurt when his brother got rid of him as fast as he could. Don was looking forward to being an uncle to his brother's kids. She hurried them upstairs as though Don was a leper or worse."

I asked, "What about you? What do you see as your future?" She looked at the floor and then sat erect. "We have it all planned. Don will graduate from the College and I will finish and graduate as well. We will do a ministry. That will really please his father. It is our only hope of his getting back into his family's good books."

I asked her about her education and her family background. She told me she had two older brothers and a younger sister. From what I could learn she had a happy childhood. "I will take upgrading in order to complete my grade twelve." She told me how she had met Don and he had swept her off her feet.

I felt this was infatuation rather than true love, but I kept quiet.

I watched the two of them and wondered what a sixteen year old saw in an older man who had been around and had been in and out of jail and on and off drugs.

The girls in the class treated her as an equal and welcomed her into the Mission and the College. She laughed along with the others and fitted in nicely. I felt she was making progress and had a desire to learn. She was quite bright and definitely mature for her age. She was not a clinging vine, but rather she took control of the marriage when necessary.

She missed a few days of College as she was sick. I thought she had a touch of the flu. An older female student told others in the class that Lorna had morning sickness. We all knew what that meant.

Don came to class three days later and broke the news. "Lorna's pregnant and we're going to have a baby, isn't that great!" he exuded.

For the next nine months everyone watched as Lorna got bigger and was about to give birth. It happened and she delivered a beautiful baby girl. Lorna cared for her and people brought clothes and blankets. The mission announced the birth and asked anyone who had a buggy or stroller to let us know and we would pick it up.

Six months later, it was second year graduation for Don and the first year for Lorna. The students loved little Patricia. She was the queen of the graduating class.

After graduation came a break. Don got a job in order to support his family. He and Lorna moved into a new apartment. I felt we were going to lose them from the College. If so, I knew they had a good spiritual foundation to build on.

To my surprise, Don and Lorna, along with Patricia, came and asked to speak to me. I was pleased to learn that they had come back to enrol in the College.

In the middle of the third year for Don, two of our other third year students , Ben and Becky were planning on planting a church in a village where we often went on student outreaches. They felt they knew enough people in that town to make it a success.

Don and Lorna were asked to be part of the Church plant after graduation. They came for my advice.

I asked many questions such as: "Do you share their vision?" "Are you compatible with them?" "What is your goal?" "Do you feel God is calling you to this ministry?" And other pertinent questions.

I wrote the questions down and told them to pray earnestly about this move. "Be very certain as it is a big step. But if it is God's will then it will be a blessing."

Before they gave their answer, I heard from Ben that Don and Lorna were going to assist them in this church planting venture.

Ben told me he had already been to this town and had secured a building to use in their church plant. He had stayed at the home of our contact persons in the town and they encouraged him to start his church.

I felt it was happening too quickly, but I wasn't going to stand in the way of progress.

I suggested that they go to the town and start a Bible Study group in the home of our contact person. As well, they could start home churches in the surrounding native reserves, as Becky is a first nations lady and has knowledge of their culture. "When you have a good solid core group, then start your church," was my advice.

Ben didn't heed my advice and he gathered together a team of eight from the College and Mission to help him launch this new church. I asked why he had chosen two who had not attended Bible College. He ignored my questioning.

I sent them off with my blessing and we prayed for them at the Bible College and again at the Mission. Don and Lorna along with Patricia went to the town and I heard they were happy to be away from the big city.

For the first year and a half there were good reports about the church plant. All was going well. The people in the town were pleased to have a place to come and worship the Lord three nights a week and on Sunday mornings.

I was distressed to hear that one by one the team began to unravel. I wasn't too surprised as I felt that Ben could be too aggressive and too self centred. At times it was either his way or the highway.

I also knew that Don was not one to be pushed around without pushing back.

Don and Lorna came back to the Mission but only for a visit. They told me what had happened with that ministry. How it fell apart. They also told me that Ben and Becky had started house churches in the surrounding native villages and a house church in the town. I nodded in agreement to this venture as this was my advice from the beginning.

Don and Lorna told us of their new venture in this town. Don was now the assistant pastor in a main stream church with a growing congregation. He was taking a correspondence course which that church denomination offered. He was due to be ordained as soon as he graduated and the paperwork was completed.

I was really happy for them. I still marvelled at a forty four year old man being married to a nineteen year old girl. But the marriage was blessed by God and that is the most important factor.

Don went from being a hard core addict and a wanted criminal to being a hard core Christian now to be ordained in a large denomination. A radical change.

We at the Mission and College are blessed by being part of this change.

CHAPTER THIRTY FOUR

BRENT

Occult Practitioner

Micah 7:8, "Tho I have fallen, I will rise. Though I sit in darkness I have seen a great light. The Lord will bring me out into the light. I will see His righteousness."

I had taught pubic school for twenty six years. During that time I bought land and subdivided it. I became a part time contractor, building and selling houses as well as teaching in a High School.

I took early retirement and pursued a less stressful career. I could work my own hours. It paid the bills. As well, I became a professional volunteer.

We joined a church and I became active. I was asked to be an elder. I was then promoted to the official board. The congregation outgrew the sanctuary and I was appointed to raise funds for a new church building.

After that we sold everything and left the small town and travelled.

We settled in this large city and became involved in a prison ministry. I met Jack and ended up volunteering at the Mission. From there I went to Bible College.

When I enrolled in my third and final year, of Bible College, Brent enrolled in his first year.

Brent is a tall, handsome, well built and well dressed young man in his early thirties.

He opted to live in the dormitory and serve in the Mission.

I live with my wife in the suburbs and commute to the downtown eastside in order to go to Bible College and serve in the Mission. I was taking my final year of Bible College when Brent enlisted in the College.

I listened to Brent's testimony to the class.

"I am married and have two children, two boys. Jake is eight and Liam is six. My wife is a teacher and highly qualified.

When I was in high school, I got a job at a construction supply company in a neighbouring community. After graduating from high school, I had the opportunity of going to university. The owner of the supply company talked me into working in his firm with the promise of taking over the business when he retired. He had no sons and no heirs. He gave me a big raise and treated me like his son. The bonuses were an incentive to work hard and increase sales.

My wife and I were financially stable and able to buy a new house, car, furniture and all the toys for the boys. A boat, motor home, two motorcycles and a four wheeled drive.

Everything was top of the line as we were living on two large salaries..

Ten years later, the owner's nephew came to work at the supply company. He started while he was in grade eleven. He came after school and on Saturdays. He followed the same work pattern that I worked at first. I was told to teach him all I knew about the business.

I didn't mind as it made my workload easier and I could spend more time going out to construction sites and drumming up business and getting big commissions.

After graduation, the nephew took over as a full time employee. My hours were cut. I worked mostly on a commission basis. I knew that I was losing my job.

My dream of taking over the business vanished. It caused me so much stress I had a nervous breakdown.

This breakdown further diminished my possibility of getting a high paying job.

For two years I applied to many employers and submitted my resume. Most ignored my application, a few said they'd get back to me if I was accepted. The interviews I had were to no avail. I was offered low paying jobs which I declined.

I became more and more despondent. My wife insisted on helping me. We sat down and went through all possible scenarios. All possible jobs that I could handle and where I could be successful.

A teacher at her school told her about a friend of her husband's who went to Bible College and now has a position in a church as the Youth Pastor. He's doing really well and loves his job.

My wife arranged for me to go and talk to him and find out how I might qualify for such a position.

He suggested that I come to this College as he felt it would be a good way to get started in a career."You get hands on training at the affiliated Mission," he encouraged. Then you can transfer to the more prestigious college.

I am living in the dormitory and will be going home on weekends."

I felt that Brent would make a good leader as he was gaining confidence and poise. He carried himself well and had a good personality.

We were studying Pneumatology which is the doctrine of the Holy Spirit. We were to the part where the teacher was informing us of the role of the Holy Spirit in the life of Jesus Christ when he was on the earth. How Jesus, as a human, was begotten by the Holy Spirit. Matthew 1:18, "...She, Mary, was found to be with child through the Holy Spirit."

The teacher went on to tell how Jesus was led into the wilderness by the Holy Spirit and cared for by angels before being tempted by Satan. And how the Holy Spirit anointed Jesus with power for his ministry.

It was all new to Brent as he had very little knowledge of spiritual matters. He persevered and gained as much head knowledge as he could.

He lived in the dormitory and often studied until lights out at one in the morning.

Many times he asked me for interpretation of lessons he was learning. I shared what knowledge I had and together we learned.

Brent attended his first Student Counsel Meeting. I happened to be the chairman as third year students take turns being in charge.

As it was the first meeting of the year, we went over the minutes of the last meeting. The first year students received the Operating Manual which laid out the procedures and the points of order. They sat along the side of the room while the second and third year students sat around the counsel table.

The next outreach was scheduled for the town where Ben and Becky were operating their native house churches. It was also where Don and Lorna were very active in a large church in the town.

I allowed the first year students to ask questions about outreaches. Brent asked if they were mandatory. I told him they were. He must attend at least three in the first year.

Others asked about duties in the Mission and about holidays. All questions were answered by third year students or the staff representative.

Brent signed up for the first outreach.

On the seven hour trip to the town of Ben and Don, Brent read his Bible and did his homework.

On the first few outreaches the first year students observe and learn. The services are the responsibility of the second and third year students.

I went on the outreach as part of my commitment. I enjoyed outreaches,

The staff representative on this first outreach fulfilled his duties.

We were to stay at Ben and Becky's apartment and at another Christian lady's place who gave up her house and stayed at her sister's house with her family.

We occupied her house during our visit.

I was to stay at the Christian lady's house .I knew her from a previous Rally held in recognition of an elder who had passed away a year before.

I talked to her on the phone from Ben's house She told me she was glad that I was staying at her house. She didn't know the Staff representative. She told me that she had a request. I wondered what this request might be.

The house was a two level newer type home on the reserve. Very nice on the outside.

Thelma, the owner of the house, was there to greet us and get us settled. She asked me to come to the living room for a chat. I invited the staff representative and had him come with me.

She told us her history and what it was like living on the reserve. She ended by telling us that her husband had committed suicide three weeks earlier in the basement of the house.

"Please pray that all those evil spirits will leave the house and never come back again," she pleaded.

We told her we would pray and have a vigil. I asked Thelma if she would like to take part. She told me she would rather not.

We enjoyed her house after we got it cleaned up a bit. We prayed that any spirit that was not of God, must leave. We also took oil, blessed it and made the sign of a cross over all doorways. We prayed that anyone entering this house and living in this house would be blessed and in the care of God Almighty and Jesus the Christ.

Brent wanted to know the significance of each action. We informed him and he was happy to learn. He told the students, "This is hands on stuff. We're really fortunate to be on these outreaches."

The next morning, Brent helped Roy get breakfast under way. He got up early and read his Bible and prayed.

I watched and knew that he was special. So much learning in such a short time.

At the Mission, he gave a testimony about what happened on the outreach.

"Imagine being in a house where someone committed suicide three weeks earlier. We prayed and drove out all the evil spirits. We prayed again and blessed the oil which we put above the doorway of each room. Man, am I ever learning a lot in the Bible College and on the outreaches.

If any of you guys wants to get right with the Lord, come and join us. It's a lot better than being on the street."

The wife of Brent never came to the Mission or the College. When Brent graduated after one year and was commissioned, I knew how much it meant to him. I was sorry noone from his family turned up for his graduation.

On the other hand this was my final graduation. My wife and a number of friends came to my graduation. I invited Brent to join our group. At first he stayed by himself. I motioned for him to come over and be introduced. He did so and the rest of the night was a celebration.

I had already been offered a position on the teaching staff of the Bible College. After much prayer I accepted. I did so as a volunteer as I knew money was tight at the Mission and the College. I'd rather see the money go to students who really are short of cash and who need what the College can offer.

I was to teach Eschatology, 'The doctrine of Last Things.' I had taken the course but I realized I had a great deal of research to do in order to teach the subject at the College level. I did a lot of research and prayed a great deal as there were concepts I didn't understand. I only had two months during the summer to make final preparations to teach the subject.

It was not only Eschatology but also Divine Healing and the Pentateuch, which are the first five books of the Bible, which were given me as subjects to teach in the first semester.

I had my work cut out for me.

Brent left the dorm for the summer and went to work. I never did ask what he worked at and he never shared that information.

The next two years Brent was in my classes. He continued to learn and be amazed at the knowledge he had stored in his brain and at his disposal.

I determined that much of the learning was not travelling from his brain to his heart. In other words, I didn't see much of the Spirit of God in his written work and in his character in general. I was too busy to do a complete analysis of where he was spiritually.

When I taught Divine Healing, I gave some examples of where God used me as a vessel and people were healed.

One example was when our drummer was working on a construction site. He was operating a pneumatic drill and hit a piece of metal. The drill jumped sideways and twisted his elbow. He told me the doctor informed him he would need surgery and he wouldn't be able to work for six months.

He asked me to pray for healing from God.

I prayed that the Holy Spirit would be active in the healing process.

I also prayed that by the stripes, (the wounds) of Jesus, healing would take place. I felt heat in my right hand. I put his elbow in my right hand and put my left hand on his shoulder. I prayed for healing. I felt the healing touch of God go into his injured elbow.

I told the young man that he was healed. "Now you must claim your healing. It must be your testimony every day."

I also told him he might feel pain for a few days, but ignore it. "You are spiritually healed. Keep your testimony positive."

He kept coming to the Mission. I wanted to ask him if he was healed. The Holy Spirit told me to keep quiet and let the healing be completed.

Three weeks later I was in the Mission. He came and told me he was healed and has been back at work for a week. I thanked God for his great power, the Great Physician at work in the lives of those who believe.

At a class break, Brent asked me if I would pray for the healing of his body. I started to pray to the Holy Spirit and told him I would pray for his healing. I asked if it was anything specific.

He told me that when he was young, he was playing street hockey.

"I got body checked and tripped over a curb. I fell and hurt my back. It's been painful ever since," he explained.

I wasn't told whether it was the upper middle or lower back. I let the Holy Spirit guide my hand as I prayed for his healing. I put my hand on his back and felt a vertebra pop out and the vertebra above pop in. I knew he was healed. God is a great chiropractor.

I told Brent that his testimony must be, "I am healed."

A day later, Brent told me the pain was not severe, but it was still there. I told him in spiritual healing, there will be phantom pain but it will go away. Only believe.

Brent went on other outreaches and asked if his son might accompany him on an outreach up north. I was the one who had to take the request to the staff counsel meeting. They felt this might set a precedence and soon the bus would be full of children with no room for the students.

I conveyed the news to Brent who accepted it gracefully.

Brent graduated after his second year. He applied for ordination and was accepted. He worked weekends and occasionally went home to visit his family.

His wife still refused to come to the College or the Mission. I believe she felt there was a stigma at being seen on skid row.

Brent was in his last year. His grades were well above average.

I had noticed for the last six months that Brent disappeared after class and didn't come back to the dormitory until late at night, just before curfew.

I asked a couple of the guys if Brent had a job. They told me he had extra cash these days.

I was happy for him as I knew he lived on an allowance from his wife.

For Brent, it was final graduation. I wondered if his wife and children would be coming to congratulate him. I was happy to see that two friends of his did make it to the celebration. These two friends, a young man and a middle aged woman were dressed rather funky. Not the type I'd expect Brent to hang around with.

Brent seemed to care for them and there was a lot of chatter and laugher.

A week after graduation, Brent came to the Mission at noon hour. I greeted him. I asked what he was doing. He told me he had a job.

"As a matter of fact I've been working telling fortunes for the past six months," he told me.

I was shocked. It was the last thing I would expect any student to be involved in.

Brent recognized my disbelief. He went on to tell me that he was really very good at it. "I have many clients who really believe I have a connection to the unknown and to a higher source. I make good money and even better tips," he bragged.

I counselled him and told him what the Bible says about the occult.

Deuteronomy 18:10, "Let no one be found among you who is a medium or a fortune teller.... as they are detestable to the Lord."

He told me he was in a hurry as he had to get back to work.

I didn't see Brent for two years except on the street once in a while. I knew he was not living in our neighbourhood.

At the Mission, two years later, I was told that Brent was in the hospital. I asked which one. They told me the General Hospital in the Psychiatric ward.

I felt it might have something to do with his getting mixed up in the occult.

I visited him. He was sedated but he knew me and wanted to tell his story.

He told me he was living in a flea bag hotel. "There are some really weird characters living in this hotel. I was afraid of them, but I can't afford luxury." He paused to think. "At times I'd hear voices when there was no one in the room. They told me weird things. They told me if I didn't take the punishment I deserve, my kids would die," he paused and shook his head.

"I was so scared. I love my kids. They have nothing to do with this. I yelled at the voice and told it to stop and go away. But it laughed and made weird sounds."

Brent stopped and looked behind him. I waited.

"I heard someone with heavy boots coming down the hallway. I didn't recognize the sound these boots made. I knew he was coming to kill me as I had to take my punishment or my kids would be killed." Brent paused. A look of dismay and unbelief on his countenance.

"I was sitting on the window sill with the window wide open," he paused.

"I was so freaked out knowing I was going to die, that I fell out the window down two storeys onto a bunch of junk people had thrown away between the two buildings. There were old mattresses, cardboard and other stuff.

Someone saw me fall. I was lying there unable to get up. They called the police and an ambulance."

He looked at me for a response.

"Were there any injuries or broken bones?" I asked.

Brent said it was a miracle that nothing was broken and there were no internal injuries.

I asked, "Can we pray together?" Brent told me he'd like that. We prayed.

I had a Bible and gave it to Brent. He told me he had a Bible but someone had stolen it.

I visited him a few times. I met his mother and father who had came over from the island. But I never met his wife or kids.

Brent and I went for coffee a couple of times and had long conversations. He told me he had been through some horrible experiences.

"It was all wrong. All so terribly wrong. It was really crazy!" he confided.

Brent was radically changed for a time. When he came to Bible College. He then slipped back and bottomed out.

When we prayed together, he told me he was grabbing onto the hand of Jesus and will never let go. I prayed for deliverance from demons that were binding him to the occult and keeping him out of the Kingdom of God.

At a later visit, Brent told me that these demons had been cast out. He told me one night he was in deep prayer. "I was repeating the twenty-third psalm and praying my heart out. I heard something fall on the floor beside my bed. I looked down and saw a black jellylike blob on the floor with one large eye in the middle. I knew it had come out of the middle of me. It wanted to come back into me. I kicked it and told it in the name of Jesus Christ of Nazareth, to leave and never come back again .It disappeared. I felt relieved. I knew Jesus wanted me back in his kingdom."

Another time when I visited Brent, it was a similar deliverance from evil spirits. Brent told me, "I was praying to God in the name of Jesus. I had been reading my Bible for two hours. I was in the presence of God Almighty. I prayed fervently. I knew something had come out of me and fallen on the floor. It looked like an armadillo with brown plates on its back and its two eyes looked at me with a pathetic look. I prayed again in the name of Jesus the Christ of Nazareth and told it to leave and go to Jesus. I had Jesus deal with it.

Brent is a prayer warrior now and I know he will never leave the Lord again.

He clutched the Bible I gave him and I know he will read it and be healed. He learned his lesson the hard way.

He thanked me for the Bible College which taught him so much. He said he still has his notes and his text books

"I'm starting all over again reviewing all I learned. I will become a spirit filled Christian and then I will pursue a career which will be a blessing to others. I owe it to the Lord who saved my life and redeemed me from the pit of despair."

I prayed that the Holy Spirit would lead him along the path which is God's will for his life.

He was released from the ward. He went to live with his mother and father until he was well enough to go home. Brent told me his wife didn't want the kids to see him in his present condition.

I agreed that was a wise decision. We have been in touch and he is now a paid worker at a detention home for young offenders. They honoured his graduation diploma from our College. He is taking a course in counselling youth and those with personality disorders.

One never knows the path God has prepared for those who will come back to Him and do His will.

CHAPTER THIRTY FIVE

PASTORS, TEACHERS AND STAFF

Volunteers

Proverbs 3:19, "My son, preserve sound judgment and discernment, do not let them out of your sight; they will be life to you, an ornament to grace your neck. Then you will go your way in safety, and your foot will not stumble; when you lie down, your sleep will be sweet."

The founder of the Mission on the Downtown Eastside, was always interested in the Native culture. When he was young and starting his ministry after his graduation from a prestigious Bible College, he ministered on native reserves getting to know the culture and the beliefs of First Nation's people.

An older man, who later ministered on the streets of the Downtown Eastside, told us in his testimony that the now Senior Pastor, when he was young, would come to their drinking house on the reserve early in the morning, before they got too drunk. "He'd tell us about Jesus and His Father, God Almighty, and the Holy Spirit."

We'd give this young man a hard time and tell him to leave us alone. I was a rebel and caused him a lot of trouble," he laughed. "The strange thing is I did listen to him and his thoughts stuck in my head. I'd have to drink lots in order to blot these thoughts out. When I was sober, these thoughts just kept coming back," he smiled."

"Look at me now. Jesus grabbed me and He won't let me go. I love that man from Galilee." This led him to sing that gospel song. "I love that man from Galilee."

One day he told us, "When I preach on the street, people tell me, "Go to hell."

I tell them, "Go to heaven," he'd laugh.

Coming to the big city, the Senior Pastor married and kept ministering, along with earning a living in the daytime. He planted churches in the big city, but none really flourished. He did gain a small following of loyal believers.

A traumatic event, the death of a prostitute near his home, broke his heart. He cried out to God and to Jesus and asked what he could do. His prayer was answered. God drew him to the downtown eastside and told him to move his ministry to the streets of skid row

He started by doing a street ministry; getting to know the people. He went into the bars and talked to whoever would listen to him about his plan to start a mission in their area. With his small band of faithful followers, he started the Mission

He scouted the area and visited the existing missions; all the time in prayer. God led him to a vacant hall, which used to be a dance hall. It had to be completely renovated to meet God's needs. The crew worked many hours in order to meet the deadline set by the owner of the building for occupancy.

It was decided to have three services a week starting at one in the morning until three. The decision hinged on the availability of volunteers.

The offering to the people from the street was hotdogs and coffee. Juice when available.

After three months and no growth in clientele and a lack of volunteers who wanted to stay up all night, it was decided to open at nine in the evening and close around eleven or twelve.

These are the hours of operation to this day

Later, a morning service from eleven until one in the afternoon became the right time to operate a second service.

The meagre offering of hot dogs is now changed to a plate of food according to whatever is donated by food wholesalers and retailers.

At first, the men and women who came to the mission talked loudly and were out of control. Upon requests from the pulpit to honour God's house and make it a quiet and safe place to meet, the noise level decreased and stopped altogether during the services. Except for the occasional outburst and disruption.

New people to the Mission are told by the regulars to be quiet when the worship service is in progress.

After three years of operation and more volunteers than could be utilized, the Holy Spirit told the founder, and now Senior Pastor, to fulfill the great commission

Matthew 28:19, "Therefore go and make disciples of all nations, baptizing them in the name of the Father and of the Son and of the Holy Spirit teaching them to obey everything I have commanded them."

The key words are "teaching them to obey everything I have commanded."

The idea of a Bible College on or near skid row was unheard of. By this time I was on staff as a volunteer. I had taught in the public school system at the High School level and had a Master's Degree. The Senior Pastor's wife was working on a Master's Degree and the other teacher had a Bachelor's degree. We felt we had competent teachers to teach at the College level.

Talks with a prestigious college operated by the same denomination earned us the right to have our courses recognized for credits in their system.

They helped set up the curriculum and the standard of teaching.

The calibre of teachers along with a College level curriculum attracted persons from all areas of the region. We didn't advertise, except in the Mission, as we had enough students to fill all the spaces available.

Most of the students walked in off the street.

Our quota for them was higher than for those who could afford to go to another College.

By then we also had a dormitory for students who desired to live in a Christian community.

I went to Bible College and graduated then taught at the College. I am still teaching at a College on skid row; training students for the ministry. I am a volunteer in the Mission as a preacher a worship leader and pastor in charge. God has supplied my needs adequately for these past fourteen years.

The joy of teaching is reward enough in the Downtown Eastside on skid row.

There are times of excitement and achievement and times of trials and testing.

Our students are trained at the Mission to work in the kitchen, clean up and carry in supplies. After one year of training in the College, the students preach and lead worship at the Mission. They also control the rowdies and witness to them.

This is all chronicled in the mini biographies of the students.

It is not always smooth sailing and without challenges. There are conflicts which face the staff, pastors, teachers and students. Three of the teachers are also pastors as we preach, teach and work in the Mission.

****

At one point in time, when I was in the Mission, a young first nations man would glare at me. I didn't know him and he had no reason for his actions. He would stand at the entrance and if I preached, he would glare as if he were angry or hated me. It is very disconcerting to have someone act in such a manner especially when you have to preach in the Spirit.

I thought I should confront him and ask him if he had a problem with me or with the ministry. I had second thoughts as I had been cursed and verbally abused by others like him. The other thing is that I had to go home after eleven at night on the skid row. If he met me outside, would he beat me up?

One night I was at the Mission to evaluate a sermon being preached by one of the second year students. I sat in the middle of the second row. Other students were gathered in the side seats near the front.

Without provocation, I was hit hard on the shoulder. I turned and saw the one who glares at me sitting behind me. Some of the students saw the attack. They yelled at the glarer, "Don't you dare hit our pastor. Get out of here, you coward!"

The glarer, who was already angry, went in amongst the students and pommelled Nick who was sitting and yelling at him. Three students forced him to leave the mission. Others asked me if I was alright. I checked my physical condition and there was no pain. I apologized to Nick for taking the beating. He said it was not a problem.

****

The Senior Pastor was not without such incidences. He decided to go down the row of men waiting to be served and shake hands welcoming them to the Mission. One big man, for no apparent reason, hit the pastor as hard as he could in the solar plexis.

Anyone who has been hit in this region knows you lose your breath and the pain is severe. The perpetrator was pushed out of line by the regulars and told to leave.

This happened three times over a six month period. The man came dressed differently and was not recognized by the pastor. The last time the pastor was so distressed, he got in his car to go and find this man. Upon thinking about it he wondered what he would say if he met him. He forgave him and came back to the Mission and enjoyed the service.

****

Another time I was in charge of the Mission. All was going well. There were no outbreaks of violence , cursing or loud shouting. I took my ususal look around the Mission to see who was present. I was horrified at what I observed.

Old Mike, a big first nations man, had a young sixteen year old boy, the son of a volunteer, pinned against the wall by the scuff of the neck. The boy's feet were a foot off the floor. I rushed over and grabbed the left arm of Old Mike and pushed him away, allowing the boy to escape. I told Mike we don't do those things in God's house. I grabbed him by his shirt and walked him backwards to a vacant chair and sat him down.

Later, one of the regulars, who witnessed the incident, told me that the boy told old Mike, "You stink." It was true, but you don't mess with old Mike.

****

One night, the Senior Pastor of the Mission was near the kitchen and a man was unruly and using the 'f' word among other expletives. The pastor told him if he was going to keep acting out and talking like that he could leave. The man was a big burly guy and was under the influence of alcohol. He asked the Senior pastor rudely, "Who the hell do you think you are?" The pastor stood his ground and told him, "You've been warned." The big guy started to tussle with the pastor. He tore the shirt off the pastors back.

****

All staff members work in the kitchen in order to show others that we are servants of God. Mission policy is that each person gets one cup of coffee and waits in line for another cup of coffee. We don't fill thermoses or other containers.

A man came to the Mission with a large container, an ice cream bucket. It would probably hold forty cups of coffee. I offered him a cup of coffee, he presented me with the container. I poured the cup of coffee into the bottom of his container. He was livid. I told him, "You have your cup of coffee." I was about to serve the next person. He grabbed for me but I saw it coming and stepped back. He saw a kitchen knife on the side counter. He lunged over the counter to grab the knife and stab me. A regular grabbed his leg and pulled him back onto the floor. He left the Mission threatening me as to what he was going to do to me when he caught me outside.

****

I had another confrontation over the coffee and toast rule. A man from the street asked for four slices of toast. "I need them for my girlfriend," he demanded. I told him to bring his girlfriend to the Mission. I broke the rule by giving him two slices of toast and his coffee.

I was about to serve the next in line when I saw a frisbee flying toward my head. It turned out to be his second slice of toast. I ducked just in time.

****

It wasn't just the men who caused trouble with the rules.

The unbreakable rule was you lined up and didn't sneak in line in front of a friend or someone you knew.

Laura, a lady of the night, would never stand in line. She knew I was watching the line up on a Saturday morning. Deliberately, she came in and found a person she knew who was about tenth from the kitchen. She wiggled her way in front of him. I walked over and told her she must wait in line. In her coarse street language she told me where I could go and how to get there.

I went to the kitchen and told them not to serve her.

She already had a litre pop bottle of coffee from some other church or mission. When she was told she wasn't going to be served she took after me with her coffee. One hand holding the bottle and the other at the spout ready to drench me. In self defence, I stepped behind a young man from the street. He had coffee running down the front of him. By now some men were helping her out of the Mission.

I apologized to the young man. He told me he didn't mind. I looked at his clothes. He had on a leather jacket and greasy pants which were oily from sleeping in them for a month or two. The coffee ran off his clothes onto the floor..

****

We often have groups of university or college students come to see what it is like living and ministering on skid row. They learn and experience a great deal..

One late afternoon, a group from another country was in the Mission getting ready to do the service. At the same time a delivery of food for the kitchen arrived. Young men and a few girls started unloading and hauling the food into the mission. A man from the street helped by bringing in a few boxes.

When someone from the street helps we give them something special.

This man from the street helped carry in boxes. He saw the beautiful young girls at the front deciding which gospel songs to sing and what scriptures to use in the message that night. He went to the front and started flirting with the beautiful young ladies. Being rude and obnoxious.

Matthew moved in and told him to leave the girls alone.

He wasn't having any success, so I went over and told the man to quit bothering the girls and go to the back of the Mission He punched me in the throat. I fell backwards and landed on a big speaker.

The girls were shocked. They had never seen this kind of behaviour in a church.

Three of the male students with the group witnessed the attack.

The pastor in charge told the three young men to usher the man outside.

They had never had to usher anyone out of a church but they gently moved him to the door. On the way out, the perpetrator asked them in amazement, "Where am I?"

They told him he was in a church. He told them, "I thought I was in a whore house with all those gorgeous prostitutes."

****

The mission was open twenty-four hours during the cold weather. I signed for afternoon duty. When I arrived there were three men sitting near the front already drunk. I told them not to drink in the Mission. I went to the kitchen and had a coffee. A young, curly haired blond man I had known as an addict for five years, came in for something to eat. He told me for the tenth time that his uncle owns the Orange Lounge, which I know is a strip joint. He always goes on to tell me that he can get money anytime he needs it.

I heard one of the drunks say, "He's the rat."

Another man said, "He's the one!"

The young man rushed into the kitchen and hid behind me. I told him, "Don't get me involved." The young guy was holding onto my shirt. He told me I had to protect him. I told him to go to the back and open the big door and run down the stairs into the alley. He was off like a shot. Now the drunks were angry at me for letting him get away. They were pointing at me and making threats. I prayed for protection and for favour in this tenuous situation.

A big man, six foot two wearing a Stetson hat, jean jacket, jeans and boots came into the Mission for a coffee. He observed the situation. Standing between the drunks and myself, he said, "We don't want any trouble now do we?" They looked up at him and one said "No." He told them to get their things and leave. They complained about the cold outside. After the door was shut, I turned to thank the man who saved my life, but he was gone.

When I prayed, I imagined that a wrestler type with bulging muscles would come to my rescue, but God sent me a cowboy.

****

Just before the service began, on a bright summer day, a man came into the Mission with blood dripping onto the floor. I asked him what had happened. He told me he was walking on Hammel Street and a young guy pulled a knife and stabbed him twice in the arm. He had on a short sleeved shirt, so I immediately pinched together the wound that was oozing blood. I had him pinch the other wound that was only dripping blood. I asked him if he had hiv, aides or hepatitis C. He told me he was on medication. I had a panic attack as I tried to remember if I had any open wounds. Not remembering any, I stayed with him until the paramedics arrived and took him away. I washed my hands and arms three times in hot water and then applied rubbing alcohol. He went away very distraught.

I went to the pulpit and preached a sermon on forgiveness.

****

A fight broke out in front of the Mission. There have been numerous fights over the years. Sometimes a combatant will be thrown against the plexiglass window and make a big thud. I saw that they were taking turns punching or kicking a tall, skinny young man. I asked the doorman what was happening. He told me the tall guy was preying on seniors who lived on skid row. He would steal their wallet, watches rings and glasses, beat them and make them bleed. "People down here don't like guys like him," he informed me. I had heard this was happening and felt he deserved what he was getting.

A police siren whined. I saw the patrol car jump the curb and park on the street. Men scurried to get out of danger. They handcuffed the predator and took him away. I felt a bit safer knowing he is behind bars.

****

One weekday night I was on duty. Near the end of the service I heard the rapping of a stick on the plexiglass window. I saw a man I have known for eight years making threatening gestures, with the large stick, to someone inside the mission.

A young man came beside me and told me he needed police protection from this man.

I had my cell phone and I could phone the police, but I figured I would talk to the man outside the Mission and keep him from doing more damage and getting himself in more trouble with the law.

I opened the door half way and told him to quit bothering us and go away. "Leave this young guy alone!" I demanded.

He grabbed the door and opened it wide. Standing in the middle of the doorway he turned on me. "Get out of the way or I'll beat you to pulp. I'm not kidding I'll tear you apart," he said threatening me with his big stick.

With the help of two volunteers, we pushed him outside, closed and locked the door.

I phoned the police as he was still threatening the boy, myself and everyone in the Mission.

I had to make a report which I did.

For a month or so I would walk on the other side of the street from where he was living.

After that, I would see him now and then. He came into the mission in the mornings and at night. One night he was there waiting for the service to begin.

That night, a man was being vulgar to some young girls who were volunteering as part of a church group. I told him to smarten up and go sit down on the other side of the aisle or leave the Mission. He refused to obey and kept bothering the girls.

George, the man who threatened my life with his big stick, came to my rescue and escorted the vulgar man to the door.

George, disappeared after that. I can only surmise that he threatened to kill someone else and landed up in jail.

Two years later he came to the mission looking healthy and clean. A sure sign he had been incarcerated for the tenth time. I greeted him kindly and asked how he was doing. He told me just fine.

****

It is not only the pastors and teachers that are abused. We have a doorman whose duty it is to turn away potential trouble makers, drunks and those high on drugs. It's a job for the big and strong.

I have had to do the job of doorman if no one else is available. I'm only five foot eight which is not that big. I keep in shape by doing weight lifting and cardio vascular exercises every day in order to be fit to act if necessary.

The doormen are to be diplomatic and kind as they are volunteer members of the Mission.

Luke, our big six foot one doorman, was doing his job when he turned away a trouble maker who was banned for two weeks. This man was not allowed in the Mission until he could behave and apologize for his bad behaviour. He kept yelling at the preachers and harassing them, causing trouble. He did this when he was drunk.

The man cursed Luke and threatened him. He came back and was pounding on the door. Luke opened it to tell him to go away. The man wielded a knife and slit Luke's throat. Thankfully no artery was severed.

So many good memories and a few I'd like to forget. Life is like that on the streets of skid row. We have to take the good with the bad.

Six weeks later, big Luke was across the street from the Mission. He had just received his money from the government. Three men knew he had come from the bank. They attacked him in order to steal his money. He put up a fight. The three knocked him down and kicked him in the head, ribs and legs. When he was unconscious they stole his wallet, pants, glasses, wrist watch, shoes, shirt and left him on the sidewalk to die.

Luke was in a coma for four days and in the hospital for two weeks under observation

When a nurse told him he could go home he asked for his clothes. The nurse told him he had no clothes when he came to the hospital. He had to phone his son to bring him some clothes.

Luke told me what had happened. I told him not to come to this street as it is too dangerous. He told me the street was his territory. "They're not going to win this battle," he said defiantly.

A few months later, Luke died of a heart attack from the trauma he had suffered.. His family phoned and wanted a memorial service at the Mission. They knew he loved to come to the Mission and listen to the worship in song and the Word of God.

I told them we'd love to have the service but they would have to take part in it. We asked that they provide a picture and flowers or whatever they would like to do. Some provide sandwiches and cakes. We like to have a member of the family speak and give a eulogy. I explained this to his brother. He told me we should do everything.

I told him we would do the music and give the message, advertise and bring people to the service as his brother was dearly loved by all in the Mission and people on the street.

Sadly, the brother never responded and we did our own service without a picture or a proper eulogy.

****

Where drugs are sold there are suppliers and dealers. There are also gang turf wars.

Our Mission is in the middle of this menagerie.

Every evening on my shift, I open early in preparation for the service. A tall young, good looking, well dressed man came into the Mission.

Near the back of the Mission is a storage room. A person standing in front of the storage room can't be seen from the street.

This young man stood with his back against the wall in this area.

Most people come in and sit down. They read Bible tracts or Christian magazines. This young man stood with his back to the wall.

Ten minutes later a shorter and stalkier man I had never seen before, came in looking around the Mission. He spotted the young man. He went at him with fists flailing and curses filling the air.

The young man fought back. Three regulars ushered the assailant out the door.

The young man was going to leave. I told him to stay in the Mission as the man outside would beat him up. The assailant was outside motioning for the young man to come out. I didn't want the police to be involved as I knew it was gang related. To get involved is to put yourself at risk of being killed.

The young man told me he must take what he deserves. He was about to leave. I talked him into staying or he would be beaten to a pulp. He stayed for the service.

Four days later, the young man came to the Mission. Both eyes were black and blue and he had a bandage on his face. I wondered how many ribs were cracked and how badly bruised were his legs. Broken and bruised by kicking when he was knocked down.

He still comes to the Mission occasionally and sits in the same area. Still involved in the gang which beat him up so badly.

****

At the morning service, we have drug suppliers come into the Mission with their blackberries set on vibrate. They are waiting for drugs to be delivered by the gangs. They then sell them to the dealers. They sit at the back of the Mission playing games on their hand held machines. The Mission is a warm place to wait for their deliveries.

I watched as one man played a game on his blackberry. He won. During the sermon he got up and celebrated his win. "Yeah, I did it." I looked at him and shook my head. He sat down.

****

We also have some strange things happen. I was in charge of a morning service. A grey haired, middle aged woman came in and talked to me. She wanted to know about the service and if I was preaching. I told her I would preach. She told me she had heard me preach before and would stay for the service. I knew her from years past.

I know hundreds from years past. She sat in the second row near the middle.

After the music in song and the offering, I was called to give the sermon. I started with prayer and read the Psalm of the day. I looked down to greet the congregation only to see this woman with her sweater pulled up to her neck with no bra. She was smiling as if proud of what she was displaying. I was shocked What could I say? I saw Roy sitting beside her smiling and laughing. I asked him to escort her to the back of the Mission. I prayed and delivered my sermon.

****

We had a first nations young man come to every service and sit in the same place morning and evening His name is Dustin. Every day I acknowledged him and many times I would speak to him before the service. He liked to talk and joke. When I asked a questions during my preaching, he had the answer. He alway carried his Bible and followed the scriptures which were being preached.

One morning I came early. Dustin was always at the door waiting to come into the Mission. This morning he was late. Just before the service started, I received the news that when Dustin was on his ways home after the evening service around eleven thirty, the night before, he was dragged into a nearby park and beaten to death.

I still feel sad when I think about this incident. But I feel happy knowing that he knew the Lord. I figured that over the three or four years he came to both services, he had heard upwards of one thousand two hundred sermons and heard over seven thousand gospel songs. The words of the songs are displayed on the screen.

He is always in our thoughts and in our prayers.

****

One rainy morning, a young first nations regular came in and draped his wet jacket over a chair next to him.

Later, a middle aged man came in asking if we had a jacket that would fit him.

I watched as he eyed my jacket. I put it in the office and went searching for a jacket. We often get jackets, socks and shoes as well as shirts and pants donated. This day I couldn't find a jacket that would fit him.

I went to tell him the results of my search. He was talking to the young man. I watched as he tried to divert the young man's attention by pointing to something on the other side of the room. Slyly he put his hand on the jacket and was sliding it off the chair. The young man looked to see his jacket being stolen.

He got up and started fighting with the culprit. He knocked him to the floor and kicked him in the head. I was already there to break up the fight. I grabbed the young man's shirt with both hands and pushed him away from the downed man. I told the man to get up and get out of the Mission. All the time I am dancing with the young man telling him not to fight in the Mission. He tried to get by me but I hung on. He wanted more of the man who tried to steal his jacket. I got him settled down and let go. He sat down and enjoyed the service.

****

When there is no bouncer, we fill that position.

Many times I have had to stop fights in this manner. Sometimes I'm not so lucky and I get thrown to the floor.

One time, I had to escort an angry man who wanted to fight with one of our regular patrons, to the back of the Mission.

The Mission was almost full. This man saw a vacant seat in the third row. He was ready to take the seat. Elliot, a regular at the Mission, told him he was saving the seat for his friend. This provoked an argument.

I heard a challenge from the man wanting the seat to have Elliot come outside and fight.

I told the man we don't fight in the Mission. He told me, "There is no saving seats." I offered to get him a seat further back.

He complied and was moving along in front of me. In his anger he turned on me and threw me across the aisle. I ended up draped over a pew. Nursing a sore shoulder and an injured knee.

Three men escorted him out of the Mission.

It was summer and the door remained wide open. He stood in the doorway and yelled insults calling Elliot a loser, coward and chicken. Cursing all the time.

Elliot is a weight lifter and a trainer in a gym. He ran down the aisle and outside. I didn't see what happened, but I was told he grabbed the man and threw him in the gutter.

Elliot and his friend came back and stayed for the service.

****

After our Sunday morning service, where I had preached, we celebrated our fellowship meal together. While the students were cleaning up and preparing the evening meal, I went to the back of the Mission and watched the snow begin to come down. I like to watch the clean white flakes make their way onto the sidewalk and the street. As I was enjoying the sight, a man on the street motioned for me to open the door. I thought he wanted to know about the services and the Mission. I opened the door and he spit in my face and on my shirt.

I never felt so dirty. I rushed to wash my face. I washed myself three times. I took off my shirt and put on my winter jacket and rushed home to have a shower.

I have forgive him, but I still remember. I had never seen him in the Mission or on the street. I often wonder who he is and what is his problem with the Mission.

****

One night, we had a group of teenagers come with their leader to the Mission. They came to see the seamier side of life. We tell the leaders to make certain they are paired off with a buddy for safety purposes as there are predators waiting to lure them onto the street.

This particular evening a young boy of about fourteen sat on one side of the Mission where I sit when I preach. He sat beside me. His group sat on the other side.

A man in his forties, who I didn't recognize, came and sat beside the boy. I heard the conversation and told the boy to go sit with his group on the other side of the Mission. He told me he was ok where he was. I listened and realized the pervert was trying to pick up the young boy.

I told the boy again to move over with his group. He shook his head.

Later, the pervert started swearing and cursing when the young boy refused his invitation to go with him to his hotel room.

I grabbed the predator by his jacket and backed him up to the door. I told him we don't allow that behaviour and swearing when in the Mission.

The man kept telling me "You can't kick people out of a church!"

Two students saw that I was evicting someone for good reason and they took over.

****

On the brighter side, when I am on the street, people come running over to me and hand me money for the Mission. One man always takes the opportunity to give his money in person. He rolls up fifteen or twenty pennies in plastic and presents them as his offering to God. I thank him and ask God to bless him. He goes away happy.

****

One night when I was on duty, we had a group of fifteen or so young people from a church in suburbia. They came to prepare the evening meal, do the worship in song and present the sermon, serve the meal and clean up. After their duties they socialized for longer than most groups. I closed the Mission and let down the metal gate. I hurried across the street to catch my bus. As I walked towards the bus shelter, I noticed three six foot men standing watching me arrive. I stopped twenty feet away. I observed that the man in the middle of the three was manifesting demons. He had a look of hatred and anger. I stood transfixed. I knew if I ran they would knock me down and beat me to a pulp. I stood and prayed for protection. That was my only defence against these three tall and mean looking guys. The man on the right said, "Not him, come on lets go. Leave him alone." The man in the middle wasn't going to leave without killing me. The man told him, "Let's go. Come on." The three turned and walked away. I thanked God and Jesus for His protection. Perhaps he had seen me at the Mission and knew I was a Pastor. I can only surmise.

After that I always had two or three escorts when I waited at the bus stop at eleven thirty at night.

****

Last week, after the morning service where I preached, I was waiting on skid row, for a green light in order to cross the street. A young, handsome, well dressed man stood beside me. On the way across the street, he asked me what I liked. I knew he was a male prostitute and I was being hustled and propositioned. I told him I liked preaching at the Mission across the street. He told me he didn't know there was a Mission. I invited him to come and join us in worship. He agreed that was a good idea.

****

When I first came to the Mission for the evening service, I wondered how I could make it safely to the bus stop at eleven thirty at night. I remembered my encounter with a big man trying to sell me rock cocaine when I came to the Mission that evening.

I didn't drive my car down to skid row as I felt it might be vandalized.

I prayed to God for protection on this night. I needed a guardian angel..

As I walked down the street filled with men and a few women a wide path formed and I walked unharmed toward the bus stop. The people on the street looked at me in awe as I walked by. I knew God had sent one or two angels in the form of wrestler type, body builders to walk with me and protect me. It was the answer to my prayer.

****

It was a Thursday morning and a worship team and a guest preacher were doing the service. I went to the back and talked to the new doorman. He is an intellectual and we have some great discussions.

I also greeted Maurice who volunteers each day to clean the sidewalk outside the Mission and do whatever he can. He told me he had asked a man who had his merchandise for sale on a blanket in front of the Mission, to move his store out of the way. It was blocking people who were entering the Mission. He said the man cursed him and wouldn't move his goods.

I wasn't in the mood to be cursed at so I ignored the issue. I looked out and saw that this man had twenty or more random items for sale. If the police came along they would give him a ticket which equated to a hundred dollar fine.

The worship in music had started so we quit talking. People are allowed to come into the Mission while the music is being played and the singing is happening.

Most people come in quietly, respecting the Word of God in song.

The door burst open and the man who owned the merchandise rushed in. Yelling, the man exclaimed, "He stole my measuring tape and ran in here. He's a thief."

I told him to be quiet and go find the man and I would speak to him. He looked at everyone in the Mission. He came back and accused the doorman of witnessing the crime. The doorman told him he didn't see anything. I knew he saw nothing as he was talking to me.

The man's voice was getting louder and louder. He was disrupting the service. I told him to leave. He then turned his anger toward me telling me I encouraged the men on the street to be thieves.

Maurice and another man from the street came to our assistance. They, along with the doorman, moved the man out of the Mission.

I told Maurice and the others to get back into the Mission. The doorman and the other regular came back in but Maurice was still arguing with the outraged man. A crowd of thirty or forty men from the street started gathering sensing their might be a fight. They didn't want to miss the action. Maurice had had enough of the fouled mouth man. He popped him on the nose. There was no blood, just a bruised ego.

I told Maurice he shouldn't have done that. He agreed.

When calm returned and everyone was back in the Mission. I looked outside. I noticed that the man whose goods were left unattended had lost half of them to people passing by.

The police on patrol were told of the incident and came to investigate. They talked to the man who had the merchandise for sale. He showed them what remained of his goods. The police gave him a hundred dollar ticket for selling goods without a license.

The man pointed out Maurice as the one who punched him in the nose. They had Maurice come outside to tell his story. They cuffed him and did a computer check.

By now I was outside to give my account of the event. I heard the officers tell Maurice that he had two outstanding warrants for his arrest. They put him in the police car. They then asked me to write out a statement and take it to the police station. They gave me a number which I must put on the statement.

I was sad to know we had lost Maurice, a nice guy who loved to come to the Mission and do whatever he could for the Lord. Many others have warrants from other parts of the country or locally. Computers tell the story.

****

One night after the service, a couple of students and a volunteer were with me when I locked up. That night a man from the street, who often caused trouble, mopped the floor. I kept watch as he would steal the brooms and mops and sell them for drug money. He would also steal from the kitchen as he put the mops away. I didn't want him to volunteer, but I couldn't wrestle the mop from his hand. I was busy that night and wasn't able to watch him as I had to check the Mission before leaving. I started to lower the metal gate and I stopped. I asked the students and volunteers if they had seen Victor leave the Mission. Nobody recalled his leaving. Darryl volunteered to go and check to make sure everything was secure. He found Victor hiding in the bathroom with the lights out. He brought him to the door and told him never to do that again.

If we hadn't caught him in the act, he would have opened the back door and stolen whatever would bring a good price. We have had our sound system stolen and sold to a pawn shop. It was recovered as they were marked and bore the name of the Mission.

****

These are only a few of the incidences which happen regularly at the Mission on the Downtown Eastside skid row of a large city.

Using what opportunities we have at our disposal, we help those who have no hope .We help them to regain their self esteem and regain their self worth. We give them the spiritual tools to rise up and take control of their lives. They are encouraged to strive to reach their potential.

When they know who and what they are in the kingdom of God, they will help others lift themselves from the gutter and get on the path of righteousness that leads to the Kingdom of God.

Hundreds have come to the Bible College in order to learn how to have a relationship with their Lord and Saviour. They have all been changed to some degree. How much change depends on the individual and what goals they set for their life and how deep is their relationship with God Almighty and Jesus the Christ.

We pray for those who are being built up in their faith and are being regenerated into the likeness of Jesus their Lord. Our hope is that we will all meet again in the coming New Jerusalem where God will be our God and we will be His people.

God bless everyone who reads this book and becomes part of our family, the family of God.

LaVergne, TN USA
02 August 2010
191779LV00002B/1/P

9 781449 081461